FOUR KINGS

The story of Paddy 'K____' O'Brien, Jack Quinn, Mick Lyons, Darren Fay an____ All-Ireland triumphs

FOUR KINGS

The story of Paddy 'Hands' O'Brien, Jack Quinn, Mick Lyons, Darren Fay and 7 All-Ireland triumphs

PHILIP LANIGAN

HEROBOOKS

HERO BOOKS

Published by Hero Books
1 Woodville Green
Lucan, Co. Dublin
Ireland
www.herobooks.ie
Hero Books is an imprint of Umbrella Publishing

First published, 2013

A CIP record for this book is available from the British Library

ISBN 978-0-9526260-8-4

Printed in Ireland with Print Procedure Ltd

Cover design and typesetting: Jessica Maile

Front Cover photographs: Paddy O'Brien and Jack Quinn (The Peter McDermott Collection), Mick Lyons and Darren Fay (Sportsfile)

Back cover photographs (top left): Mick Lyons lifts the Delaney Cup after defeating Dublin in the 1988 Leinster final.

Back cover (bottom right, photos clockwise from top left): Mick Lyons tackles Dublin's Vinny Murphy; Darren Fay wins the ball against Kildare; Jack Quinn fields brilliantly against Galway; Jack and Martin Quinn in their official Meath blazers before heading to Australia in 1968; and Paddy O'Brien and the Meath team before the 1949 Leinster final victory over Westmeath.

Inside photographs: The Peter McDermott Collection and Sportsfile

To mam and dad ... who left our lives too early

AUTHOR'S NOTE

The hours spent in the company of the four subjects at the heart of this story were an absolute pleasure.

It was fascinating to listen to Paddy O'Brien - always dapper, always welcoming – talk through his life and times, and with his wife, Kay always ready to chip in with colourful anecdotes to give a fully rounded portrait.

Their son, Garry was the first point of contact and a great help along the way and was quick to pick the brains of his brothers, Padraic, Tony and Gabriel for all other relevant background information. So thanks to one and all.

Frankie Byrne too – another legend from the '49ers' – gave great insight into the breakthrough years and a lot more besides.

There's a reason Quinns pub is so well regarded outside Trim. Thanks to Jack and Mary for their hospitality – and to the former for lugging the suitcase full of clippings down from the attic at various stages. There are few better men to tell a story than Jack, who is a natural raconteur. Rarely is interviewing so much fun.

Brothers, Gerry and Martin played starring roles too along the way, as did Gerry's daughter, Janet and husband, Darren Feldman - Darren still making a name for himself as one of Ratoath's Wednesday night 'veterans'.

Knocking on Mick Lyons' front door for the first time, you get a sense of what many full-forwards must have been experiencing as they took a deep breath and prepared to go to battle with Summerhill's iconic full-back.

Except off the field, Mick is one of the game's true gentlemen. Great company and with a droll sense of humour, thanks to Mick for finally telling his tale. Paraic Lyons too, for fleshing out the family story so vividly.

To Darren Fay as well for being so open and honest about his time in the fabled No.3 shirt and articulating it all so brilliantly. And for the box of scrapbooks, cuttings and photographs to mark a stellar career that were such a help along the way. His father, Jimmy added to the full picture.

Seán Boylan is the closest thing to a living, breathing archivist of Meath football and shared some wonderful memories of the four subjects.

Bernard Flynn, Mícheál Ó Muircheartaigh and GAA president, Liam O'Neill too offered their time, and Brendan Cummins helped firm up the record of championship appearances.

To my wife, Mary and the two lads, Jack and Will for all the support and encouragement along the way – and staying the course when so many other things were put on hold.

To Mary's parents, Margaret and Mattie McCabe for providing a refuge when the kitchen in Meadowbank Hill was under demolition – not to mention the odd 'snack' along the way.

Turns out Mattie, another gentleman who won an All-Ireland junior hurling medal with Meath, had a very brief outing at full-back for Meath back in his day.

To my brothers, Don and Brian and all my friends for their support – Don might yet have a second calling as an editor.

To the *Irish Mail on Sunday* for continuing to give me the opportunity to write about the best games in the world.

Finally, I'm indebted to Liam Hayes and Hero Books for making it all happen and bringing it all together so well.

ACKNOWLEDGMENTS

Paddy O'Brien's status is such that *The Irish Press* ran a serialisation of his life and times during the 1950s and Padraig Puirseal's chronicle provided an invaluable source.

The photographs used come courtesy of Ray McManus and Sportsfile as well as the Peter McDermott collection housed in Navan Library, the latter providing a treasure trove of black and white images from back in the day.

Thanks to John Donohoe of *The Meath Chronicle* for his help and assistance with the viewing of the original newspaper archives.

The archives of the *Irish Independent*, *Irish Press* and *The Irish Times* in particular were also an important source of information.

Thanks to Gerry Kelly, Sideline, for helping to secure the DVDs of Meath's All-Ireland finals and to Ronan O Coisdealbha of TG4 for supplying the collection of Laochra Gael programmes featuring a host of Meath legends.

To anyone with an interest in the history and evolution of Gaelic games, the 'GAA Gold' series produced in conjunction with the IFI provide a wonderful collection of highlights from the All-Ireland finals of the 1940s and '50s. And thanks to Darren Frehill for pointing me in the right direction. To sit down with Paddy O'Brien as he watched the old footage back for the first time was an experience in itself.

A number of books too provided a frame of reference. The most pertinent included Brian Carthy's *Football Captains: The All-Ireland Winners*, along with his *Championship* collection, Colm O'Rourke's *The Final Whistle*, *Out Of Our Skins* by Liam Hayes, Con Houlihan's selection of essays, *More Than A Game*, and *The Boylan Years* which I had the pleasure of working on and interviewing a long line of Meath greats.

Dave Carthy's two-volume history of Skryne GAA club is something that deserves a place in the GAA museum as a piece of history in itself, a superbly crafted labour of love that is a valuable record of not only the club's but the Royal County's history.

CONTENTS

CHAPTER 1

ALL-IRELAND DAYS

Croke Park
Sunday, September 26, 1999

Darren Fay sits in a corner of the Meath dressing room, eyes closed, towel draped over his head, a portrait of intense concentration. There is no chit-chat with the rest of the team, no wise-cracking to wish the nerves away.

The click clack of studs on the hard floor tells him it isn't long now, not long before the call comes and the roar of the crowd on All-Ireland final day greets him.

For days, weeks, he has been wracked by a nervous energy, building himself up for just this moment. Back in Trim, he can be like a stranger in his own home. His wife, Rhona will hear the doors open and close in the house as he paces from room to room or up and down the stairs, turning over the endless possibilities of the match in his head. She knows him well enough to just let him go through his own routine, his own way of channelling his nerves into an intense concentration.

On the morning of a Championship match, he has been known to grab the keys of the car and go for a spin, sometimes as far as Kells, a puzzling sight for any Meath supporters who happen to catch sight of their full-back whizzing by with the boot down.

But that's how he is in the build-up to the big days, consumed by thoughts of the game. And this is no different. Don Davis is listed to play full-forward for Cork. But what if he goes walkabout?

He can't afford to be surprised if there's a plan to pull him from the edge of the square and the plot of ground he has made his own. In 17 Championship matches that he has started at full-back for Meath, he has never conceded more than a single score to any opponent.

And yet he is still wracked by nerves and self-doubt.

When his father, Jimmy calls over and sees his son with his game face on, he'll roll his eyes to heaven. 'It's just a game!' Jimmy played for Meath on and off for 14 years and never worried about anything, a 'happy-go-lucky guy' as he describes himself, who enjoyed the friends and the banter just as much as his football.

Life pitched himself and Mick Lyons together on the same Meath team and the pair became buddies for life. On the face of it they looked like Meath football's 'Odd Couple'; the carefree, mischief-maker and joker in the pack, Jimmy paired with the Meath full-back with a reputation for chewing up opposition full-forwards and spitting them back out again.

But Jimmy's quiet drive and ambition was matched by Lyons' different persona off the field, the same fondness for the post-match pint and craic, the sense of pride and belonging that comes with playing football and representing your county.

After Championship matches, they'd share a few jars and often land back in Jimmy's house to entertain themselves and an awe-struck Darren who would try and gatecrash the adult conversation. It felt cool to grow up with one of his idols knocking around as a regular. Who just happened to be best pals with his dad. And he wonders why he ended up as a Lyons' heir to the No.3 shirt.

Now here he is, trying to match his exploits.

The call comes.

It's time. Seán Boylan draws the players close around him and reiterates the same message from the team meeting the night before. Captain Graham Geraghty too keeps it short and to the point.

And then they're out and gone.

They may be different characters but one thing Darren has inherited is his father's sense of superstition, not surprising given Jimmy rounded off his career as a goalkeeper with Meath after a long and storied career between the posts with Trim Celtic.

So he blesses himself before leaving the dressing room. Makes sure to be second or third out the door when the team exits. As he strides out, he always carries an

'O'Neills' under his arm and gives it an almighty thump as his studs hit the grass, just to get that first feel of ball on boot. Makes a beeline for the bench where he usually sits down in the front row for the team photograph. He's standing this time, but no matter.

When the ball is thrown in, that's when he leaves the rest of the world behind, when anything outside the whitewash might as well cease to exist.

Meath cling to a three-point lead in the final moments of the game. Substitute Michael O'Donovan takes a line-ball, bangs it in towards the full-forward line. Don Davis took him on a tour of Croke Park for spells but didn't produce a score.

Cork need a goal and it's Joe Kavanagh who is now shifted inside on him. Both contest the punt down the line and Fay uses his strength to win the breaking ball. So composed and confident, his bullet-proof persona on the field is so at odds with his other self. Handpasses it out to Paddy Reynolds who transfers it to Trevor Giles who gives it a thump upfield as referee Michael Curley blows the final whistle.

For Meath supporters, it's one of those days in footballing terms when hope and history rhyme. Fifty years, almost to the day, since Brian Smyth became the first Meath captain to lift the Sam Maguire Cup. A half-century brokering seven All-Irelands.

Four men lined out at full-back on those winning teams, four men who shared the No.3 jersey for Meath for the guts of half a century combined. Four of the greatest full-backs the game, never mind one county, has borne witness to.

Four Kings.

✦ ✦ ✦ ✦ ✦

With Mick Lyons a familiar feature around the house growing up, little wonder Darren Fay's career followed its designated path. In July of 1988, at the very time the Summerhill player was in full battle mode for the Leinster final against Dublin, a step away from captaining Meath to back-to-back provincial titles, Fay too lined out that day at Croke Park in the schools match at half time. It seemed pre-ordained.

So much of it did.

Before Lyons came Jack Quinn, the prince of Meath full-backs.

Twenty years before Lyons captained Meath to All-Ireland final glory against Cork, Quinn was a charismatic rock-like presence on the team of

1967 that vanquished the same opponents.

When Fay married in August 2002, Lyons and Quinn were guests.

And the first among equals, the Meath man who was named full-back on the GAA's 'Team of the Millennium' in 1984, Paddy 'Hands' O'Brien. Part of the history-making '49ers', the men who broke the mould in 1949. King of the square too against Kerry as Meath added a second title in 1954.

Four men whose lives were to intertwine in ways they could never have possibly imagined. None of them even dreamed of playing full-back for Meath. All four were natural midfielders who ended up there as much by accident as design.

Four men, four full-backs, whose life and times span that 50 years of grace, 1949-1999. Whose combined story is the story of Meath football, from Croke Park to Wembley to Melbourne Cricket Ground to Gaelic Park, New York. From shooting the breeze with Charlie Haughey on the steps of the Hogan Stand to playing cards and singing songs with Hollywood royalty, Marlene Dietrich. Playing football for Meath would allow them to travel the world, and involve all sorts of incident and accident.

Their story is the story of Meath's golden era.

♦♦♦♦♦

In Paddy O'Brien's dining room in his house in Santry, on the north side of Dublin, a harp hangs displaying his medal collection, with a neat trim his wife, Kay added as an adornment. It takes a keen eye to pick out the two Celtic Crosses amidst the multitude of different honours, the five Leinster medals, two National Leagues, the three Railway Cups with Leinster and assorted others.

He hands you the first one that made history, won with the famous '49ers' as the team became known. Etched into the medal is the year in question, a milestone in so many respects.

Even now, at 88 years old, the man christened 'Hands' exudes a calm and a presence that made it easy to understand why he stood apart as a No.3 in his prime.

In terms of his preparation for big matches, his demeanour was closer to

Jimmy Fay's than that of his son's. Ask if he ever felt nervous and he replies? 'No … just took it all in my stride. There were no motions or commotions.'

His wife, Kay and son, Garry sit in as he recalls his life and times and can't remember him ever being fazed heading out for a match.

'You were rushing one day and you had a pair of black shoes and yellowy coloured socks,' says Kay, ' … and somebody said, "Oh my God, wouldn't you think he'd dress better than that." First thing he could get … he put on.'

He shows you the broken finger on his right hand, sustained on a famous trip to America, the same adventure that helped earn his famous moniker. Christened 'Hands' by New York commentator, 'Lefty' Devine on the 1951 visit to New York for the National League final, it stuck. The nickname said all you wanted to know about his fielding.

'Because I used to claw in everything with my hands. I used to get up above players. I had a great spring off the ground … I caught so many balls over their heads.'

As Garry puts it, 'The American commentator christened him, because all you could see were these hands coming out of the bunch.'

That New York trip is one he recalls fondly, the Polo Grounds venue unique in the history of the GAA for hosting the only All-Ireland final to take place outside Ireland, the iconic meeting between Cavan and Kerry in 1947.

'That was a hard match,' says O'Brien. 'There were a lot of Kerry fellas playing – 'Gega' O'Connor for one. They had a fair side. There were baseball mounds in front of the goal. I used to use them to spring off.'

A trip to Boston then followed as part of the tour, where O'Brien broke a finger. All in all, it was an eventful trip. 'That's one thing that stands out in Boston. Whatever car I was in, four or five of us were dispatched back to the hotel for the meal after the match.

'Jack Fitzgerald, Lord have mercy on him, he was one of the mentors. He said, "We'll go in here, have a drink" in what seemed to be an ordinary pub. The hotel was next door. We went in and sat down at a table.

'There were two Galway fellas who were at the match and came back with us. They started singing *Galway Bay* and Irish songs. There was a gang of fellas sitting at another table across from us and they had inserted their coins into a jukebox. So they had their own songs.

'But our fellas were belting out, drowning out their music. The next thing was ... a glass was fired from their table ... struck Paddy Dixon on the forehead. And the blood started flowing down his face. It happened so fast, we didn't know what was going on.

'The police were called.

'There were five or six in their party and they got out the back way. They got away. Poor Dixon had to be patched up.'

As he watches a DVD featuring highlights of the 1954 final against Kerry for the first time, compiled as part of the wonderful GAA 'Football Gold' series, he has one distinct memory from that day.

'In the second half, Kerry were pressing. On the Cusack Stand side a big high ball came in. There must have been half a dozen fellas went for the ball, including yours truly. But I sneaked in from behind and I made a colossal jump, a huge leap, and with one hand I took the ball clear from all the other fellas who went up for it. I took it into my arm ... got a clear kick on it down the wing.

'It was the greatest feat in my life of playing football I felt. It was talked about by fellas who were at the match, a lot of them would always recall it.

'We beat Kerry by six points that day which was a colossal achievement. They were hot favourites. It was a great victory for the underdogs.'

The fact that he lined out with a big bandage around his neck to cover a carbuncle that threatened his participation only added to the legend.

✦✦✦✦✦

Jack Quinn didn't have a nickname bestowed on him, he'll admit that much. Instead, he had a song borrowed and reworked in his honour.

When Bob Dylan wrote *The Mighty Quinn*, he probably didn't expect it to be aired at Croke Park by hordes of delirious Meath supporters. But the Kilbride player's feats on the field led to regular renditions, and one line in particular ... '*You ain't seen nothing like the Mighty Quinn.*' Over and over.

The 1975 National League final was one of those days.

Meath 0-16 Dublin 1-9. Heffo's Army brought to a halt, at least temporarily. At 31 years-old, his last great stand in the No.3 jersey.

In his long established pub on the Dublin road just outside Trim, he digs out an old suitcase full of clippings, match reports and photographs, and hunts for the notices. In the quarter-final against Kerry, the semi-final against Mayo and the final against Dublin, he picked up a 'Sportstar of the Week' award in the national newspapers. For a man who played such a key part in the 1967 All-Ireland triumph and captained Meath in the 1970 decider on a day when Kerry took the honours, it's still a source of pride. Especially coming 12 years after making his senior debut. Remarkable.

Little did he know either that it would be a decade and more before Meath were contenders again, before Seán Boylan lit the touchpaper on another revolution.

Funny how it works. Jack Quinn was at the 1955 Leinster final when the curtain came down on Meath's first great team, and on Paddy 'Hands' O'Brien's career. O'Brien's stature was such that he was an idol to Quinn, as he was to most of the kids of his generation with an interest in football.

He just never dreamed he would feature on the next Meath team to lift the Sam Maguire Cup and become a worthy successor to O'Brien. Older brother, Martin was the full-back in the family, Gerry the corner-forward and Jimmy the sterling wing-back, who, for various reasons, just never transferred his talent from the club stage to county.

Jack Quinn, like O'Brien, Mick Lyons and Darren Fay, was a reluctant No.3 who spent the bulk of his club career playing midfield.

Apart from a Dylan song appropriated in his honour, he would also have a racehorse named after him. For someone who runs a successful bar-trade business, it's no surprise that Jack Quinn is affable in company, full of fun and stories which he peppers with a raucous laugh.

Over the course of a career that spanned from 1963 to 1976, he developed his own big match rituals, especially when it came to playing at Croke Park. Like Fay, he had a single-minded focus when it came to preparing for games.

'The one thing I do remember is that I didn't want to be talking to anyone, even at home where we all were at the time. I'd go for a bit of a walk by myself.

'We'd go to Croke Park and before any match all the team would meet in Barry's Hotel … have a cup of tea there. Then the mini-bus would bring us down to the stadium. But I always used to walk to Croke Park on my own.

All the time … kept my gear … I didn't want to talk to anyone. I'd my own routine, I'd be thinking about the game.

'I'd just tell whoever was driving us at the time, whether it was Jackie May or whoever … just to let him know. You'd be walking down with the crowds.'

It's an arresting image: Quinn, gear bag slung over his shoulder, strolling down Gardiner Place, across the top of Parnell Square, a short step down Fitzgibbon Street to mingle with the match-going crowd.

Imagine. Sometimes, he'd bump into his own supporters who would see him striding down towards the ground before the game and have to do a double-take.

'People would come up to you asking, "How's it going? Are you not Jack Quinn?"

'And you'd say, "Ah, I'm just killing time."'

It reached a stage where the lads on the gate at Croke Park knew him personally. Sometimes, they'd usher him in and he'd take a seat in the stand to watch a bit of the curtain-raiser before heading to the dressing room and meeting up with the rest of the team. Typically, it was against the Dubs when he nearly ran into bother, that famous National League final day of 1975.

'There was some match on before it and a few Dubs came in to sit beside us. A few things were said. Lucky enough a few more of the lads I knew came in or I think I could have been in trouble!'

Just like Fay, he had his preferred spot for the team photograph, except he liked to stand in the back row. Waiting for that first touch of the ball, and the release.

'You'd always feel a certain kind of a tension building up. Nervous energy. Lucky enough, when I went out on the field it always left me. Any tension I had in the dressing room or that morning … even in the house I wouldn't want to talk to anyone. But as soon as I started kicking a ball around on the field it left me.'

+ + + + +

During his own time in the Meath dressing room, Mick Lyons gravitated towards the corner of hard chaws. His first cousin, Liam Harnan invariably sat one side of him; his brother Paraic, three years his junior, was always close at hand as well. Liam Hayes and Colm O'Rourke too.

There are full-forwards who spent time in the company of Lyons who wish they could have that time in their life back to try and do something else more productive with it - scrambled physically and mentally by the Summerhill full-back who created a mythology around the square that he had to guard.

Famously private in terms of giving interviews, the radio silence only added to the mystique as the Lyons' legend grew. But his reputation as a fearsome character on the field - iron-willed, unbending, indomitable – was always at odds with his persona off it. To pal around with Jimmy Fay, sure you'd need to have a sense of humour, to be able to look on the light side of life.

Off the field, he is easy and engaging company. You get a sense that he's happy to talk about his career now as much because of the men he shared the No.3 jersey with, not out of pride in his own achievements. Few players with such a big reputation could have such a lack of ego.

His recall of dates and matches isn't his strongest suit but that's because he was able to let it all go when he retired.

In his house in Oldtown, Summerhill, there are only a few giveaways in terms of his feats on the field.

In the hall, a photograph of him lifting the Sam Maguire Cup as Meath captain in 1987.

And beside it, one capturing 'The Block', that iconic moment in the 1987 final, a career-defining intervention - the shot of Lyons diving full-length just as Jimmy Kerrigan swings his right boot for the goal to kill off Meath.

There's one more photograph, tucked away in the bottom corner of the back room of the house where he talks through the highs and lows of his footballing life, a lovely picture of him being presented with the Delaney Cup in 1987 by the Leinster chairman … 'my old friend Jack Boothman' … who has his arm around him sharing the moment.

For a man who refused to write an All-Ireland speech, arguably the most famous photograph of all came in that very same spot on the Hogan Stand later in September, just as the Sam Maguire Cup was ready and waiting to be presented.

In the break between the madness of the pitch invasion and climbing the steps of the Hogan Stand, he plonked down beside then Taoiseach Charles Haughey, like two ordinary Joes just shooting the breeze. The rogue in Charlie would have loved the untamed element in Lyons and the pair chatted away just before the latter was called to lift the Cup.

'I just saw the seat and sat down,' says Lyons. 'It wasn't the fact that I wanted a picture taken … general chit chat. I don't think we were planning the country or anything like that!'

What did they say to one another?

'We had a conversation about the match and things in general. It certainly wasn't politics because my family was the other side. My mother wouldn't have liked to see me sitting there!'

Only Lyons, with his lack of pretension could pull it off and make it seem like it was the most natural thing in the world. It was more a case of 'Well Charlie … ' rather than bandying official titles about.

'I wouldn't have called him "An Taoiseach" anyway. He called me "Mick" … said well done. The usual.'

Like Paddy 'Hands' O'Brien, he kept his pre-match routine simple, bereft of any superstition.

'Just get all the thoughts in your head clear.

' … and just get out there.'

Thinking back, he recalls how simple things were in terms of preparation, how different even the logistics of match day were compared to the modern day when the choice of music track on the coach is designed to be of a specific purpose.

'Myself, Paraic and Liam Harnan, we'd always travel together. We were lucky in that we played in Croke Park most of the time.

'We never went on a team bus. Everyone drove their own way to Ashbourne … to the hotel where the players would meet and have breakfast or whatever. It was the same before a Leinster final. For the All-Ireland final we drove over to Malahide.

'From Ashbourne then, everyone drove in in their cars. You'd have a pass and you'd get in the back of Croke Park. We parked out the back of the Hogan. Or across in Clonliffe.

'It's all team buses now, which is right.

'Kevin Foley was late one time. He'd no pass and the fella wasn't letting him in and time was running out … sure he nearly took a lad in on his bonnet! He nearly missed the start of the match.'

For someone who played in such a fearless manner, Lyons admits to having the same routine nerves and doubts of most players. 'You would be nervous … yeah. You'd be nervous that you're going to get roasted.

'I would have worked all the week, even the week of an All-Ireland. It wouldn't be strenuous stuff but I wouldn't like to be sitting around Thursday, Friday waiting for the match … filling in time.

'Saturday is nearly always taken up with a bit of training, Mass … bit of everything. The next thing you knew it was half ten that night and time to go to bed.

'When it came to the match I wouldn't be jumping around the dressing room. Just sitting down. A bit nervous. You'd be wondering what was going to happen.

'Con Houlihan said one time, "When you play in your first All-Ireland you don't know the pitfalls. But when you go for your second and third, you know the pitfalls, you know the hurt, you know what can happen."'

✦ ✦ ✦ ✦ ✦

Darren Fay used to turn the potential pitfalls over in his head relentlessly. He shakes his head in bemusement at the example of Tyrone star forward, Stephen O'Neill, who a teammate once revealed is so relaxed before games that he can sometimes be spotted with a book in his hand in the dressing room. The nerves and doubts were always part of the build-up.

'It was head down … and just don't talk to me. That's the way I had to be to get myself into the mindset. Football came so hard to me that I had to get so focused on doing it.

'The likes of Trevor Giles could breeze into a match, kick six points without breaking sweat. Because he was that gifted. Graham Geraghty the same. I found … because I wasn't naturally gifted … everything that I did was pure commitment. Trying to get a hand on the ball or making sure I was first to the ball. That takes huge focus.'

As much as Lyons is private, Fay is naturally shy. In a dressing room, nobody ever confused him for the joker of the pack. But he always had that presence about him, that will to win that pushed him to the very top.

And like Lyons, he talks through his career with a lack of pretension, unflinchingly honest at times in his assessment of the good days and the bad.

Turns out the man he used to idolise as a kid had an impact on his own career, right down to what he had for breakfast on match day during his breakthrough All-Ireland winning year in 1996.

'I used to eat a steak every morning, because Mick Lyons used to eat a steak every morning!' he reveals, laughing. 'Every Championship match that year I had a steak. It was a gesture from Kepak where we were all given steaks every Thursday night. As a young lad I used to love it.'

'I think it was before the Laois game ... the Leinster semi-final ... my father says, "You should eat one of them Sunday morning ... Mick Lyons used to eat one every morning of a match."'

'It was purely down to that.

'Just steak on a plate ... you weren't going to pack it with spuds or anything. It was just a superstition. So I used eat a steak about half nine in the morning, and then go to the County Club with the rest of the team! You'd go up then with Conor Martin who was living in Ballivor at the time. Barry Callaghan used to come in, Mark O'Reilly ... the bus used pick us up in Trim. Boylan used have a bus go around Meath bringing everyone up early in the morning. There'd be a bite there in the County Club ... but I never needed it!

'That's what I had for breakfast on the morning of the All-Ireland final.'

And Mick Lyons confirms that it was no tall story, his younger brother, Padraig and himself tucking good and early in the day.

'When we were playing football in the early days alright, that's what we did,' remembers Mick. 'Before we started getting good ... we definitely ate a steak then! Certainly when we were living at home. That was back in the '80s.

'Myself and Paraic. At home in Oldtown, in our home house ... just up the road. On a Sunday morning, for breakfast ... steak ... and there could be eggs with it. Anything at all!'

✦✦✦✦✦

It's still remarkable how close the bond between the two families now runs. Mick is godfather to Darren Fay's sister, Jamie. A regular guest on family occasions, including Jamie's wedding.

Mick and Jimmy are still good pals and it's little wonder either that Darren developed his own particular pre-match superstitions.

Seán Boylan tells a story about Jimmy Fay. For anyone not acquainted with Meath football, Boylan is the man who made it all happen in the modern era, a ball of positive energy who took on the job that nobody wanted on a caretaker basis and stayed for a golden era that spanned 23 years.

He leans forward in the chair in his home in Dunboyne where they come from all over the world to his herbal clinic, and mentions the landmark Centenary Cup win of 1984. 'I knew Jimmy really well. He won the Centenary with us. He had been there but wasn't there in my first year ... had drifted from it.

'Great fella. Had the superstition. First League match, if we won it, he'd never take the socks out of the bag. So you can imagine seven matches or seven months later, the smell of the socks! Lord Jaysus, will you stop!'

By 1999, Fay had started another post-Championship match ritual that most of his teammates probably never even noticed. 'At that time, as a release, I used never go training on the Tuesday afterwards. It was just a break. Because I used to get myself so riled up for Championship games. I couldn't talk to anyone two hours before a game and I couldn't talk to anyone for an hour after either ... until I brought myself back down. It was just a release for me then to miss the Tuesday ... to stay away.

'Seán Boylan knew. How many Championship matches do you play? And it was just that following Tuesday. It was five matches to win an All-Ireland back then.'

That cocoon that he enveloped in the build-up to match day, and on the big day itself, meant that he didn't fully connect to the sense of history in 1999, the result book-ending a storied half century since Paddy O'Brien played at full-back on the first Meath team to win an All-Ireland in 1949. .

But he knew that something special had been achieved. 'When we had our meals in Dalgan Park after training, Sean was always inviting members of the old Meath teams in,' explains Fay, 'so we were a bit aware of it. Just didn't really dwell on it.'

When Boylan stood down as Meath manager on August 31, 2005, he wrote a letter to his Dunboyne mentor, capturing the impact he had on his life. In the 15-page appendix of tributes at the back of Seán Boylan's autobiography 'The Will to Win', it's the first letter printed.

'It was only on Thursday evening, sitting out at the back of my house with my wife, Rhona, that I realised how much I owed you in life. I have a wonderful wife and two lovely kids, with another on the way. That certainly would not be the case had you not guided me so well or given me the opportunities that you did …

'For the first 19 years of my life I never had won a football accolade – not one. And then when I was 20 I won 'Young Footballer of the Year' and an All Star award, but most of all I had an All-Ireland medal … I matured overnight and was able to appreciate what we had achieved as a team …

'That new personality helped me to plan my life the way it is today, because before that I was arrogant, immature and disrespectful to myself and others and would not be mature enough to be married with kids today. I thank you so much for that …'

It was a poignant appreciation from a player who actually decided to bow out of inter-county football at the same time, the news only featuring in the fine print beside Boylan's decision to officially bring an era to a close.

But Fay would be back. Another chapter had still to be written.

CHAPTER 2

BEGINNINGS

For anyone growing up in Skryne, Father McManus Park was the field of dreams. Still is in fact.

'I defy anyone to be born in the parish of Skryne, as I was, and not be Gaelic football minded,' is how Paddy O'Brien evocatively puts it.

His father, Michael may never have played competitive football but instilled a deep-rooted passion for the game that caught hold of Paddy from the first time he 'knew what a football was'.

On his mother, Brigid's side there was form too. Two of her brothers, the Fays of Tullaghanstown, being well regarded members of their local team.

Skyrne village housed the Gaelic pitch, now Father McManus Park, with the O'Brien farm on the outskirts of the parish. And it was in a back field where any budding footballers used to gather for a kickabout.

The second eldest of eight children – sister, Carmel the only girl in the family to go with the long line of brothers Mikey, Seamus, Vincent, Cyril, Donal and Colm – O'Brien was born on February 24, 1925. The local national school fostered his love of the game, particularly his teacher, Brian Smyth who fanned the flames of his interest with tales of Tony Donnelly's exploits on the field for the Meath senior team.

School breaks became the place where they enacted out their dreams of wearing a county jersey and where O'Brien's natural talent came to the attention of Smyth, the schoolmaster.

'I was in his section of the school. He used to organise matches and he had me as one captain. We had to pick our teams before we'd go out to lunch. We went up to the football ground, across one field up towards the Hill of Skryne and we murdered one another for a half an hour.'

His feats in the schoolyard soon went beyond the boundary of the school gates. When Dublin came to play Meath in a juvenile game in Navan, three of the home team hailed from the Skryne school – Tom Browne, Mick Devine and O'Brien. That day he lined out in the very same position he would later make his senior Meath debut, midfield.

What put paid to any chances of lining out at minor level was the outbreak of World War II, when most inter-county competitions were disrupted or put on hold.

September 3, 1939.

The day Britain and France declared war on Germany after the latter's invasion of Poland and the day of the famous 'Thunder and Lightning' All-Ireland hurling final. Three weeks later, O'Brien made his first trip to Croke Park along with his first cousin, Micheál, to see Meath's senior footballers line out in only a second All-Ireland final.

'We cycled to Croke Park to most of the important matches, the Leinster finals or All-Ireland finals,' he explains.

Mattie Gilsenan scored a famous solo goal that day against Kerry but it wasn't enough.

'One thing I do remember especially about the '39 final. Kerry were given the benefit of a goal that never was. In fact, myself and Micheál were lined up with the Railway goal, from the corner of the Cusack Stand. The ball came down and the ball banged off the toes of goalie Hughie McEnroe.

'He was on the line and the ball shot out off his football boots, out the field. Play went on and the umpire pulled it back and said the goalie was over the line when it hit his boots. And that cost them the All-Ireland. They were beaten by two points by Kerry that day.'

The whole occasion made a big impression. 'Of course. I don't believe I ever thought I'd make it the way I did however.

'I had the pleasure of playing on a Meath team with Mattie Gilsenan before he retired. I don't know what it was in aid of but it was played in Virginia. Mattie was playing in his usual left half-forward spot. I was brought into the team. He was a wonderful man. We always kept in touch. He'd ring at least once a month.'

Sadly, in April 2013, Gilsenan would become another of his old teammates to pass away, fondly remembered as someone involved with Meath, whether on the field or part of management teams, through the decades.

Despite Ireland's neutrality, the country couldn't escape the pall that hung over Europe because of the war.

'It was a dangerous time. People were a bit scared. In fact, I remember one incident at school where a German plane crashed up near Skryne Castle and we all went up to view the damage that was done. I can't recall whether the pilot survived or not.'

O'Brien's brothers, Cyril and Seamus also represented Meath at different stages but it was his first cousin, Micheál and himself who were in it together from a long way out and who were to later form two-thirds of a famed Meath full-back line – Kevin McConnell the missing remaining member of the 'Old Firm'.

'Micheál lived on the same road. We trained together at home in our front field. Often there might be up to 100 young fellas kicking ball in that field every summer's evening.' With the disruption to football competitions, he spent his days bounding around the farm, vaulting ditches … 'even doing a bit of high-jumping' when the opportunity presented itself.

'When I was a young fella in my early teens and up to my late teens, I used to win all the sprints in the local sports, and sports all over the country. I won a lot of high jumps too in the local sports.

'I could always jump my own height, and that was supposed to be the same height as Our Lord … six foot one!'

He beams a wide smile as he delivers the last line, his son Garry pointing out that the 'Fosbury Flop' had yet to be popularised.

That ability to sail through the air would soon stand him in good stead on the football field.

After leaving school, Paddy O'Brien answered an advertisement in the paper looking for a full-time gardener. Interested in agriculture, he decided to check it out and ended up being posted to Wexford to tend a large residence.

'I went down to Wexford with my little bag on my back on the bus and I remember my mother crying when I was leaving,' he says. 'I was barely 18 at this stage.

'I only stayed 12 months but we did a great job with the gardens. I took six first prizes at the show in Enniscorthy that year with produce that I had grown.'

And he played a bit of football too into the bargain. Lined out for Ferns one day at centre-forward and scored four goals. And still lost.

Even at such a tender age, the strength of personality shines through in one story he tells.

'The parish we were living in was a place called Castledockrell, not far from Ferns. We used to go to Mass there on Sundays. I cycled in.

'We had been knocked out playing for Ferns so here I was, out on a limb again. I went around a crowd of young fellas outside the church … you know the way they'd be standing there, yapping … and I said, "Any of you fellas interested in playing football?"

'I told them who I was, that I'd like to start a team in the parish. So I did. Got fifteen fellas together and didn't we make a go of it in the same competition the following couple of Sundays. I was playing midfield. We were knocked out in the semi-final. I came back to Dublin then.'

Paddy ended up leaving his beloved Skryne for a permanent move to Dublin, club officials from the Sean McDermotts club paving the way. 'I had been approached by some of the Sean McDermotts officials to play for them. I came home from Wexford and had given myself time to decide what I was going to do.

'But the chairman of the club came down to the house in Skryne, persuaded me that he'd get me fixed up with a good job in Dublin if I'd come up and play for Sean McDermotts.

'So I did. And I never looked back.'

Worked various jobs, starting out with a bakery. Then bought a van and went out on his own selling confectionary wholesale. 'Travelled county

Meath from one end of it to the other,' he recalls with a smile. Called on all the shops at different times. And made a great success of that.

'I was going places I felt.'

Went on to open the first supermarket on the north side of the city, in Drumcondra, just down the road from Croke Park.

There was a good reason Sean McDermotts targeted him for a move to Dublin, to live and work. With Skryne, his first senior appearance came at the tender age of 16 and a half in 1942.

When the club won an epic county final against Parnells of Navan in 1944, O'Brien was corner-back. And encountered a player he would soldier long and successfully with for Meath, Frankie Byrne. He feels those games had a major knock-on effect in terms of the county team's fortunes.

And the three matches proved to be the springboard for him to make his mark with Meath.

The fact that the National League was in abeyance was a sign of the troubled times. Football continued on instead with a more parochial Leinster League, divided into four sections.

Group opponents, Louth had already been put to the sword in the first round game at Navan but were confident of turning the tables in the return encounter. This was a milestone day in O'Brien's career … his senior debut for the county.

While he quickly learned to take wearing the Meath jersey in his stride, little wonder his nerves were stretched as taut as a violin string on the road up to Dundalk. Sharing the car with him that day were the other players from around his area, Jackie May, Matt O'Toole and Tony Donnelly, and the trip was notable for one particular incident. Heading down Kilmoon Hill on the road to Drogheda, a black cat dashed across the road in front of the car. O'Brien was no bag of superstition but given the day that was in it, took it as an auspicious sign.

Little did O'Brien know that his career would merit serialisation in *The Irish Press* and his memories coalesce with Padraig Puirseal's later chronicle as he thumbs through the bound copy that first carried his story to a national audience.

'I said to the rest of the lads that this must be a good omen for me, but that cat must have meant to bring luck to my whole football career, and not to that particular day … for that first senior inter-county appearance of mine certainly did not set the furze ablaze on the Hill of Tara.'

When the ball was thrown in, he had Willie Halpenny for company as his midfield partner, with Sean Boyle of Louth his direct opponent.

The pair would square off on many future occasions but O'Brien felt the pressure of being a raw recruit. 'Right from the throw-in I was over-anxious and could do nothing right.'

And so the selectors shunted him around the field, trying to make this latest piece of the Meath jigsaw fit the overall puzzle. So he was moved from midfield to centre-forward, from centre-forward to wing-forward, from the wing to the corner and, finally, from the corner to full-forward.

On a day when teammates such as Frankie Byrne, Sean Ludlow, Tony Donnelly, Willie Snow, Peter McDermott, Paddy Meegan, and Willie Halpenny carried the fight to Louth, Meath were still in touch with time running out, trailing by three points.

And then O'Brien made a name for himself in the very last minute, scoring the goal to tie up the match, 2-4 to 1-7. The result meant victory in that section of the Leinster League, and that O'Brien would have a second chance the following Sunday in the final of the Three Counties League.

Once more, he struggled to make an impact on a day when he remembers the duel of two grizzled veterans taking centre-stage – big Tom O'Reilly at full-back for Cavan and Tommy 'Boiler' McGuinness at full-forward for Meath.

'Boiler', full-back on the 1939 team defeated by Kerry in the All-Ireland final, was making a comeback after a long lay-off with a broken leg. And while Meath ran out 3-9 to 1-8 victors, McGuinness decided to call time on his career after that outing in Virginia.

The upshot? O'Brien was handed the No. 14 shirt in a challenge against Derry the next week. This time luck went against him, a collision with an opposition defender forcing him to be carried from the field.

Anyone taking odds on the young Skryne man going on make the grade as full-back on the GAA's 'Team of the Century' would have got long odds indeed.

Thankfully for O'Brien, 'those Meath selectors showed plenty of patience where I was concerned.' In November 1944, Meath took on Louth once more in the final of the Cairns Cup in Drogheda. Once more, O'Brien was included, this time at midfield. To all intents and purposes, he felt like a gambler with one roll of the dice left before he was asked to leave the table.

With Paddy Meegan as his partner, it all began to click. 'I had what was described as an "inspired hour", and scored a goal into the bargain. We beat a good Louth fifteen by double scores, 4-4 to 2-2. I was a Meath "regular" from that on.'

✦ ✦ ✦ ✦ ✦

Jack Quinn doesn't hesitate in recalling his first memories of travelling to Croke Park to see Meath play.

The year?

1955. Two jousts with Dublin that would bookend Meath's first golden era.

The first came in the National League final in May when Meath, the All-Ireland champions, were made to look as if they had aged a decade in the months since capturing the Sam Maguire Cup. A match forever remembered as the day a swashbuckling, young Dublin full-forward by the name of Kevin Heffernan gave notice as to his talents, and hint at why he would go on to be regarded as an innovator, one of the game's thinkers, when he later turned to management.

Rather than sticking with the fashion of catch-and-kick, the St Vincent's player went walkabout, taking the 30 year-old O'Brien on a tour of duty far from his usual territory in front of goal. Rather than serve up the high ball that was meat and drink to 'Hands', Dublin worked the ball short and ran at the Meath defence in waves, targeting the legs of the full-back line. The Dublin forward line, and Heffernan ran amok.

A 12 years-old Jack Quinn was there to see it all unfold.

The man who Jack Quinn put up on a pedestal – O'Brien was his idol – was reduced to having feet of clay. When the sides met again in the Leinster final a matter of months later, it was like watching history repeat itself, Gaelic football's answer to Groundhog Day, with Heffernan again the focal point of a globetrotting attack.

'I'll never forget it,' says Quinn. 'We were sitting down in the Cusack Stand – my mother, God rest her, and myself beside her. At that time there was no dug-out underneath the Cusack Stand so the subs on the team were actually sitting with the crowd.

'A lot of the Meath team at the time had won two All-Irelands, were there 13 or 14 years, and were at the end of their days, including Paddy O'Brien. And the next thing Kevin McConnell came off. Sure he was hardly able to stand up … he was at the end of his years as well. And he sat down right beside me.

'You wouldn't see that nowadays!

'I never imagined I would get to know him so well because he became a selector during my time with the Meath team.

'Micheál O'Brien was missing that day. And he would have been a great corner-back. So that certainly didn't help because himself and Paddy were so used to playing with each other. They just met a smashing young Dublin team coming up. Every team has their day, I suppose.

'I used to say, "I'll revenge that!"'

It was O'Brien's last ever time to line out for Meath, an ill-fitting end to such a celebrated career. But Jack Quinn, still only a boy, had made that silent vow to himself.

And boy was he going to try and do his best to keep it.

Jack was the youngest of four Quinn sons who quickly inherited their father's passion for the game - daughters Gertie and Brenda completing the family line-up.

'His two great loves in life were farming and Gaelic football,' says Jack of his father, James who grew up in Kilbride before working for a time as a barman in Dublin, coincidentally in a pub called Quinns, in the Liberties. A flu epidemic that swept across Ireland had devastating consequences for the family. His brother, Martin died as a direct result - James too very nearly succumbed – so he moved back home to take over the running of the family farm.

And that's where the four sons grew up with a ball always near to hand.

Back then, Kilbride, one of the smallest parishes in Meath, had few football pretensions. Instead, it became famous during the 1960s and '70s for being home to 'The Riordans' – the chapel and local pub landmarks in the long-running RTE television series and its fictional county Kilkenny 'Leestown' setting.

It was the Quinns who played a large part in putting Kilbride on the map in football terms.

Martin, the eldest of the four sons, a granite-shouldered presence. Gerry, the quick-thinking forward who could conjure a score out of nothing or pick a pass out without looking. Jimmy, the wing-back, who they all agree 'coulda been a contender', but who was content to wear the club jersey. And Jack, the baby of the four, who would become a man with the Meath jersey on his back and would eventually be mentioned in the same breath as Paddy 'Hands' O'Brien in terms of celebrated full-backs.

To all of them, O'Brien held a special allure. 'I remember being in Jackie May's shop over in The Ward around 1951 or '52 as a young juvenile,' says Gerry, 'and going in to buy a pair of football boots. Jackie May was a great Meath footballer. Going in to his shop … and who came in only Paddy O'Brien.

'Jackie May introduced me to Paddy O'Brien and it was like meeting your hero. To shake hands with Paddy!

'So whatever size boots I was taking then, Jackie May of course must have winked at Paddy and Paddy picked the boots. He said, "These are the best boots – put those on. Oh they look well on you."

'At that age, to be meeting your hero. Coming home and telling everyone … "Paddy O'Brien picked these for me!" They were all heroes to us – Paddy Meegan, Brian Smyth, Christo Hand. They were legends. Sure … "the '49ers!"'

Jack was too young to remember the '49 final but Gerry can recall it vividly. 'Oh I remember '49. All of us listening on the radio. They became 'the 49ers' … great name! You'd think they were in the American Civil War!

'Meath beat Cavan … and all the shouting in the house! Straight out to the field then and we were all 'Paddy O'Briens' and 'Paddy Meegans' and 'Brian Smyths'. It was all radio then so they were all heroes. The publicity in the papers wouldn't have been as big at all. I was nine.

'I remember the excitement and everyone there saying, "Be quiet, be quiet … what's he saying?"

'The older people would talk about the match as if they were at it - "that was a great solo run… that was a bad pass' - just the same as people talk about it now on television. The parents and uncles and aunts were all excited so it went through the neighbourhood, the whole parish.'

No matter that there was little in the way of organised competition, not even a Kilbride team to tog out for. The boys found a way to hone their skills.

'There wasn't enough juvenile players to have a team,' explains Jack, 'so we used to go over and play a team called the Flat House. There was no actual football team – it's St Paul's now – but we called them the Flat House.

'Played them generally in seven or eight aside … in a local field. And they used play on our farm at home. That was going on every few weeks and it would be great craic. All unofficial.'

At times they were like football nomads in search of temporary home.

Jack played minor with Dunboyne and Kiltale before linking up together at adult level with Kilbride. '1960 was the real start for Kilbride when we won the Junior Championship,' says Jack. 'Two years later we won the Intermediate. Two years later again we won the Senior.'

At the heart of the meteoric rise of Kilbride were the four Quinn brothers.

It's hardly a coincidence that Meath's fortunes began to rise again right around the same time. Martin played minor for the county in 1956, Gerry in '58 and Jack, somewhat questionably, was overlooked in 1961, watching from the grass bank in Navan as Dublin squeezed past Meath, courtesy of a few scratchy goals. His omission looked even stranger when a year later he would line out at midfield on the Meath team to win a Junior All-Ireland, Gerry featuring in the full-forward line.

The very same Kevin McConnell, who plonked himself down beside Jack after being substituted in the 1955 Leinster final, was a senior selector with Meath.

By 1963, Jack joined Martin in the senior set-up before Gerry followed suit.

'When Kilbride won their first Junior Championship I think Jack was 16, 17 … in at corner-back,' explains Gerry. 'By the time we won the Intermediate in '62 he was dominating midfield. He just took off … became a great footballer almost overnight.'

'Martin was there a few years before me,' says Jack. 'He was full-back for years. He was probably a bit unlucky in that Meath went through a bad spell. From '54 to '64, Meath didn't win a Leinster title. And Martin was full-back not that long after Paddy O'Brien went. He was unlucky to be playing with a middling team because he was a smashing full-back.'

In the spring of 1963, Jack got his first big chance.

'Meath and Cavan played in a National League divisional play-off, to see who'd go into the final of the League. We played Cavan in Drogheda. I was a sub at the time, and Ray Carolan was dominating in the middle of the field.

'Now Ray's a great friend of mine … still is. I came in centre-field on Ray and had a right good game. From that moment on I never lost my place.

'That was the start of it.'

+ + + + +

It's not such a stretch to think that Mick Lyons' father, Paddy could have been part of the famous '49ers'.

Instead, that year, he actually lined out for Kildare *against* Meath in the first round of the Leinster senior football Championship. Lined out full-forward. Marking Paddy O'Brien. Imagine.

Back then, club and county boundaries were more blurred.

Where Mick lives now is just a matter of 100 yards down the road from the family home at Oldtown, at the back of Summerhill, a stone's throw from Kilcock and the Kildare border.

Growing up, his father went to school in Kilcock and played plenty of football in the county too.

'He played with Cappagh … that's just across there,' Mick says, pointing out the back window of his house. 'He played with Kilcock. Summerhill then as well. Back then, players moved around a lot. Sure you'd nearly play with two clubs in the one year.

'He played centre half-forward. If he'd played with Meath that year, he could have been on the panel to win the first All-Ireland.'

As for the idea of Mick ever thinking of following suit? 'Oh no ... I never went across the border! Martin McDonald used to do a bit of football in school,' which was Coole National School. 'I started playing then in Summerhill.'

One of Jack Quinn's contemporaries on the 1967 All-Ireland crew, Mattie Kerrigan, was a leading light when Lyons was coming up the ranks. 'Mattie Kerrigan was very big in Summerhill then. Huge. He was way ahead of his time. Go back to the early '70s – they won the Championship in '74, '75, '76 and '77 - Mattie had masseurs and everything at that time.

'He had a great way about him to, an air about him. If he said to do something, lads would believe him. Half of it mightn't be true ... but they'd follow him! That's all a good manager is half the time.'

Mick was the second eldest of five Lyons children. Along with sisters, Mary and Brenda, younger brother, Paraic and Terry, a couple of years younger again. Padraig remembers that Mick seemed to take pride of place when it came to travelling with his father to matches.

'I always remember, he'd be told to disappear. He'd go out the yard, across a field and my father would pick him up out the road. Because there would be a row if he was brought and the rest of us weren't. You'd be told he's gone up to the neighbours to get something. And you'd forget ... next thing he wouldn't be back for a couple of hours!'

Even then, the underage club scene was a bit haphazard. 'The first team I started playing with was under-14,' says Mick. 'You were lucky if you played two or three games. The next thing was under-16, then you went to minor.'

Rarely did he feature at full-back.

'You moved around everywhere.'

When he left Trim Technical School early to go on to start his own plant hire at the age of 18, he actually continued to play football for the school at the request of one of the teachers. Went back in to play and train every

Wednesday. He remembers seeing Mister Moran appear at the house one day and worried, "I hope they're not coming to take me back to class!"

A Meath minor in 1976, his raw-boned athleticism and fearlessness soon led to him to break onto a Summerhill senior side that had taken over Kilbride's mantle as the kingpins of senior football.

'A year playing corner-back, maybe two. Then a year or two at full-back. Then midfield all the way … with a brief spell at full-forward. A very brief one!'

The hearty laugh gives it away as an experiment that Summerhill would be loathe to repeat. 'I'd say they were looking for someone to win the ball inside. It wasn't a success. On all fronts!'

By 1979, he was drafted in to the Meath senior set-up, making his Championship debut in low key circumstances, a victory against Kilkenny that was farcically one-sided. At centre-back. Meath's stock was such at the time that the club held nearly as much allure.

'I wasn't that excited. Summerhill were going that well, all I wanted to do was play with the club. Because they were winning Championships. The training with Meath then was terrible. Terrible! Let's call a spade a spade. There was better organised training in the club in Summerhill.

'You'd go to Navan in the early days, well before Championship and there'd be 10 one night, 12 another, 15 a different night … different fellas. A week or two then before the Championship match … all in! It was certainly no better than club training. I'd say worse, actually.'

Still, there was always a certain allure to being a county footballer. 'Ah you'd like to be one alright. Once you start playing a sport you always look up and see how far it can take you.'

Even if it seemed, on certain Sundays, like the road to nowhere.

'Back then, playing for Meath, you wouldn't tell anyone. If you were out somewhere working, and someone said, "Do you play football?" you'd say, "Yeah, I play for Summerhill."

'You wouldn't be going highlighting that you were playing for Meath.'

Despite the tradition of Meath's All-Irelands? It must have been 15, 16 years since there was an All-Ireland won … 1967! That's a long time.

It would take Seán Boylan to shake it all up.

And one of his first acts was to drop Mick Lyons.

+ + + + +

The Fay name always seemed to be part of the furniture in Trim. Darren's grandfather, Paddy ran the hotel on the main street and the local chemist, and even the cinema as well passed through family hands. Later then, his father, Jimmy ran the Emmet Tavern before Darren made a brief venture into the pub trade, setting up the Willow Oaks pub on Emmet Street before realising the bar trade wasn't for him.

And the football bloodlines ran deep. One of the record scores put up in an All-Ireland final belonged to Jimmy's brother, Mickey who banged over 10 points in the 1970 decider, from all different angles. Upped sticks later and moved to London where he ran a bar for a spell.

A fresh-faced Jimmy was part of that Meath squad which happened to be captained by a certain Jack Quinn.

The eldest of four – brother Aaron and sisters, Janice and Kylie coming after him – Darren then, didn't lick it up off the ground.

The first memory that made an indelible impression was Meath's Centenary Cup win in 1984, Meath's first serious trophy under Seán Boylan. Dad, after all, had reinvented himself as a goalkeeper by that stage and Darren will never forget the buzz around the RDS where the post-match function was held.

'I don't remember the match because I would have been only eight at the time. When you're young, you don't pay too much attention to the matches. But I remember afterwards … Cork had won the centenary hurling and we had won the centenary football. And I remember running around getting a heap of autographs in my first autograph book.

'I kept it for years. Jimmy Barry-Murphy was in it, Bernard Flynn and Robbie O'Malley. Ford gave them keyrings and I came home with a bag of keyrings because I was robbing all the keyrings off the tables!'

Already, Mick Lyons was someone he looked up to, particularly being a familiar face about the place at home.

'My father was usually in goals and Mick was full-back. After the Meath games they used to go drinking in Trim, and come up to the house and have a feed afterwards. We'd be allowed stay up late on a Sunday night because the babysitter would be with us. Mick and Paraic Lyons would actually come in with my father.

'I remember it so well because they were always in together and they might be half cut, and there would be a bit of craic and we'd be allowed stay up late.'

Mick Lyons admits that the social aspect went hand-in-hand with the football back then. 'Ah sure, back then you could do that. After a match you'd go drinking ... everyone did. As we went on, we got different. You might have had a few drinks that evening, but that was it.

'I knew Darren as a kid alright from being up in the house. When he started playing football first I knew he was the real deal.'

Little did either realise then how much their lives would intersect.

'It's amazing actually,' says Fay. 'I remember being in a summer camp in 1984, over in St Pat's in Navan. It was like the Cúl Camps now. You stayed over there for a week.

'We got Meath jerseys. And we had the old transfers with them, the old iron-on transfers.

'I remember getting a Meath jersey at that summer camp and ironing on a number three, just because of Mick. I had three on my back going around. My brother had number five, I think he was a Padraig Finnerty fan. It's amazing how things pan out.

'I had No.3 on my back from eight years of age ... but I never played full-back. Say with under-14 teams and being 11 or 12, you might be stuck in corner-back. But I was never, ever full-back. The only central position I got then was centre-back. And then midfield. So it never dawned upon me that I would follow in Mick's footsteps.'

Still, with Lyons palling around with his father and a regular guest in the house, his senior career path was half ordained.

'My father was a huge influence on my career and so was Mick. When you have a legendary figure close to you, sure he'd have to be.

'When Mick was on the Meath team, and then winning the All-Irelands and so much else, you aspire to be like him. It's not even that I wanted to be a full-back; I just wanted to be like him.'

If the 1984 Centenary Cup filled an autograph book, the 1986 All-Ireland semi-final is another one of those days as a kid that he'll never forget.

Meath's big breakthrough in Leinster, throwing off the shackles in what proved to be an era-defining provincial final victory over Dublin, was followed by a shot at the greatest team the game has ever seen and a place in an All-Ireland semi-final.

Jimmy had drifted from the county scene by the time the big breakthrough came around but was still keeping goals in soccer.

'I remember going to the Kerry game,' explains Darren. 'My father was playing soccer with Trim Celtic in Dublin that morning.

'I remember the soccer match well. He was after getting knocked out in the goals. I was standing on the sideline and when he came too he was on the sideline as well! And he kept giving out to the referee. I was embarrassed then. But the referee sent him off the pitch ... or off the sideline, because he wouldn't stop abusing him!

'After the game, myself and my father and a few from the soccer team went to Croke Park for the big match. We were standing on the Canal End. I would have been 10. It was the first time Meath had won Leinster in my lifetime.

'When you'd see the Kerry team at that time, you just thought Meath weren't going to win.

'I remember going to the game and asking my dad, "Why didn't Meath win Leinster last year and they wouldn't have had to play Kerry?"'

Even for a rapt young Meath supporter, Mick O'Dwyer's team of all talents had gold dust sprinkled all over it.

Little did he know that the soap opera surrounding his father would be a precursor to the senior game. This time, it would be Mick Lyons who was dazed momentarily in a clash that would almost have been funny if the stakes weren't so serious. Denis 'Ogie' Moran thumped a ball in, and Joe Cassells and Mick Lyons went rushing back for the same ball as goalkeeper Mickey

McQuillan advanced to clear. Kerry forward Ger Power, who was meant to be the meat in the sandwich, stepped out of the way, to leave a three-man Meath pile-up, McQuillan clobbering Lyons as he tried to punch the ball.

'The one thing you remember about that game, because you were so far away, is "The Collision," says Darren. 'It's the only thing I remember clearly about the game. It gave Kerry a chance and Kerry didn't need a chance, not at that time.'

Ten years later, Fay would control the same square space as Lyons en route to All-Ireland glory.

It was always mapped out.

CHAPTER 3

PADDY 'HANDS' O'BRIEN

Winter, 1948.

Paddy O'Brien has long since established himself as a midfielder of renown since first breaking onto the Meath team in 1944 in that very same position. But a quirk of fate changed his career path as a Meath senior footballer and, arguably, the course of the county's footballing history.

A trip to Breffni Park to take on All-Ireland champions, Cavan in the National League was always going to represent a challenge ... that's without losing a car load of players along the way. When Meath gathered at the ground, Paddy Meegan, Willie Halpenny and veteran full-back, Matt O'Toole were nowhere to be found, along with several substitutes who had crammed into the car.

'It never reached its destination,' explains O'Brien as he recalls the confusion that reigned.

With the clock counting down to the throw-in, the SOS went out among the crowd – all told, Meath only had 14 players present and correct. Against the reigning All-Ireland champions.

'An army man, Lt Rooney from Carlanstown, who was among the spectators on the sideline, had to volunteer for duty to enable us to take the field at all. We had to make up fifteen. Sure he played in his stockinged feet. He hadn't come prepared to play!

'Sure the whole team was re-jigged. Fr Tully put me full-back as a temporary measure. I stayed there until I finally hung up my boots nearly seven years later!

In his *Irish Press* memoirs, he recalled the finer detail of a landmark day.

'To ensure I got a proper baptism of fire in my new position, I found myself playing on Peter Donohoe, then the most famed and feared full-forward in Ireland. But that black cat from Kilmoon Hill must have been working overtime, for Peter failed to get a score from play, even though Cavan beat us as they pleased, 3-10 to 0-3.

'When the game ended the late John Joe O'Reilly, who was not only the greatest centre half-back but the grandest sportsman of all - and many good sportsmen I have met on Gaelic fields – came over and congratulated me on my display.

'As we walked off together he discussed the Meath team, and, after allowing for our absentees, expressed the opinion that we would be "down" for many a year to come.

'Now I replied that there was good reason for it today, a carload of players didn't turn up. So we had a bit of an excuse anyway.

'Still, I suppose I had to agree with him, but the next few months were to prove just how wrong even the shrewd John Joe could be.'

O'Brien's swansong as a midfielder came on a Leinster side beaten after a replay by Munster in the Railway Cup final at Croke Park on St Patrick's Day 1949. 'So that day saw the departure from the Gaelic scene of Paddy O'Brien, midfielder, while Paddy O'Brien, full-back had yet to prove himself.'

And boy did he prove himself.

It took time to make a name for himself during the first part of his Meath career. After 1944 closed with O'Brien establishing himself as a regular on the Meath team at midfield, the mix of new blood and old had supporters thinking of a strong Championship run.

Back then, the rivalry with Louth had an added dimension all of its own. For the first round Leinster Championship match in Navan in 1945, it was somehow fitting that he made his Championship debut at midfield in the company of the player with whom he had spent his youth kicking a ball around, first cousin Micheál.

From a position where they were under pressure at half-time, trailing 2-5 to 1-4, Meath took over, the midfield dominance matched by the displays of Matt O'Toole and Tony Donnelly in defence and the brilliance of Peter McDermott, Frankie Byrne and Paddy Meegan in attack.

'That, I think, was the first time I received favourable mention in the Dublin "dailies", but my vanity was cooled by the fact that the Metropolitan scribes then, and for some time to come, always referred to me as "P. Brien."'

A 2-9 to 2-7 victory set up a clash with Dublin at Drogheda in what turned out to be an epic two-match saga, not quite on a level with 1991 but another series of games that took on a life of their own.

Six points up and cruising in the first match, Dublin's Mick Culhane rifled home two goals to force a replay.

The next day out, O'Brien remembers the performance given by the tall, fair-haired Johnny Gibbons of Parnells, and another see-saw battle ended level. In extra-time, Meath's superior stamina was the distinguishing feature and they ran away with it in the end, 2-16 to 1-10.

His direct opponent for most of the two games was Paddy Neville, though his replacement Batt McCarthy left a lasting impression when he came on late in the second game.

'Batt had barely arrived on the field when he gave me the heaviest fall I ever sustained in Croke Park. I was kicking the ball, just on the touch-line, when Batt crashed into me full force.

'I was travelling fairly hard myself at the time and landed in the second row sideline seats. Fortunately, the spectators broke my fall, otherwise my football career might have ended then and there.'

Whether it was tired legs or tired minds after the extended saga against Dublin, or whether Meath felt 'cocky' on the back of it, the following Sunday in the Leinster semi-final O'Brien admits they got the 'shock of our lives'.

And so his first Championship summer ended prematurely with a 1-8 to 0-5 defeat. There would be better days.

+ + + + +

The end of World War II restored a sense of hope and optimism across Europe, not to mention normality to everyday life in Ireland. One of the things peacetime signalled was a resumption of the National Football League.

Even now, memories of the first round game against Fermanagh in Enniskillen bring a smile to O'Brien's face. Heavy rain in the build-up to the match left the field a quagmire. With the players ankle deep in mud on the field, floodwater washed up to the edge of the pitch. But there was one other person involved that day who lent a certain air of comedy to the whole affair.

'There was a lake one side of the pitch. They actually had a fella on a boat out there when the ball went in ... it was his job to retrieve the ball.'

When Meath were awarded a penalty, O'Brien himself added another light element of farce to proceedings. 'I came up to take the kick but so soft was the surface at that particular spot that my foot stuck in the ground and I fell over the ball!'

It hardly mattered though as Meath coasted to victory, the performance of one Fermanagh player sticking with O'Brien. 'There was a great player, he was a banker here in Dublin afterwards, in College Green, Alf Breslin ... lovely fella. He was playing full-back for Fermanagh. I remember the length he was able to get with his kicks that day.

'I'll never forget the muck. When we came into the hotel afterwards it was a scramble to get to the bathrooms ... the dirt on the players. There were no showers then, it was baths ... or a bucket of water.'

So much mud was washed off the players that it clogged the pipes, threatening to flood the hotel for good measure.

'I enjoyed those days all the same,' he adds gently.

That National League campaign of 1945-46 was to prove a memorable one for Meath as the team began to show real promise, taking the scalp of All-Ireland finalists, Cavan en route to the final.

A date with reigning Leinster champions, Wexford in May of 1946 brought O'Brien up close with the celebrated figure of Nicky Rackard. While the third tier All-Ireland hurling Championship that is currently in place is named in honour of the famous Wexford man, back then his reputation was as a footballer of note, having lined out at full-forward in the Railway Cup final a matter of weeks before the League final.

'He played full-forward on me several times,' recalls O'Brien. 'He was a big fellow ... big and fit ... hard to master. I had great tussles on him. I didn't lose my place as a result of our first meeting – I remained full-back.'

Indeed Wexford's failure to score a goal in a hard-fought final was telling, Meath lifting only their second ever National League trophy on a scoreline of 2-2 to 0-6, 13 years after the only other success.

A truncated Championship campaign saw Meath actually beat Longford in the first round in the Leinster Championship before that League decider, and then crash out to their old nemesis Louth in the next round.

What made 1947 an iconic year in the history of the GAA was the decision taken at annual congress to play the All-Ireland final in New York, a decision 'to put fire under the heels of every footballer in Ireland'.

'I tell you, that made us tuck up our sleeves in Meath and make a silent vow ... that, when the time came to cross the Atlantic, we would be there or thereabouts.'

They were as good as their word.

A harsh winter played a part in Meath surrendering their National League title, forced to let it go by default when snow forced the abandonment of too many of their games, but the Leinster Championship was a different case, Wicklow dispatched with ease in the first round.

If the manner of the second run victory over Westmeath wasn't overly convincing, there were mitigating factors, two in particular. The timing of the Dublin Championship meant that Paddy O'Brien and Christo Hand were actually lining out the same day at Croke Park for Sean McDermotts in the Dublin county final.

O'Brien captained the team from midfield. How much he values his time playing football there and that landmark success is that the Sean McDermotts team photograph hangs proudly in his sitting room.

With both back in harness for Meath's next match, the nature of the rivalry at the time and the perception that Meath were a coming team led to a record crowd for a Leinster semi-final, almost 30,000 travelling to Croke

Park. A failure to translate possession into scores cost Meath in the first half, especially when Louth got a goal on the break to lead 1-2 to 0-4 at half time. 'Two more points for Louth on the restart made it look very much like "Farewell New York," as far as we were concerned.'

Not for the first time, the livewire presence of Frankie Byrne, just 5' 8" in height but bold and brave and a blue-chip free-taker to boot, hauled Meath back into contention. O'Brien too seemed to thrive when the stakes were highest and chipped in with a point, and Meath were ahead 0-9 to 1-4 by the finish, Byrne accounting for two-thirds of his county's total.

Yet another record crowd came to Croke Park to bear witness on a day when the Heavens opened. The pulling power of Tommy Murphy for reigning champions Laois – a 'genius' is how O'Brien describes a player who later joined O'Brien on the GAA's official 'Team of the Century' – played its own part.

'He was one of the most outstanding footballers I ever saw,' he admits. 'He was on a par with Paddy Kennedy of Kerry. A star centre-field player.'

Laois's efforts were backboned too by 'an amazing attempt by the great-hearted Bill Delaney to be in all parts of the field at once'. Apart from O'Brien, Meath had their own stars in Matt O'Toole, Tony Donnelly, Christo Hand, Victor Sherlock, Paddy Meegan, Peter McDermott and the irrepressible Frankie Byrne.

A late goal was of little consolation to Laois, Meath winning on a 3-7 to 1-7 scoreline.

For the first time since 1940, they were kings of Leinster.

'It was marvellous to be part of that team,' recalls O'Brien. 'We were making a name for ourselves during that period. Now we were in the All-Ireland semi-final, only one step away from those New York tickets and the sky-scrapers … and the Polo Grounds.'

A barrier to those precious flights across the Atlantic came in the predictable shape of Kerry, reigning All-Ireland champions.

To give an idea how much the pairing had captured the imagination of the public, the attendance hit record levels once more on a sun-splashed August Sunday at GAA headquarters. The raw recruit who was a bundle of nerves on his debut just three years earlier was now replaced by a man who relished the opportunity of pitting his wits against one of the aforementioned Kerry greats, Paddy Kennedy.

'I was picked to play on Paddy Kennedy and I was having a ball on him,' says O'Brien, who recalls that afternoon with mixed feelings even now. His opponent came into the game with an ankle injury and was involved in an incident that inadvertently changed the game.

'Anyway, he fell on me. He was a bit older than me now, coming to the end of his tether. He packed up and they brought in a sub who completely knocked me out of my stride.

'I was having a ball up to that. But this fella was put in not to play football at all, just to play me. Eddie Dowling … the very fella.' With O'Brien's influence subdued and Dowling and Teddy O'Connor tilting the balance of power Kerry's way, the Munster champions took over.

'Score after score went sailing between our posts, and with every score our vision of the skyscrapers grew fainter and fainter. The tally was 1-11 to 0-5 when the last whistle found us leg-weary and disappointed, and more dispirited than I remember any Meath team before or since.

'We wouldn't have been human if the combination of that crushing defeat and the shattering of our high hopes didn't cool our interest in football for a spell.'

♦♦♦♦♦

O'Brien headed up the Meath contingent on the Leinster Railway Cup team in 1948 but losing to Ulster did little to improve the general mood. When Louth – who else? – stripped Meath of their Leinster title in the semi-final, it was another blow.

For O'Brien, the match had a significance all of its own. 'This was my last Championship game as a midfielder and I chalked up a score that I am proud of yet. Half-time was at hand, and Louth, with the wind, were a point ahead and pressing hard.

'I got the ball near our own square and went away on a solo up the Cusack Stand side of the field. I was let travel unchallenged for a long, long way, but finally I was hemmed in near the touchline about 50 yards from the Louth goal.

'I tried a left-footed drop-kick and landed the leather on top of the net for a point. Level at half-time and with the wind in our favour in the second half, we must have looked odds-on, but out came Louth and beat us.'

It didn't stop him taking a keen interest in the rest of the provincial and All-Ireland race. Louth marched on to provincial title success and were unlucky to lose out to reigning champions, Cavan in the All-Ireland semi-final.

On the other side of the draw, Mayo's drubbing of Kerry set up an attractive pairing that drew a big crowd to Croke Park on All-Ireland final day.

'I was very anxious to see the game myself, but when I got to Croke Park I found to my dismay that the gates were closed and a huge crowd already packed inside. Now I had a particular interest in this match, for my midfield partner of 1947, Victor Sherlock, who had previously lived with relatives in Navan, had meantime returned to his native county and was now starring in the Breffni colours.'

Watch the highlights on the GAA 'Football Gold' series and it's possible to catch a glimpse of where O'Brien witnessed the game, from a vantage point that no ticket covered, sitting directly over the Railway End scoreboard on a bundle of grass that the local kids were charging sixpence to avail of.

'When I got to the top, the first thing I saw was Sherlock coming down the left wing in Croke Park under the Hogan Stand side and scoring a goal. And he was my understudy when I was playing with Meath.'

With a gale blowing down the field, the proverbial game of two halves unfolded. Cavan, spurred by Sherlock's goal raced ahead only for Mayo to turn the tables in the second half, aided by the elements.

And the match ended with a whiff of controversy, Padraic Carney's attempt at an equalising free saved by Mick Higgins. Whether the Cavan star rushed the kick is a topic to animate Mayo supporters of a certain generation right to this day.

Sherlock's mazy run and rifled left-foot goal was one of a picture reel of Cavan highlights.

All it did was leave O'Brien with a wistful sense of what might have been.

'Here was Paddy O'Brien, precariously perched on a bundle of grass on top of the Railway Wall, a mere gatecrasher at the All-Ireland final, while below on the greensward the brilliance of Victor Sherlock was thrilling the overflow crowd.

'At that particular moment my own prospects of ever winning an All-Ireland medal were anything but bright.'

Little did he know what 1949 would bring.

✦✦✦✦✦

Meath's Championship campaign in 1949 will always stand apart in the annals.

Putting one over the 'bogeymen' from Louth in the first round of the '98 Tournament added to the squad's confidence. 'This competition, though confined to the Leinster counties, aroused very keen competition, because the trophies, a set of miniature gold footballers must have been among the most beautiful ever awarded.'

The first round of the Leinster Championship took place at Croke Park as Meath faced Kildare. At full-forward for Kildare was one Paddy Lyons of Oldtown, Summerhill, whose career path had taken him the other side of the border that lay within a stone's throw of his house.

It's not hard to imagine that under different circumstances, he could easily have been lining out alongside O'Brien. An injury to Kildare's blue-chip forward, Pat 'Boiler' White forced him from the field at a crucial juncture and allowed Meath to power on to a 0-11 to 1-5 victory. The report in *The Meath Chronicle* referenced a save from goalkeeper, Kevin Smyth after a Lyons drive hit the crossbar! Frankie Byrne's frees were invaluable and Christo Hand was so good in the half-back line he was chaired off the field.

The next round against Wexford produced a game memorable for the remarkable difference in scoring. 'We couldn't score a goal and the Wexford boys couldn't score a point.'

With the Meath attack on song, the points flowed from all angles. The only problem was that every time a lead was built up … bang! Wexford found the back of the net. The final scoreboard could have been mounted in the GAA museum for its eccentricity.

Meath 0-14 Wexford 4-0.

O'Brien doesn't spare himself in the verdict. 'That's a crazy scoreline. They scored four goals on us. It was a very close game all through. Our backs were very poor that day to let all those goals in.'

He does himself a disservice. The writer in the *Chronicle* showered him with bouquets.

'Paddy O'Brien's brilliant clearances were another noteworthy feature of the game. Where high balls were concerned, his timing and judgement were beyond all praise. They were matched only by his courage. We are sorry now we did not keep a tally of the number of balls he fielded and cleared. The number can be very little short of a record.

'He won the greatest roar of all when his hands appeared above the crossbar to pull down a free at a vital stage. That was a memorable save on the part of the cleanest full-back in the country today or ever.'

That was the day he marked Nicky Rackard for the first time. 'Very powerful, but scrupulously fair. The burly Nicholas was a very hot handful on the football field.' The bould Rackard finished with a sizeable haul, not enough ultimately to sway the day.

If there was a forerunner to the epic four-match saga against Dublin in 1991, it came in the next round against Louth. The trilogy of games that unfolded only added to the mythology of Meath's campaign when the dust settled.

'On a bone-hard pitch they gave us the run-around for about 40 minutes,' is O'Brien's original recollection, and the team trailed worryingly at that stage by 1-5 to 0-3. Bit by bit, Meath hauled their opponents in. At one stage, they bundled the ball into the net. As confusion reigned, one Meath supporter dashed on to the pitch, grabbed the green flag and signalled a goal! After consulting with his umpires, the referee awarded a free out. In a nail-biting climax, Paddy Meegan hit the equalising point just before the full time whistle.

Part Two threw up another drama-filled afternoon. Seven points up and cruising in injury time, the game was won. Except somebody forgot to tell the Louth players. A Sean Boyle free was barely marked up before the same player stood over a '50' moments later.

'We Meath defenders set ourselves as the ball came sailing in, but forward Frankie Fegan codded the lot of us. He feinted as through to let the ball go by, and then, at the last moment, punched the leather to the net.'

Barely 30 seconds later, Boyle launched another free goalwards and it came dropping through the air with all the danger of a hand grenade with the pin already pulled.

'Half the Louth team came tearing in after the ball. There was a fierce melee on our goal-line, with the ball bobbing above us in a cloud of dust, for a further week of sunshine had made the pitch harder than ever.

'Eventually I secured the leather, but as I was forcing my way out to clear there was an ear-splitting roar from the crowd. I turned to see the green flag hoisted. The umpire had ruled that the ball was over the line when I got it.'

On the kick-out, the final whistle blew. Encroaching spectators in a state of high agitation made a beeline for the referee, one of whom had to be taken into custody by Gardai.

What happened next only heightened the sense of drama on the day.

'Considerable confusion followed. Though the referee left, both teams stayed on the field in expectation of extra time. After a while St Vincent's and Clanna Gael appeared to play in the Dublin final which was scheduled to follow our game.

'When the referee for that match, Simon Deignan, began to blow his whistle, we withdrew. Yet, no sooner had we reached our dressing room than we were told extra time must be played, so out we marched again.

'When we were half-way to midfield we discovered that the Vincent's and Clans teams were marching around the far end of the pitch behind the Artane Band. Simon Deignan was in lonely possession of the centre-line, while there was neither sight nor sound of our referee, nor of the Louth team.

'We marched on another 20 yards or so, to the cheers of our very faithful supporters, but cheers soon turned to laughter as the three teams converged on midfield, and we had no option but to turn back to our dressing room again, feeling annoyed and foolish.'

Except for one Meath player.

Along with the likes of Paddy O'Brien and Christo Hand who had put down roots in Dublin and played with Sean McDermotts, Frankie Byrne had switched from Navan to Clanna Gael.

So he went and lined out for a second time at Croke Park on the same day – with two different teams.

'I turn around … put a blue and white jersey on me … and off I go,' recalls Byrne. 'I was playing in my stockinged feet. My feet were all blistered.'

St Vincent's won easily in the end, what was the first in their unequalled succession of seven county Championship victories in succession.

As for Meath versus Louth, the third instalment followed the same course, nip and tuck throughout, Meath leading the way for much of the game only for Louth to rally and equalise right near the end.

The final few frantic passages of play went a long way to deciding the ultimate destiny of the Sam Maguire Cup. Meath's hero came in the shape of substitute, Paddy Connell whose booming kick from distance settled a series of games that would live long in the memory of those involved.

'Louth were always a very sticky team. A very hard team to beat,' recalls O'Brien.

Few expected a Leinster final against Westmeath, scheduled for the following Sunday, to match up.

As O'Brien says, it was 'something of an anti-climax. The occasion seemed too much for our western neighbours.' A 4-5 to 0-6 final scoreline tells its own story, Peter McDermott and Paddy Meegan doing their fair share of the damage up front.

Meath's six-game odyssey might have been the talk of Leinster but the shock of the decade came in Munster where Clare ambushed Kerry in the first round.

So at least the team that vanquished Meath in 1947 were out of the picture. Mayo though, were no less worthy opponents in the semi-final.

Bouncing back from the loss of the 1948 All-Ireland final to Cavan, they drove on from a National League title success, beating Louth in the decider, to cut a swathe through Connacht.

Just like the twist of fate that resulted in O'Brien's switch to full-back, circumstances conspired to see his first cousin, Micheál repositioned. Back after missing the latter stages of the Leinster campaign due to his dismissal in the second game against Louth, the selectors had a brainwave, shifting

Seamus Heery out to right half-back and repositioning Micheál O'Brien at corner-back, with No.2 on his back. Now the two men who had spent so much of their youth kicking a ball around together togged out within calling distance of each other. Kevin McConnell had also been switched from half-back to the other corner and had made the position his own.

Thus, the 'Old Firm' of Micheál O'Brien, Paddy O'Brien and Kevin McConnell began that August Sunday in 1949 at Croke Park. For six seasons, they would hold steady together.

'Time and time again the whole line was chosen en bloc for Leinster … and all three of us, though never all three together, wore the Irish jersey.'

They proved to be the rock that Mayo's ship foundered on, Paddy in particular going a long way that afternoon to establishing his reputation as one of the game's true greats.

'In all the games we played together after, I doubt if we ever had to face a fiercer barrage than we endured that first afternoon in Croke Park, when the flashing Mayo forwards came at us backed by sun and wind. Friends tell me that this was the best game I have ever played. All I know is that it was the busiest.

'Out in front our grand half-back line of Heery, Dixon and Hand were playing like demons. On each side of me, Micheál and Kevin were never idle, and never beaten. Behind me the eagle-eyed Kevin Smyth was busy as a bee between the posts. Yet the ball was always coming right back into our goalmouth as though someone behind the net had it held captive on a long piece of elastic.'

Padraic Carney spent the early part of that afternoon dropping high balls down into the square only for the Meath full-back line to repel wave after wave of Mayo attack. With no sniff of a goal chance, a lead of four points to no score was a source of frustration as much as anything else for the Connacht champions. And slowly Meath found a way into the game. Wing-forwards. Frankie Byrne and Paddy Meegan lifted the siege with some galloping solo runs up the field, and Peter McDermott, Brian Smyth and Matty McDonnell showed a remarkable economy of purpose up front.

Five points in quick succession hit Mayo like a burst of machine gun fire, leaving their confidence shot to pieces.

Meath turned then with an unlikely lead before the score that defined the match, the freakish manner of it another sucker blow to Mayo.

Matty McDonnell booted a ball high into the goalmouth and O'Brien explains what happened next.

'Mayo goalkeeper Tom Byrne, hesitated a moment, then dashed out and dived in an attempt to smother the ball as it fell. He missed, and had no chance to recover. Without a player near it the ball hopped on to the net … and hard though Mayo tried to make up the lee-way, the game was ours from that on.'

And the legend of the 'Old Firm' Meath full-back line was born.

Cavan provided the opposition in the final having seen off Cork and for all the quality attached to a team famous for winning the Polo Grounds final in 1947 against Kerry, Meath had no psychological hang-ups taking on their neighbours.

Recognising their shot at history, Meath went on a collective training camp for a fortnight at the Gaelic Hostel in Gibbstown, just north of Navan.

A forerunner to the training camps that that have become a staple of the modern game, it laid the foundations for what was to come.

Rare footage of the players being put through their paces by Father Tully is captured on the 'Football Gold' DVD as part of the highlights reel on the 1949 All-Ireland final.

O'Brien doesn't remember any cameras being present and watches on intrigued as the younger version of himself with a thick head of hair in the footage leads the team out in the sprints.

'There were chalets for the students in what was an Irish summer college,' he recalls, his eyes lighting up. 'We all had our own quarters … God, it was a great holiday!'

Everything was geared towards getting the players in the best shape for the big task ahead and O'Brien pays tribute to one man in particular.

'It was the first time we had collective training. We had the immense advantage of being put through our paces by Father Tully who played as big a part in the subsequent All-Ireland as any man on the field.

'He was very strict … he had us out early in the morning. We had breakfast first and then we'd be out on the training pitch at ten o'clock. Running … fast sprints … that sort of thing. We'd go for cross country runs in the afternoon … there was a lot of land out there.

'In the evening we'd go for road walks. Paul Russell of Kerry was a selector at the time and he would help out. Ted Meade was another coach. Mattie Gilsenan and Joey Loughran were also there to provide a world of useful tips and tutoring.'

And the secluded nature of the spot meant that there were few distractions in the evenings.

'We used to play table tennis in the compound. There was real tennis as well. It kept all the fella amused and out of harm's way in the build up to the All-Ireland. There was no such thing as drinking or anything like that. We'd get to bed early.'

At no point, says O'Brien, were the players weighed down by a sense of history.

'I don't think we were. We were just taking it in our stride. We were very fit and ready for it.' A trip to Butlins epitomised the sense of camaraderie.

In that fortnight of preparation, the final seeds for success were sown. By the time Sunday, September 25 rolled around, Meath were primed and ready.

Croke Park, Sunday, September 25, 1949.

A record crowd of almost 80,000 pack the stadium. 'Never before had such a crowd attended a sports fixture in Ireland,' proclaims Michael O'Hehir in the commentary box.

As the cameras pick up the former Taoiseach, Eamon de Valera along with the famous Irish-American promoter, John 'Kerry' O'Donnell in the stand, the Meath players wait nervously to run out.

'I remember sitting in the dressing-room and someone saying to me, "Paddy, if you don't stop running your hands back through your hair you'll be bald before ever the match starts."'

Cavan are chasing a three-in-a-row of All-Ireland titles and like a team with plenty of big day experience, settle quickly, leading to one nervous moment for O'Brien.

'Early on my immediate opponent, Peter Donohoe went ranging out to take part in a passing movement. I decided to let him go, and fell back to cover off the goal. Peter got the ball, and tried a fast snap-shot. With several forwards racing in I caught that

ball ... and dropped it! But the ever vigilant Micheál was in to lash the ball to safety, and all Meath drew breath again.'

Jim Kearney, recalled to midfield at the last moment, is well supported by Paddy Connell as Meath kick on after trailing by a point at half-time, 0-8 to 0-7.

Frankie Byrne has Simon Deignan chasing shadows until injury slows him but his free-taking is already a key factor. And from the moment Willie Halpenny sweeps the ball to the net after a great run by Paddy Meegan to push Meath five clear, there is no way back for Cavan.

Captain Brian Smyth, another hero on the day, lifts the Sam Maguire Cup. The first Meath man. And he makes history in another way. Not wanting to jinx the day, he never prepared a speech. And never utters a word on the podium, just parades the trophy.

'It was great. We were delighted having won the All-Ireland. The first breakthrough.'

Even now, the homecoming stands out. 'There were bonfires in every village. The first stop was Clonee. I remember the speech-making. It took us a long time to get home because you were stopping to wave to all the people. Dunshaughlin was black with people. It eventually finished in Navan.

'In my memory, as in the memory of every other Meathman of my time, those victory bonfires of 1949 will blaze for ever on every hill ... and in every town and village...'

As the National League resumed, the reception afforded Meath's history boys was still a sight to behold, the first home game against Kildare leading to chaotic scenes in Navan.

'So many thousands of our loyal supporters turned up to cheer us that the turnstiles couldn't admit them quickly enough and they came swarming over the walls in all directions!'

Meath's elevated status was confirmed with the Railway Cup selection. In a remarkable show of strength, over half the starting fifteen on the Leinster team to face Munster were Meath men. O'Brien at full-back was one of the eight who avenged the previous year's defeat by the same opposition in the competition.

'Frankie Byrne gave a particularly brilliant performance that day before the home-town fans.'

Hopes of a first Railway Cup medal though were dashed on St Patrick's Day, Ulster winning out convincingly. Suffering from injury, O'Brien watched on helplessly from the sideline.

The chance of an historic League and Championship double also went west later in the spring after Cavan gained a measure of revenge, the honeymooning Peter McDermott a notable absentee for Meath.

+ + + + +

A chance to defend their Leinster and All-Ireland crowns was all the motivation Meath needed going into the Championship. Wexford very nearly pulled the rug from under them though in the semi-final on a day when O'Brien says Rory Deane, later to become Father Rory Deane 'nearly beat us by himself' in what was his senior debut.

Meath squeezed through to meet Louth in the Leinster final.

'The odds against another draw must have been at least a million to one, but draw we did, though thousands of spectators maintained that … owing to an error by the referee … the full hour had not been played.'

In keeping with previous clashes, the game was full of drama and incident. With Frankie Byrne missing due to injury, Micheál O'Brien was pushed up from the full-back line to the forwards with Paddy Dixon slotting in at right full-back. But Louth stole in for two goals to lead by 2-2 to 0-6 at half-time.

And a second half in which Meath couldn't shake off Louth's gutsy challenge built to a nail-biting finale. This time Louth had the final say, the boot of Nicky Roe ending Meath's dream of back-to-back titles, his point right at the death breaking Meath hearts.

A sign of Louth's stature at the time came in the way they disposed of Kerry in the All-Ireland semi-final before Mayo deprived them at the final hurdle.

+ + + + +

Not for the first time, the carrot of a trip to America was dangled tantalisingly in front of the players. The Polo Grounds final of 1947 had already taken on a mythology all of its own and now the New York venue would host the

1950-51 National League final.

As O'Brien recalls, 'We were firmly resolved that we were going to see that Statue of Liberty this time'.

It didn't quite match up to a trip across the Atlantic, but Easter saw Meath travel to London where they beat Mayo in the Ward Cup. Six days later, Monaghan were put to the sword at Croke Park to set up a semi-final against Cavan.

Trailing by three points at half-time, Meath conceded a second goal before pulling down the shutters on the Cavan attack and coming storming back into the game. It was all level then with time almost up when Meath were awarded a free about 60 yards out. The distance meant the call went out to one man to take it, the player who spent his afternoon's booming kick-outs down the field.

'I raced up to the ball, determined to hit it as straight and hard as I could … and away it sailed straight between the Cavan posts for the clinching point!'

For the second year in succession, Meath faced the All-Ireland champions in the National League final. This time it happened to be Mayo who were forced to start without Padraic Carney.

With the half-back line of Seamie Heary, Connie Kelly and Christo Hand 'especially masterly', the forwards turned a good supply of ball into a 0-5 to 0-1 lead.

The loss of Hand after a collision with Micheál O'Brien upset the Meath rearguard and a couple of Mayo points meant that there was only two in it when Mayo were awarded a penalty.

'As I stood waiting for the kick to be taken, I couldn't help thinking "Here goes New York again." But Kevin Smyth stood, cool between the posts, cooler indeed than was the Mayo place-kicker. As one newspaper put it at the time, "Peter Solan shot without conviction, and Kevin Smyth saved without a qualm."

'The roar that greeted Kevin's save sounded the death-knell for Mayo's hopes, and, shortly before the end, Peter McDermott punched home a fine point to ensure that we would see the Statue of Liberty after all.'

New York, at last!

The trip though wasn't scheduled until that September, after the Championship, and 'with our New York seats booked, I'm afraid that we took the early games in the 1951 Championship rather casually,' scrambling past Dublin.

Games against Louth at that time inevitably took on a life of their own and incredibly, for the third year running, nothing separated the sides at the final whistle of their Leinster semi-final. Paddy Meegan and Brian Smyth popped up to provide match-defining cameos in the replay, scoring the late points to draw Meath level before the latter provided the coup de grace with the winner on the stroke of full-time.

Even the great Tommy Murphy could do little to halt an unstoppable Meath team in the Leinster final, ballooning a penalty over the bar, an incident that summed up Laois's day.

Meath's good form continued through to the All-Ireland semi-final where they were 10 points up before Antrim staged an onslaught for the final quarter.

Indeed, the game ended 2-6 to 1-7 with Meath clinging to their lead in the final frantic moments. A disputed goal added a note of controversy – Antrim being called back for a free – but O'Brien has his own view of the incident.

'Well, we in the Meath defence pulled-up when the whistle blew for that free. I can state pretty confidently, that, had the whistle not sounded when it did, that ball would never have reached our net.'

In a re-run of the National League final, Mayo again were the opponents in the All-Ireland final.

Croke Park, Sunday, September 23, 1951.

Meath prepare with the trip to New York looming in the background. The innoculations taken in the build-up leave some of the Meath players off colour.

In the 'Golden 49ers' jubilee book 50 years later, Seamus Heery revealed, 'Some of the lads were badly affected by the vaccination. My own arm turned septic and I was in terrible pain in the final. It was a big disappointment for me as I was captain of the team. To make matters worse I was unable to play in the League final in the Polo Grounds but the lads fared well without me.'

On the day, Mayo wear the white of Connacht, Meath the green of Leinster.

Seamus McFerran, vice-president of GAA is one of the escorts to the dignitaries at the start of match, the same man who later went on a singing tour in the United States such was his talent in front of a microphone.

At full-forward for Mayo is Tom Langan, Paddy O'Brien's clubmate with Sean McDermotts. When the 'Team of the Century' was unveiled all the years later, they would be selected in the full-back and full-forward slots.

Not long in, the Mayo man bangs in a goal. The Meath defence, under huge pressure, ships another blow, Joe Gilvarry firing in a second goal.

At half-time then, Mayo lead 2-3 to 0-8.

Midway through the second half, Meath's full-back takes a ball before being fouled. 'Up goes the mighty Paddy O'Brien,' says commentator Michael O'Hehir, 'He falls - but was he pushed?'

One of the stars for Mayo is wing-back Fr Peter Quinn, who puts in a sterling hour before heading to the Philippines on missionary work later in his career.

Clearly out of sorts, Meath only muster a point in the second half, to lose 2-8 to 0-9. O'Brien though has never sought to make excuses for the final scoreline.

'We had been inoculated a fortnight before, but I don't think "after effects" had anything to do with our display. What I do think hindered us was the excitement and anticipation of the trans-Atlantic trip, which prevented us from concentrating as we should have done on the All-Ireland. In any case, Mayo were very much our masters that day, and, God knows, they owed us that beating.'

Little did Mayo supporters think that their search for another All-Ireland would stretch into the new millennium.

✦ ✦ ✦ ✦ ✦

For a team that had just lost an All-Ireland final, there was no time for the usual maudlin inquest. Instead, the timing of the trip to New York lent a surreal air to it all.

Crowds turned out to cheer the players off, first in Meath, then in Dublin, as they set off on the first leg of their prized journey, barely 24 hours after losing an All-Ireland final!

Shannon was the first destination where Meath's footballers joined up with the Galway hurlers who had also earned a trans-Atlantic trip. 'After a magnificent "God speed" dinner, off we went on what was, for many of us, our first long-distance air trip.'

Long before the time of a six-hour direct flight, the 17-hour journey involved a touchdown at Gander in Newfoundland to refuel where players sent greeting cards back home just to put the word out that everything was going as planned.

What O'Brien recounts as a 'rip-roaring New York welcome' awaited at Idlewild Airport, now JFK, before the players made the last leg of the journey to the Henry Hudson Hotel.

New York, New York.

O'Brien felt like an explorer in pressing need of charting new territory. Rather than kick-back and relax, after a quick bite he set off with Paddy Dixon and Christo Hand to explore the bright lights of the big city.

Clearly, the word had gone out about the visiting Meath team and the trio bumped into an old friend from home who offered a chauffeured driven ride through the city and out into the country. So in they hopped, not knowing that their first tourist trip would be an unforgettable one.

'Away we went marvelling at everything we saw. We must have been 30 or 40 miles from the city centre, when, in explaining or pointing out something or other, our driver took his eye off the road, and crashed into a kerbside pillar!

'None of us was hurt, but the right front-wheel was completely shattered. As you are not allowed to leave a car stationary very long on those huge trunk roads, the owner dashed away to phone for assistance, and Paddy Dixon and I feverishly began to change the buckled wheel in an effort to get the car moving again.

'Meanwhile Christo gallantly took his stand at the rear of our stalled vehicle, and though scarcely an hour in the States, valiantly set about directing the traffic! He had his hand up stalling the traffic to let us get out over to the side.

'We were on the outside lane of the particular "turnpike", the land reserved for the fastest traffic. As Dixon and myself wrestled with that stubborn wheel, I expected to see all that was mortal of 'Christo' come flying over the roof at any moment, for cars were flashing past at anything up to 90 miles an hour.

'But Hand remained cool as a cucumber and kept us safe until the owner returned with a break-down truck just as we finished changing the wheel.'

Turns out the car was beyond repair. Off went the truck, car and owner, leaving the innocents abroad to navigate a way to a police hut down the road where they were told they would be looked after.

It took another breakdown truck to rescue them and drop them at the police hut. No surprise, the policeman on duty found the concept of a touring team from Ireland hard to grapple with … 'He had never heard of the Meath team … or of Gaelic football either'. More worryingly, he hadn't a clue as to the location of the Henry Hudson Hotel.

Eventually, a bus was ordered to collect the three Meath players 'who had quite enough New York adventure for one day'.

The month's tour was to live up to the players' expectations in every other way. Feted at every turn, the Irish-American community in New York pulled out all the stops.

None of the players forgot the true purpose of their visit. 'From the prestige viewpoint, victory meant a lot to us. We had lost that All-Ireland final just before coming over and only by beating New York and "rescuing" the Cup, which the exiles had captured in Croke Park the year before, could we retrieve Meath's reputation.'

And so, the following Sunday, New York and Meath met at the Polo Grounds.

Kerry star 'Gega' O'Connor, who lined out for his county in the Polo Grounds All-Ireland final three years earlier had since emigrated and was just one of the stars on show for an extremely talented home selection who powered into a double scores lead, 0-8 to 0-4.

It still didn't look good for the visitors who trailed with 10 minutes to go but a few familiar faces turned up the heat.

Frankie Byrne pointed two crucial frees, and then Matty McDonnell blazed through for a goal. For a player standing 5'8", Byrne was fearless, deciding that 'David' would have a shot at 'Goliath' at one stage in the second half, except instead of a sling-shot, Frankie had a football boot.

'The biggest man playing football at that time was Pat McAndrew. Big Dessie Taaffe lumbered into him and then I came across and blocked him,' recalls Byrne.

'Well, whatever he did, the next thing I'm getting up and I feel this pain across my back. The Meath jersey was like a sack cloth, thick and awfully woolly. And the temperature was in the nineties.

'I didn't even think. Just got up and ran and gave him a kick up his arse as hard as I could.

'I said to the referee, "That f**ker is a little bit big for me but if he goes on the ground again it's his head I'll kick!"'

Play on, waved the official.

Further points from Byrne and Des Taaffe, and Meath were National League champions. The Cup was going back to Ireland. With Galway's hurlers coming through as well, the double had been secured.

O'Brien was to carve out his reputation in stone against the hosts, his display earning the nickname that would last for life. 'Hands' O'Brien proclaimed the commentator 'Lefty' Devine.

Byrne kicked six points in another exhibition of scoring. But his cameo with McAndrew didn't go unnoticed.

'I'm in the bar afterwards drinking a 7-up and a Yank came up to me,' he tells, eyes shining as he relives it, donning the American accent to suit the part.

"Are you the little guy who kicked that big guy up the ass?"

'Yeah.'

'Let me buy you a drink.'

'I don't drink.'

'I don't mind staying in your company.'

'The next thing he says, "Put it there." And in his hand ... 10 dollars. He got such a kick out of it!'

Another player for New York, Bill Carlos, penned his own version of events.

'He was writing something for the *Irish Echo*. He wrote that they should have won it but for the departure of big Pat 10 minutes from time with concussion.

'So I waited around and I said, "I read your article Bill. It must be the first time in medical history that a fella got concussion for a kick in the arse!"

'So I got my own back. It was great!'

And he lets out a laugh that tells you he'd do the same all over again.

A trip to Boston then followed where Meath took on and beat a local selection by 4-8 to 2-6. Unfortunately for O'Brien, that's where he broke a finger. 'Boston proved every bit as hospitable as New York but Dixon, Hand and myself took good care that we didn't go on any long distance car-drives to view the country this time!

'I was sorry to say goodbye to New York, and it was a memorable experience to play in the Polo Grounds with its wild enthusiasm and its huge three-decker stands. But I think the happiest moment of the whole trip was the tumultuous reception we got from our own folk in Meath when we arrived home again, safe and sound, and with the League Cup carried aloft by our captain Paddy Meegan.'

+ + + + +

That injured finger took time to come right before a second knock forced O'Brien out of action as Meath progressed to a divisional final against Dublin in the National League.

And they paid little respect to Meath's tag of defending champions, a 1-9 to 0-2 scoreline suggesting a shift in the balance of power in Leinster.

'This was the first time we in Meath realised that the Dubliners had really "arrived",' he recalls.

It certainly focused minds for the Championship campaign when Meath turned the tables, before scrambling past Longford in the semi-final.

Louth - who else? – awaited in the Leinster final and 'again the game was as good as a heart test for the 50,000 spectators'. Meath trailed by a point at half time and the game-changing moment came when Brian Smyth cut through for a goal.

Still Louth came back, O'Brien and company in defence holding firm, until the final whistle blew with just a single point between the sides.

Roscommon had burned such a trail through Connacht that they were actually favourites going into the All-Ireland semi-final and played like they believed it.

'Their veteran midfielder, Eamonn Boland, who was living in Meath at that time, flew back from his honeymoon to play, and gave a classic exhibition.'

Meath fought a rear-guard action, a battle between the young legs of Roscommon and their experience. Under pressure around the middle, the switch of Paddy Connell out from full-forward helped give Meath a winning platform, holding out for another victory by the narrowest of margins. Just like 1949, Cavan awaited in the final.

Croke Park, Sunday, September 28, 1952.

Back to their old training haunt in Gibbstown they went to put the final touches to their preparations. But nothing could have prepared them to play in the monsoon-like conditions that broke across Dublin that September day.

'So bad was the weather that the minor game was not staged, and every player on the field must have felt as rain-swept and as miserable as I did while we waited for the throw-in.'

And Cavan had a plan to combat the aerial supremacy of the Meath full-back.

'I was soon up to my neck in trouble, for that was the first time I was really faced by the problem of the roving full-forward. Cavan had Tony Tighe on the mark. I would rank Tony with the fastest, cleverest and most dangerous forwards I have ever played against, and he was at his best that day.

'I had to make my choice between following him on his excursions outfield and staying "at home". Rightly or wrongly, I decided to follow him. It was a thankless task, but my two "old reliables" closed a lot of the avenues that Tony opened up. Even so, Tony streaked through for a goal and a couple of near misses.'

'That goal is a cracker,' particularly given the day that is in it.

On one occasion, Cavan's celebrated attacker Mick Higgins slips as he goes to take a free, the conditions making it a test of will as much as skill. That's why a piece of skill by Brian Smyth still stands the test of time, a brilliant chipped flick-up into his own hands at full flight showcasing his class.

Connie Kelly's authority at centre-back is key and the Meath forwards' scoring is a lesson in economy. Turning level and with the breeze now at their backs, the omens look good. Cavan snatch a goal but it stays nip and tuck right to the game's climax.

When Peter McDermott pounces for a goal roughly 10 minutes from the end, O'Brien says, 'I gave a sigh of relief for that looked like the decisive score.'

Instead, the final would be remembered for a 'wide that never was'.

Even now, over 50 years on, O'Brien gets animated by the memory of it, the series of events never before or since witnessed at Croke Park.

With Meath leading by a point, the clock is ticking down on the final few minutes when Tony Tighe launches a ball high into the wind. Seeing it tail off target, the umpire Micheal O'Rourke moves to signal it wide.

O'Brien, already thinking ahead, 'strolled past him in order to have a good run for the kick-out'.

His walk is checked by a 'thunderous roar' from the crowd. Turns out a huge gust of wind caught Tighe's kick before it hit the ground and brought it straight back into the hands of fellow forward, Edwin Carolan. He, in turn, spirals a kick on the breeze and this one turned and struck the upright and dropped over the bar. Level!

Tighe's original kick even fooled the match cameras who went to track the kick-out. 'Everyone, including our camera man, gives up on that ball,' intones Michael O'Hehir.

'A Kerryman was the umpire on the Nally Stand side,' explains O'Brien. 'He walked out and signalled the ball wide and we all stopped playing.

'Apparently, before the ball hit the ground – I didn't see this now because I was walking back in to the goals getting ready for the kick-out – the wind took the ball back into play.

'Next thing the ball came in and I could see it hitting the far upright and going in, and the umpire on that side raising his white flag. Notwithstanding the fact that the umpire on the other side had already signalled wide!

'It was wide … it just blew back into play. It was unbelievable. Sure I witnessed the umpire walking out and making this big signal wide.

'God I said, "What's going on here at all."'

The equalising point is allowed.

Piqued by a sense of injustice, and 'determined not to let the wind rob us of an All-Ireland in such remarkable fashion', O'Brien's kick-out is worked up the field. When the ball is blocked out for a '50', up goes the call to the Meath full-back to take it.

One kick for the All-Ireland?

Forty nine years before Stephen Cluxton jogged up the field to slot the winning point for Dublin against Kerry in the 2011 final, here comes O'Brien striding up with a chance to be a hero in similar circumstances.

On a heavy sod and with a rain-soaked ball, the elements again do much to undo Meath. O'Brien gives it a good thump but it tails off. 'It was a sorry sight,' sighs O'Brien.

As the ball is booted out, the final whistle sounds.

'It was the worst day's weather I ever togged out in. it was dreadful. Played in a storm.' That is the very day the three Maguire brothers line out on opposite sides. Brendan Maguire of Oldcastle puts in a serious shift at midfield for Meath, while Liam and Dessie Maguire backbone Cavan's challenge.

Brendan would later move to California where, more than 25 years later, he would be reunited with some old colleagues on Meath's tour of Australia and the world.

Ask Paddy O'Brien if 1952 was the one that got away and he answers, 'Oh absolutely ... we were really done out of that. When a ball is signalled wide ... That was a terrible robbery as far as I'm concerned.'

Croke Park, Sunday, October 12, 1952.

Whether or not it is a carry-over from seeing the chance of the county's second All-Ireland deprived in such bizarre circumstances, Meath never hit the same heights in the replay.

A low-scoring affair sees Cavan run out 0-9 to 0-5 winners. The free-taking of Mick Higgins plays an instrumental part, the player accounting for all but two of his team's scores.

For O'Brien and Meath, it's the one that got away.

✦ ✦ ✦ ✦ ✦

1953 was punctuated by various battles with an emerging Dublin team. First Meath 'regained heart – and some lost prestige' by putting one over their border rivals early in the League campaign at Navan. A place in the semi-finals beckoned then if a point could be secured against Louth, but their neighbours took great glee in winning comfortably.

A play-off against Dublin at Croke Park was the result. 'This time we were completely overrun by the smooth-moving Dublin machine,' 3-13 to 2-3 the final scoreline.

Still, the spring contained a milestone in O'Brien's career. On St Patrick's Day 1953 he lined out at full-back on the Leinster team that defeated Munster 2-9 to 0-6. Not only that, but the fabled 'Old Firm partnership' of Michael O'Brien, Paddy O'Brien and Kevin McConnell were selected en bloc that day, as they were in the two years following.

'I could now claim to have gained every major honour in the game.'

When Meath met Dublin in the Leinster Championship at Navan, the celebrated trio showed exactly why there wasn't a full-back line in Ireland to match. Dublin came with the swagger of National League champions, cock a hoop after crushing Cavan in the final.

Jim Reilly, Paddy Connell, Paddy Meegan and the recalled Frankie Byrne led the charge as the match first swung Dublin's way, then back to Meath.

In the final quarter, 'they fairly bombarded our goal' is how he remembers it. But the 'Old Firm' weren't for shifting.

A point separated the sides at the finish. Meath were like a seasoned boxer, taking a pummelling at times on the ropes but still able to get out of a tight corner.

Louth made light of Meath's fancied status in the semi-final. In a typical encounter of fine margins, they had the point to spare this time at the finish.

For the first time since 1948, Meath did not grace a Leinster final.

✦ ✦ ✦ ✦ ✦

By early 1954, the feeling that the team was in decline prevailed. O'Brien recalls a mood of pessimism when Mayo came to Navan for a National League game and were simply too good.

'Players, officials and spectators alike agreed, after that game, that Meath were down and out, and anyone who saw us in the first round of the Championship at Croke Park some four months later, must have gone away shaking their heads and expressing the view that ours was as lucky a victory as was ever recorded at GAA headquarters.'

It wasn't all down to luck though.

When the Sam Maguire Cup was being paraded in Navan later that September, it would be remembered that the odyssey truly began with the thumping right boot of Paddy O'Brien. In the '52 final against Cavan, the elements conspired to make his last ditch '50' to try and win the game all but an impossibility.

This time, Meath's full-back copper-fastened his legend.

With Gerry O'Reilly and Jim Rogers leading by example, Wicklow were two points up going into injury time and on the verge of a famous Championship victory. In keeping with the county's never-say-die mentality, Meath continued to press, earning not one but two successive '50s'. Up jogged O'Brien to launch both between the posts to tie the match. Inspired by their full-back's heroics, Meath then had the temerity to thieve the victory via a point from substitute Paddy Meegan.

'You wouldn't be thinking of winning the All-Ireland at that stage, struggling against Wicklow,' he admits.

But on such cameos All-Ireland are won.

And 1954 proved to be a milestone year for another reason - on April 24, Paddy married Kay O'Connell, at the Church of the Visitation of the Blessed Virgin Mary in Fairview.

They took off to France on honeymoon.

'We flew to Paris. Did a bit of travelling around France. Even got down to Lourdes.

'We were to be back on a certain date, got the train back to Paris, arrived at midnight. Got a taxi back to the hotel and the hotel wouldn't let us in because we should have been back the night before.

'So we went downtown at twelve o'clock at night, found a different hotel, a beautiful place, and stayed there. But our baggage was in the original hotel and we had to pay for the night we weren't there just to get it back. Spent two weeks over there.

'I remember coming back, getting off the plane at Dublin airport ... Sean McDermotts were playing a match at Croke Park. Of course I played for them. Some of the lads from the team, some of the officials, were waiting at the airport to meet us. I had to go down then and play the match. It was an evening match ... a Championship match.'

Kay knew the man she married.

Off she went with her new husband to Croke Park.

'Fella playing on you that evening ... a small fella,' recalls Kay. 'There was a Meath fella watching and he said, would you look at O'Brien patting him on the shoulder saying, "You poor little old innocent playing on me!" I thought it was so funny.'

After scraping past Wicklow, Longford provided a decent test in the Leinster semi-final, with Offaly the opposition in the final after ambushing a much-heralded Dublin outfit.

Like a pacemaker determined to run a race on his own terms, Meath hit the front early and kept driving on. Then Tom Duff fractured his leg in a collision and had to be carried from the field, a real slice of misfortune for a new player who had been flying it at midfield.

'Then there came a heart-warming roar from the crowd as Peter McDermott, donning that famous cap, came running on as a substitute.'

There must have been a few Meath supporters wondering if their eyes were deceiving them. 'The man with the cap' had officially retired from inter-county football. Not only that, he had made a transition from player to officialdom, having been appointed Meath county secretary some months before.

'Here he was back in harness … without quibble, when the need arose.

'Off McDermott went to his customary corner-forward position where he set up one goal and scored another to give Meath a match-defining lead.

'Peter had the experience in a tight corner like that,' explains O'Brien.

A sign of how it was Meath's day? Goalkeeper Patsy McGearty saved Paddy Casey's drilled penalty.

The All-Ireland semi-final pitted Meath against Cavan. Both sides had introduced new blood since the 1952 final and the Leinster champions' selection now included the likes of Kevin Lenehan, Ned Durnin, Michael Grace and Tom Moriarty.

Tom O'Brien partnered Paddy O'Connell at midfield, and Peter McDermott kept his place at corner-forward, now captaining the team as a representative of county champions, Navan.

A low-scoring first half saw Cavan go 0-4 to 0-1 clear before Brian Smyth 'waltzed through for one of those inimitable and invaluable surprise goals of his' to stun the opposition. As the match reached end-game, Meath clung to a one-point lead and O'Brien injured himself in making a last ditch intervention.

Out went the ball, only for a free in to be awarded to Cavan for a foul. Brian Gallagher stepped up to take it. Around 30 metres out on the right, it looked well within his compass. With three frees under Gallagher's belt already, O'Brien's mind was already drifting to a replay as he underwent running repairs from the sideline. In a denouement that carried echoes of the drawn '52 final, this kick too failed to hit its target.

Meath were back in the All-Ireland final.

Croke Park, Sunday, September 26, 1954.

Frankie Byrne also could have been the one to lift the Sam Maguire Cup. Navan O'Mahonys were crowned county champions meaning that either Peter McDermott or himself would normally be in line to captain Meath. But both retired that winter.

Now, McDermott had answered his county's call and Byrne too suddenly found himself thrust back into the frame, from a position where both were involved in picking the team.

'I retired but, like Peter, I'm a member of the selection committee,' Byrne remembers. 'Then in the Leinster final, one of our players breaks his collarbone. So now there's a problem for the All-Ireland semi-final. Someone has to go into training. So in I go.'

When it comes to the final, he is right in the mix. 'There was talk that Michael Grace would have to go midfield and I was to go right half-forward. So I train like hell for the final and I'm first sub. But for the first time in history that I can remember there was no substitution on the Kerry or Meath teams.'

'The team who led the way for the first All-Ireland was on the wane at that stage,' says O'Brien candidly. Eight of the famous '49ers' are still on the go and O'Brien is one of six survivors from the team well beaten by Kerry in the 1947 semi-final.

The fact that Kerry are chasing back-to-back titles says it all about their status and ambition.

And Gibbstown isn't an option for Meath in the build-up.

'This was the first year that the ban on full-time training came into effect. The Kerry mentors had no hope at all of getting their widely scattered side together and some of our fellows felt we should steal a march on them by meeting each evening at Navan.

'But, to tell the truth, none of us felt like doing any training at all. We did gather at Páirc Tailteann once or twice. But I'm hardly betraying any secrets when I reveal

that our only spell of organised "training" lasted less than five minutes, and was put on solely for the benefit of an Irish Press photographer!'

'Our trainer, Father Tully, rightly believed that rest, rather than work, was what we needed but to keep our hand in, and our feet as well, we played Louth on two successive Sundays before the All-Ireland ... and Louth beat us sick each time.

'So, though we had often been outsiders before, even some of our most faithful followers began to shake their heads every time they dared think of what Kerry were going to do to us.'

It's hard not to believe the smoke signals from the ashes of those defeats didn't carry on the wind to Kerry. The champions must have been rubbing their hands with glee.'

Typical Louth to rain on Meath's parade.

Nothing about the build-up is mundane. O'Brien's nuptials back in the spring didn't quite equal the drama of another teammate.

'Paddy Meegan got married and departed for the south on his honeymoon, leaving us the cheery assurance that we'd see him in the Croke Park dressing room at match-time.'

Just to add another note of tension to the mix, O'Brien develops a nasty boil or carbuncle on the back of his neck a few days before the game. Laying him low.

'The infection quickly spread and, by Thursday, there I was in bed, chock full of penicillin. I couldn't care less about all the All-Ireland medals that were ever made.

'I was still so ill on Friday that the folk who came to see me, and they were many, went away convinced that, if Paddy O'Brien was well enough to be allowed out to see the match, he'd be a lucky man.

'The funny part of it was that, on Saturday morning, I woke up feeling in the pink and when the teams marched around Croke Park on Sunday afternoon, there was I in the midst of them, with a fine fat bandage around my neck. And there too, was Paddy Meegan, who, true to his promise, had arrived back dead on schedule.'

In Hollywood, scriptwriters have been fired for less outlandish plots.

And the real drama is only beginning ....

The way O'Brien looks at it, 'We Meath lads had nothing at all to lose. Kerry looked a certainty to beat us any way, so we went on to that field determined to do the best we could for as long as we could.'

Kerry line out in the blue of Munster; Meath the green of Leinster.

Facing into the breeze, O'Brien, with Micheál O'Brien and Kevin McConnell *flanking him, felt like three frontline troops waiting for the heavy shelling. Except it never materialises. With every passing moment, the truth seeps into O'Brien's brain. 'I suspected Kerry were not nearly the force we had expected them to be. The Kerry forwards were getting plenty of ball, but with the exception of an occasional flash from Tadhg Lyne, and some testing centres from Paudie Sheehy, there wasn't very much sting in their attack.'*

Honeymooner Meegan is at the heart of the action. Married life is certainly sitting well with the Meath forward who is in the form of his life, flighting over points from an array of angles.

O'Brien remembers thinking, 'If we could hold them till half time, we have it.'

Just at that same moment, Paudie Sheehy launched in a high ball from the right. 'I got to the leather all right, but it went off the tips of my fingers.'

John Joe Sheehan is there ready to pounce.

Goal!

Quick-fire points from Tadhg Lyne were like further sucker punches and suddenly one behind, Meath regrouped in the half-time dressing room.

One more heart-in-the-mouth incident is still to come though. 'Patsy McGearty, who, all through, played brilliantly in goal, fisted out a hot shot from a Kingdom forward early in the second half, only to see the ball rebound off Kevin Lenehan, who was tearing back to his aid. With unbelievable agility, McGearty just got across to save again by the far post, but, from that on we had not many uneasy moments.

'Seven years before I had galloped vainly all round midfield while Kerry hammered home point after point to shatter our New York hopes. Now I could stand at my ease in front of the Canal goal watching Brian Smyth, Paddy Meegan, Michael Grace and Matty McDonnell send ball after ball sailing towards the Kerry posts.'

There is even time for an amusing aside involving referee Simon Deignan, again captured in O'Brien's original memoir. 'He was following the play very closely, and was racing up around midfield in the midst of a Kerry movement when from a mis-directed pass, the ball landed right into his arms.

'For a moment it seemed as though Simon was going to catch and kick – under the mistaken impression that he was among his own Cavan men again. But, in a flash, he tooted his whistle, hopped the ball, and play was on again.'

The Meath players could afford to smile.

'Meath's Paddy O'Brien, playing the game of his life, fields well' declares Michael

O'Hehir at one stage in the match commentary.

Peter McDermott then plays in Tom Moriarty who picks his spot in the Kerry goal as Meath simply take over. A punched effort over the bar from captain McDermott puts Meath into an unassailable position with the clock counting down.

Cue delirium at the final whistle ... Peter McDermott making a point as he raises the Sam Maguire Cup.

'"To beat Kerry in a final is as good as winning two All-Irelands," said Peter as he accepted the trophy, but to those of us who remembered our defeats by the same sporting opponents in 1939 and '47, that 1954 victory counted the same as winning three!'

Before the players returned to the dressing room, the 'Old Firm' full-back line are pulled aside by some amateur photographers.

The reason? A picture of 'our last time in togs'.

On the day that is in it, the much-vaunted trio pose for posterity.

'Fantastic ... to beat them so convincingly. They were favourites of course to win. That was one of my best games even though it was doubtful whether I was going to play with my neck.'

That is the day Paddy 'Hands' O'Brien also made the famous one-handed catch, rising above the crowd to pluck down the ball in spectacular fashion.

To line out with a big bandage around his neck only increases the size of O'Brien's legendary status.

'I made a rapid recovery in the finish I suppose.'

As for the big bandage worn around his neck? 'It didn't stop you from getting up in the air!' he answers with a devilish smile.

Peter McDermott decided that nothing could match the manner of his comeback and turn as All-Ireland winning captain, and promptly retired a second time. Paddy Meegan followed him.

But with the League campaign of 1954-55 starting up even as the celebrations continued, O'Brien found himself carried along, 'turning out again, largely, I suppose, from force of habit.'

One Dublin man in particular tried to get him to break that habit.

He could have walked away then; indeed he should have walked away then. Instead, he felt the same pull of the jersey that so many have found hard to resist.

'I found, and I'm sure most players will agree, that it's not at all easy to bid farewell lightly to the game you love … at least not until you are convinced that your days in the top class are over.'

So the good ship Meath sailed on with him still on board.

A chance to cut Mayo, just back from New York, down to size, then meant that a trip to Castlebar couldn't be missed. Humbling the hosts didn't go unnoticed as the 'Old Firm' – along with goalkeeper Patsy McGearty – were all selected for Leinster for the Railway Cup. Just to top it all, O'Brien filled the role of captain. And history beckoned as on St Patrick's Day 1955, Leinster captured the trophy for a fourth successive year, a record that still stands to this day.

To the less discerning supporter, the bandwagon was still rolling along nicely, Meath doing enough to set up a League final meeting with Dublin. O'Brien though, was beginning to heed the warning signs.

'Owing to business calls I had no hope of keeping up to the standard of fitness on which I had long prided myself. And, at this stage, I could notice … what nobody else but our own midfielders and half-backs seemed to discern, that my goal kicks were getting shorter and shorter in every match.

'In addition, when I did make mistakes now, I had a feeling that Kevin and Micheál were not as quick as of yore to repair the damage, and that, behind us, Patsy McGearty was seeing more and more action in every game we played.'

The National League final - and subsequent Leinster final rematch – were to book-end an era for Meath football. In the first of those encounters, Kevin Heffernan lined out nominally at full-forward but Dublin had no intention of banging high balls in on top of his marker 'Hands'. Instead, the St Vincent's man had licence to roam out the field, tempting his older adversary from that comfort zone around the square.

'And what a day out he had!' admits O'Brien. 'He ran riot.' And so the roving full-forward was born. Not for the first time, the cerebral St Vincent's man would look to reshape the game in tactical terms.

'Sometimes they shot points from far out; sometimes they came racing in, three or four together, in criss-cross passing movements. I have often since been asked why I did not follow Kevin out that day? The answer is quite simple … I had not the speed to do so.

'Rightly or wrongly, I thought it better to stay put on the square and do what I could in that position. Dublin scored two goals and twelve points. Had I tried to go chasing outfield after the fleet-footed Heffernan I felt the score might well have been twelve goals and two points.'

With Ollie Freaney, Des Ferguson, Cathal O'Leary and Johnny Boyle all on top of their game, Dublin took great pleasure in taking apart the All-Ireland champions.

On a personal note, the day was to end on an even more disappointing fashion as injury forced him from the field. 'The game was all over bar the shouting, when 10 minutes or so from the end, I had to retire with a ricked back, leaving an able deputy, young Jim Ryan to take over instead. I stress this fact of the back injury, which made it very painful even to walk, because many people chose to believe I left the field that day just because I was being beaten.'

On the field, he always had the stomach for battle. To suggest otherwise was, in a way, the ultimate insult.

'I opted to go off. There was something wrong with my leg, and I was suffering from my back. The Meath officials were all in a bunch on the sideline, sitting on the benches, I was calling them over to give me a hand around to take me off.'

To no avail.

'They thought all he wanted was attention,' explains Kay.

'I shouldn't have played at all. I knelt down at the goalpost and I was beckoning Jack Fitzgerald or Father Tully or the officials sitting on the bench. I was looking for support to get me back around the pitch but, by God … I got such a doing from the Dubs. I had to walk around in front of the Dubs in Hill 16 and they gave me such a bashing. They hated Meath. Meath had beaten Dublin so often.

Kay adds, 'I was in a flat with my friends in Richmond and I know when you were going around some of the Dubs were saying, "Ohhh, we'll get you tonight in Richmond Road. We'll dip you in the Tolka."'

'I ignored them completely,' says Paddy. 'Meath were out of the game long before that. It was finished for that Meath team. They had been played out.'

That back injury – first picked up in the first round of the 1951 Championship against Dublin in Drogheda - still troubles him to this day. 'I remember it well. Lord have mercy on the fella I was playing on, Terry Jennings ... he played for Dublin full-forward on me. The two of us went up for a ball in the square and I got up very, very high - I over-balanced myself on his shoulder believe it or not. When I came down off his shoulder I crashed my spine against the butt of the goalpost.

'In those years there was no such thing as physio or doctor to look after the injured. I was 10 minutes recovering. I played on would you believe ... when I shouldn't have. And I still suffer from that today.

'My biggest problem today is my back.

'Even now, my left side in particular, I can't get down to lace my shoes. I've been suffering from it ever since. It's a struggle ... all from that fall.'

And yet the prospect of defending Leinster and All-Ireland titles seemed to re-invigorate Meath. Even without hitting top form, the champions found a way to scrape through against Kildare – by a point in extra time in a replay – and then stumble past the challenge of Westmeath.

Never mind the National League final posturing, this time it would be different against Dublin ... at least that's what the Meath players told themselves as they walked out. Instead, it was another rout.

'That day, we were up against the fastest and fittest team Croke Park saw in 1955.' That's O'Brien's view, despite the fact that Kerry would go on to ambush Dublin in the All-Ireland final.

During the lightning pace of the first 10 minutes when Meath held their own, staying tight to Heffernan was like trying to catch a hold of quicksilver.

'Once our early dash faded we were fighting a hopeless battle. Twice inside five minutes Kevin Heffernan fairly flashed past me to score terrific goals, and that started the debacle which only ended when we retired, stripped of our All-Ireland and provincial crowns and beaten by the biggest margin ever recorded in Leinster final.'

Dublin 5-12 Meath 0-7.

If only he had taken the advice of that amateur photographer on the field moments after the final whistle of the '54 final.

A slight factor in mitigation was the absence of Micheál O'Brien, but Paddy was big enough to describe the unvarnished truth: 'He was missed but one man or even more, would have made little difference. We were whacked by a great Dublin team at its peak of perfection, and I, for one, see no disgrace in that.

'That was the finish for me. I was determined never to put on a Meath jersey again after that. I felt I was past it. I'd given them what? From '44 through til '55.'

Watching on from a prime position in the stand that afternoon was a young Jack Quinn, the biggest thrill of the day coming when Kevin McConnell was taken off and actually sat down in the seat beside him where the Meath substitutes gathered. In his own head, he was already thinking of how he would avenge the hurt if he ever got the chance.

In an era when full-backs had a licence to throw their weight around, O'Brien lived by his own code. The consummate ball player, he is proud to proclaim, 'I never hurt anyone in my life playing football.'

To those who asked him why he didn't resort to more unconventional marking techniques where Heffernan was concerned – in other words, why he didn't try to blackguard him – he answers, 'That wasn't part of my game at all. I never hit anyone either directly or indirectly. I never intentionally went out to hurt anyone playing the game.'

That principle was important to him.

'It was. Absolutely.

'Again the question was asked why I didn't "stop"' Kevin Heffernan that day, when, as one fan put it … 'he was making a show of you".

'I couldn't "stop" him within the rules of the game, and, if I couldn't, I wasn't going to "stop" him any other way. I had known Kevin Heffernan as an opponent and a Leinster colleague for six or seven years.

Why should I, just because my own career was ending, have to resort to pulling down or tripping, or even more robust and unsporting action to "stop" him and thus "make a show" of myself?

'In my day, I had "made a show" of my own share of full-forwards and none of them had taken drastic action as a result. When a full-forward "made a show" of me for a change, the only thing I could do was my best, inadequate though that best may have been for the occasion.

'To my way of thinking there could never be any shame in being beaten by a better man. It would have been shameful, and very shameful, if I couldn't take that beating.'

That's why his legacy remains pure and untainted.

'Wending my way through a jubilant Dublin crowd to the dressing room on that glorious July afternoon, I sadly realised I had come at last to the end of the road that had begun on Kilmoon Hill a dozen years before. It was time … high time, to hand on the torch to the younger men who have, God knows, proved well worthy to bear it.

'But that day of disaster provided one bright moment. A Dublin supporter, whom I knew by sight, but not by name, approached me as I left the field. More than once in the past he had loudly let me know that he was no admirer of mine, but he stopped me now, and to my surprise, shook my hand. "I'll say this for you, O'Brien," he said, "win or lose, you always acted the man."

'I couldn't ask for any finer epitaph to my football career!'

And yet, it's a nod to his magnanimous nature that a photo of the Dublin team of 1955, the team that ended his career, hangs from the wall in his living room. If sport can be said to reveal character, well then that was a day he stood tall, stayed true to his beliefs of a lifetime.

CHAPTER 4

JACK QUINN

Playing full-back on the Meath team that won the Junior All-Ireland in 1962 provided the launching pad for Jack Quinn's senior career. Never mind the aberration of being over-looked as a county minor the previous year, by the spring of 1963 his talent was such that he was an automatic starter by the time the Championship came around.

If Meath's rivalry with Dublin began in earnest during O'Brien's latter years, Jack Quinn's career too would be defined in so many ways by Dublin.

As a Kilbride man living within a few fields of the county boundary line, there was a heightened dimension on a personal level. Sure his father, Martin used to run Quinn's pub in the Liberties before moving back home to take up the running of the family farm.

June 2, 1963.

Meath versus Dublin in the quarter-final of the Leinster Championship. Another day for the annals ... and the Quinns at the heart of the battle.

Martin, full-back, a 'thou shalt not pass' presence on the edge of the square. Jack, centre-field, slugging it out with the inimitable Des Foley, Dublin's blonde-haired talisman.

It was Jack's first Championship start after making his Croke Park bow in the League semi-final against Kerry a matter of weeks before, when he made hay in the absence of the legendary Mick O'Connell. *'A new star was born at midfield,'* declared *The Meath Chronicle.*

But despite a blistering opening half against Dublin, his return to Jones' Road wasn't a happy one.

'They robbed us,' says Martin, bullishly. 'Well, they didn't rob us ... but the referee robbed us! He gave Dublin a penalty just before half time when it should have been a free out.

'John Timmons, the Lord have mercy on us, laughed at me. "Ah Jaysus now ... you wouldn't begrudge us a score?" Dublin got nary a score at all before that.'

Jack agrees that it was a dubious call. 'It was a shocking decision. John Timmons got the ball and did nothing bar charge at Martin. It was a blatant free out.'

Timmons himself stuck the ball in the net to give Dublin some sort of a lifeline, their only other score against the breeze coming from a free. So Meath lead 2-5 to 1-1 at the break and looked to be well on their way.

Jack announced himself as a force to be reckoned with in that half, dispossessing Des Foley no less at one stage and racing through to drive a rasper to the net from fully 25 yards. An opportunistic goal from John Nallen just before the break helped them into that seven-point lead.

'And they came out in the second half and they switched the whole team around,' recalls Martin. 'Lar Foley switched from the full-back line down to full-forward on me.'

Ask him what it was like to mark one of Dublin's fabled dual stars and it prompts a deep, rolling laugh at the hell for leather nature of it all. The unstoppable force versus the immovable object.

'God ... he was an awful hardy strong fella. No punches, but hard hitting. Definitely ... hard hitting.

'The man wouldn't give up! He was so determined to win that match.' Foley's two points were crucial to Dublin's fightback, but the decisive intervention came from his brother Des.

'It was a ding-dong match,' adds Jack. 'Time was practically up. Des Foley kicked the ball with his left foot, which Lord rest him, he very, very rarely kicked with, and he put the ball over the bar with nearly the last kick of the game.

'So there wasn't a kick of a ball between us. But I don't think we'd have done it if we had won. Dublin were ready … that bit more experienced. But it was that close. Of course we met in the Leinster final in '64 and we got our revenge!'

✦ ✦ ✦ ✦ ✦

For the first time, the Quinns tell the story behind the 1964 Leinster final.

By turns heart-rending and bitter-sweet, it's a story that goes to the heart of the county's proud footballing history and illustrates how the game has such a hold over its people. How the game is bound up in the parish, in the community, in a way of life.

With Martin, Gerry and Jack all part of the Meath starting line-up, the Championship draw set the team on a collision course with Dublin, the Leinster final this time providing a fitting backdrop.

But what should have been a landmark day for the family, the three brothers lining out together for the first time in a provincial final, carried an oh-so-poignant sting. Emotions were running high in the Quinn household in Kilbride that weekend for a very different reason.

'My father was in failing health,' explains Gerry.

'On the Saturday he became critically ill and we thought he wouldn't last. Father Healy came to the house at twelve o'clock. Anointed him. We all said our goodbyes. All the uncles and aunts were in tears. And he was fading.'

In a matter of hours, the three were expected to backbone Meath's challenge in a provincial final. Their father, James, only 73, had been in ailing health for some time. But the sudden downturn in his health shocked the whole family to the core. Nobody outside the front door knew what the Quinns were going through that morning.

'We thought about all the things you'd naturally be thinking about,' admits Gerry. 'Your father is dying, should you be leaving? What would he do? He'd let you go.

'But that's a big decision for three men to walk out of the house, and leave my mother and the rest of the family at home with all the aunts and uncles.'

His voice catches as he recalls the time when it came to do just that ... walk out the door with kit bag in hand, and get ready to meet up with the rest of the squad.

'One thing that stands out in my mind that day leaving the house in such turmoil ... the determination. There's a job to be done - let's f**kin' do it.'

Their mother's words left no room for doubt.

'Go, go... Meath, Meath.'

'It wasn't easy,' says Martin, 'but we all knew that if he was alive, he'd be saying ... "Get out there and play the Dubs!"'

'He was very sick at the time,' adds Jack. 'It really was tough. But he was a fanatical football follower. The one thing was, it made us more determined than ever to go home and show him the Cup.

'We went to the match ... arrived in the dressing room, and Father Tully comes with word that he was still alive.'

Just to heighten the nerves and sense of worry, Martin's fitness was a big concern, a twisted ankle forcing him to miss the Leinster semi-final.

'I had an appointment to go see Dr Kevin O'Flanagan. He played rugby and soccer for Ireland. He was based in Fitzwilliam Square. I went over to him and he bandaged me up and said, "You'll be perfect for playing, agin I'm finished with you."

'I took that as a bit of bravado. Well, after he bandaged me from my toe to my knee I felt perfect. No pain, no nothing ... played the whole game. Never felt a thing.'

For the three of them to be lining out together when Amhrán na bhFiann was sung on Leinster final day was a special achievement in its own right.

It was actually Meath's first appearance in a provincial final since 1955, that fateful day when Dublin signalled a changing of the guard and Kevin McConnell plonked down in the seat beside Jack Quinn in the stand after being taken off as the sky fell in on Meath's first All-Ireland winning era.

The 12-year-old Quinn vowed to 'revenge' that day. Well, now he had the chance.

Just to up the stakes, he was tasked with going one-to-one with Dublin's match-winner from the previous year and force of nature around the middle, Des Foley.

'I was marking Des that day alright … one of the greatest midfielders. Lar would more have the laugh with you after – when it got going he'd be great craic. Des was quieter. But on the field he'd be the same sort of competitor. He'd go through you.'

Meath started like a steam train, pulling away into the distance to lead by five inside the first quarter, only for Dublin to respond and gradually peg back the difference as the exchanges became hot and heavy. Referee John Dowling booked three players in that period alone.

'Martin had become involved with a very tough Dublin forward line at the time,' explains Gerry. 'He was the tough man in the Meath back-line. A Dublin player went down injured and Martin got the blame. But Martin had a lot of blood running from his nose from another Dublin player.'

Gerry reminds his older brother that he wore the scars of battle like a badge of honour: 'You had blood on your face coming up to half-time.'

Asked whose blood it was, they both look at each other before cracking up. Let's just say, nobody is too sure if it was actually Martin's.

'You had a run in with Bill Casey,' adds Gerry. 'And Bill was a nice guy. Once there was trouble down that end though, I was in trouble down the other end. When you're from the same team it's bad enough, but when you're brothers! It's causing havoc. I was down at Hill 16 and that's where the craic was with bottles coming in over your head. If you've ever played in that corner under Hill 16 you'll know all about it!'

So did Martin realise he was getting Gerry into trouble by throwing his considerable weight around the full-back line?

'I had enough trouble looking after my own patch!'

Meanwhile, Jack was sailing through the match in his own trademark style, plucking balls from the sky and eclipsing Dublin's go-to man. With Peter Moore alongside him dominating Simon Behan, Meath had a crucial platform, and Ollie Shanley's peach of a goal helped them into a 1-6 to 1-5 lead at half-time – Brian McDonald punching in an opportunist goal in return for Dublin.

In the dressing room at the interval, the news was passed on to the Quinns:

their father was still alive. The manner and style and spirit of Meath's second half performance would have made James Quinn proud.

Gerry though, didn't get to see a large chunk of the second half, or the trophy presentation. Early in the second half, he jumped for a ball that Lar Foley, Ollie Shanley and the Dublin goalkeeper all had their eyes on and ended up in a heap on the ground, knocked clean out.

His brothers were so caught up in the frantic nature of the game, they didn't even realise Gerry was concussed as he was stretchered from the field.

'We were hoping that everything would be alright naturally,' says Jack. 'But the sheer tension of the match and with things so tight, you nearly hadn't time to think. Obviously you'd be worried but you had to try and concentrate on the rest of the game.'

With Pat 'Red' Collier inspirational in a defence that was completely on top, Meath turned the screw. Substitute Paddy Mulvaney reacted quickest to Jack Quinn's blocked goal effort to fire home and they powered home from there on, picking off Dublin almost at ease.

In *The Irish Press*, Peadar O'Brien wrote about the futility of Dublin's attacking threat, *'They may as well have tried to take a high ball off the top of Nelson Pillar as take it from Martin Quinn, Dinny Donnelly and Peter Darby'*.

Dublin's decision to switch Lar Foley up front again on Martin provided theatre all of its own, getting the crowd going by gesturing at his old adversary to come join him as he jogged down the field to lock horns.

'You called him down,' recalls Gerry.

'I wasn't looking forward to meeting him,' replies Martin. 'That's the truth! Definitely one of the hardest, most determined men I ever played on.'

But this time even Foley's best efforts couldn't spark Dublin.

'The last 10 minutes was played out with Meath on top,' adds Martin. 'It was won. There was no goalmouth scrambles or anything like that.

'All through the second half I felt we were going to win. We were playing that well they were never going to beat us that day. We were the top dogs.'

'Apart from Lar, Dublin had given up. But Lar never gave up. Or Des.

'You stood there and thought, "We've done it!"

A decade without a Leinster title, the famine was over.

The pitch invasion.

Dinny Donnelly's victory speech.

The captain chaired off the field by jubilant supporters with the Cup in his hand. Receiving medical attention in the dressing room, Gerry missed it all.

'I could hear the doctor giving me the smelling salts saying, "He's coming around all right."

'And when I came around, there wasn't a sinner in Croke Park - the team had already gone from the dressing room. Everyone was down in Barry's Hotel celebrating.

'The first thing I remember Fr Pat [Tully] saying is, "Great news. Your father is still alive... and we've beaten Dublin."'

His brothers have a quick reply as to why they didn't wait for Gerry to come to in the dressing room. When we saw he was alright, says Jack, we said, "We want a pint quick!"'

Fires back Martin, 'We don't win too many Leinster finals!'

When Gerry eventually joined up with his brothers in Barrys, the party was in full flow.

'Croke Park was empty. Everyone was gone. Winners and losers. We went straight back to Barry's Hotel.

'I remember joining in with the conversation and asking, "What happened? Who scored?" You had supporters hugging and kissing you, the usual craic after a match. It was massive.'

But the constant updates from home only added a poignancy to the occasion.

'The extraordinary thing is that we knew he was alive, that he was alright,' says Gerry. All the Quinns will never forget the generosity of spirit of team captain, Dinny Donnelly.

Jack remembers, 'He insisted on us bringing the Cup home so the father could see it. It was a lovely gesture. And we did that ... we showed it to him that night.

'We brought it up to Sweeney's then ... they were delighted all around Kilbride to see the Cup there sitting up at the bar. And it right on the Dublin border!'

Word of the famous victory seemed to revive their father's spirits, if only briefly.

'He came around on the Monday,' says Gerry, 'and took it all in. My mother read him the newspaper and he said, "that's fantastic", or words to that effect. And he died on the Wednesday. It was emotional.'

On the Friday, in the cemetery adjoining Kilbride Church, James Quinn was laid to rest. Glowing tributes were paid to a man who had an unbridled passion for the game, for his club, Kilbride and for his county. Peter McDermott, Frankie Byrne and Paddy Dixon were among the host of county stars, past and present, who came to offer their condolences.

His passing hit all the Quinns like a hammer blow, the days and weeks that followed a heavy and tear-filled blur.

And yet football gave the family, and the three brothers, a much-needed routine given that their world had been turned upside down with their father's passing. All knew that he would have given anything to have been there at Croke Park on Leinster final day, to watch with pride as his three sons played their part in such a famous victory. Especially to put one over the Dubs.

There was only one way to honour his memory.

'The elation of beating Dublin and the sorrow of being at home and your father gone and not being able to talk about football,' says Gerry. 'All that goes with a death in the family is serious. But the great thing about it was that the hype and the football kinda carried you through. Because it was a hard time.'

It said everything about the character of the Quinns that Martin, Gerry and Jack pledged to do everything they could to drive Meath on.

Amongst supporters, there was a growing feeling that the team could go all the way.

Gerry agreed. 'Absolutely. It was a different ball game then. All of a sudden this Meath team had made the breakthrough. After being unlucky in '63, beating the All-Ireland champions in the Leinster final, that was big stuff. Sure we played in front of a huge crowd in the Leinster final – it doesn't get any better than that.'

Just like Mick Lyons who proclaimed, 'I'd live and die to play the Dubs.'

Martin Quinn admits, 'We all feel that way.

'The atmosphere with Meath and Dublin, right up to the present day, is fantastic,' adds Gerry. 'That tension is in the air ... it's only when you arrive outside of Croke Park that you realise Meath and Dublin is different.'

'I read a piece recently where someone was going on about the atmosphere when Barcelona were playing Madrid. The same guy said, "Well he must never have been at a Meath-Dublin match."

'For me playing at corner-forward and Martin dishing out a bit of hot stuff at the far end … with the bottles and the noise and the craic you could hear nothing. The supporters would be throwing all kinds of gear in.

'The gardai were always down there. The young lads would be there and the paling would be half pulled down … marvellous atmosphere.'

One thing he never did was experience the thrill of scoring a goal into the Hill on such an occasion. 'No. Unfortunately! I scored a goal against Kildare and Westmeath, but it's not the same. '

And Meath and Dublin were able to recognise the best in each other.

'I'd a great chat with Lar Foley around those times,' says Gerry, 'and he made the comment, "As a full-back, wouldn't it be great to be kicking the ball out if you had Jack and Des in the middle of the field. Wouldn't it be a long time before it would be back!"

Before the Meath fans christened the square patch of ground in front of the goalmouth at Croke Park 'The Lyons Den', the eldest of the Quinn brothers knew what it was like to play the character of the hard man in front of Hill 16.

'I loved it!' proclaims Martin, with a grin that tells you he milked the part of villain in the piece for all its worth. 'The more they booed you the better you'd play.'

At times, he gave them reason to get riled. His approach was the no-nonsense side of Mick Lyons. In keeping with the moniker of the formidable Tipperary full-back line of the time, Martin could be a one-man's 'Hell's Kitchen'.

The question as to whether he ever felt intimidated with the Dublin supporters baying for his blood in the Hill draws broad laughter once more. 'Oh, Jesus no! You'd never hear clearly what they were saying … just this bloody big droning!'

Any year Meath dispense with Dublin is one in which the county believes itself credible All-Ireland contenders.

The summer of 1964 was no different.

If there is one game that influenced Meath's fortunes in that entire decade, Jack Quinn believes it's that semi-final in '64 against an emerging Galway team, a game laced with controversy. Not for the first time at Croke Park, a referee was at the heart of the drama.

For the first time, both minor and senior matches were televised in full and the big game was also broadcast by Radio Eireann.

'We met the start of the great Galway team who went on to win three-in-a-row,' says Jack. 'I was centrefield at the time. I think the course of history was changed big time with that game. We were a point behind, and I had a goal disallowed.'

The 'ins' and 'outs' of the game up to that point are easily told. Mattie McDonagh's gem of a goal threatened to be the defining moment in a finely balanced game that slowly tilted in Meath's direction as Peter Moore and Jack Quinn again controlled the midfield against the pairing of Mick Garret and Mick Reynolds.

Five minutes into the second half, however, came the incident that gets Jack up out of his kitchen chair to re-live the finer details with great animation. 'A high ball dropped about 30 yards out ... dropped out of the sky. I came running in.

'There were two or three lads jumping for the ball. I said to myself, "This ball could break." And luckily enough it broke straight into my hands. So I took it on the run, no-one near me ... no-one within yards of me, and I buried the ball in the far corner of the net.

'When I was kicking the ball, I went back this way,' he explains, as he stands upright from his seat and acts it out. 'For some reason I actually lost my balance. But there was nobody near me. And I ended up nearly sitting on my hunkers. So whether that caused the referee to blow, I simply don't know.

'But the reason I ended up like that was that I tried to keep the ball low. I was delighted with the shot because I was after beating one of the best goalies that ever lived in Johnny Geraghty. One of the greatest ever.'

As the roar went around Croke Park, the whistle of referee Seamus Garvey was almost lost in the confusion. The truth came dropping slow on Quinn; the goal wasn't going to count. To his astonishment, the official was calling the play back.

For what? 'Absolutely nothing,' insists Jack.

'I don't think the ref even knows.'

Even more galling for Meath is that the referee gave a free-in for Meath, rather than some offence committed by Quinn.

'We don't know what he blew for because he never said. The whistle went when the ball was half way to the net … not before I kicked it. In fact, it was practically in the net.'

On the wall opposite his bar, just outside Trim, the photograph of that very moment is captured – Johnny Geraghty diving despairingly to his right as the ball nestles in the corner. Jack too is captured, arching his body so as to make sure to keep the ball low as he unleashes the shot.

There is nothing in Geraghty's pose to suggest the play had been stopped, his full-length dive in fact suggesting just the opposite.

When Jimmy Walsh stepped up and then missed the resultant free, the confidence seemed to deflate from the team like a balloon after the smallest of pin pricks.

'It was a very, very inexperienced referee,' explains Jack. 'He'd never refereed a top county match before. He was put in at the deep end and it must have got to him.

'That would have been the winning of the game. And Galway went on to win three All-Irelands. Who knows what we might have done? It was a great Galway team at the time.'

A moment they all felt changed the course of Meath's history.

'That was the day, all right,' adds Martin. 'All the play was up at the Galway goals. The ball was going only the one way the whole time but it kept going wide.

'Then to kill it all … Jack's goal.

'I had a perfect view of it. Sometimes you wouldn't know what's going on but not this time. Jack went straight down the middle of the field. Let go from 25, 30 yards out. I could see the line of the ball … back of the net. Everyone was roaring: Meath goal!

'It wasn't 'til 20 seconds later that we all realised the goal had been disallowed, he'd given a free in.

'All I can remember is him getting the ball and going straight for goals. If someone fouled him, he never got near him.'

In the photo in Jack's pub he is in clear space, not another player in the shot.

'I was close to it,' adds Gerry. 'The ball flew in as Johnny dived. At that stage the Galway backs, particularly the late Enda Colleran and John Donnellan were really laying in to one another as to who was going to mark Jimmy Walsh because Jimmy was destroying them.

'How would you describe it? A team that was rail-roaded out of a win over Galway. The most dire refereeing decision probably ever recorded in Croke Park. I always wonder did he accidentally blow the whistle and then couldn't go back on it.

'Johnny Geraghty was a great goalie at the time – no goal scored against him in three All-Irelands – but that was a goal scored from the guts of 30 yards.

'The ball was in the net and the referee blew his whistle.

'Sure it was in the net!

'The free was to him, not against him … the free was to Meath!'

But Meath had themselves to blame in other aspects. A string of missed frees didn't help and Gerry puts his hands up to for another missed opportunity.

'I know I missed an open goal … not long after Jack's goal was disallowed. Either effort would arguably have turned the match. I don't want to remind myself of it! I still think about it. Winning that All-Ireland made that Galway team.

'But they shouldn't have been there.

'Apart from the goal, that famous Galway forward line could only score eight points against Meath. Meath had a brilliant back-line and a brilliant midfield. Jack at that time was virtually unplayable.'

Jack's performance that day added to a quickly flourishing reputation.

'Jack was probably the best midfielder in the country at that stage,' says Martin. 'Between himself and Des Foley. Jack was a big loose footballer who didn't care who was in front of him or going for it as well. He went into the clouds and went off with the ball. That's the type of player he was.'

With barely two minutes remaining then, and Meath failing to make their superiority tell on the scoreboard, Galway won a '50'. Mick Reynolds stepped up and showed serious nerve to stroke it over the bar. A fisted point from Sean Cleary wrapped it up.

Galway 1-8 Meath 0-9.

As if the personal trauma off the field wasn't enough to handle, the playing field was no longer a sanctuary.

'To lose your father and then lose in that manner to Galway, that was the pits,' admits Gerry.

But football was to provide succour again in Kilbride's remarkable odyssey to a first county senior title later that year, a team that included four Quinns, Jimmy joining his three brothers.

'It was always tinged with the sorrow that he was missing for the two biggest occasions, the Leinster final and winning the senior Championship, that he wasn't around to see either,' says Gerry sadly.

+ + + + +

'In the pub quiz, the question was always asked, "What had Bobby Moore, Bobby Charlton and Martin Quinn in common?" Gerry grins as he delivers the punchline, 'They all went up the steps in Wembley to collect the Cup.'

In 1965, the Meath team spread its wings. On Easter Sunday, they travelled over to Coventry to play an exhibition match.

And then in early June, an historic appearance at Wembley Stadium beckoned as they flew to London to take on Galway in the eighth annual tournament at the iconic stadium, a match-up that featured the All-Ireland champions against top quality opposition. The double-bill of fare saw Galway take on Meath in a re-run of the controversial semi-final, while Tipperary took on Kilkenny.

Captain of the Meath team for that historic trip? Martin Quinn.

A weekend of drama and excitement ensued, on and off the field, as Jack recounts.

'Martin and myself and a few more – I'm not sure if Gerry was with us – went on a boat ride down the Thames … didn't realise how far away we were. It suddenly dawned, then, that to get back to the hotel, get our gear and get to Wembley wasn't on. So we had to ring back to some of the lads in the hotel before they left to go up to our rooms and bring the gear for us.

'Lucky enough, we took to the Tube and made it!'

. For an exhibition match, Meath had plenty to prove after the 'what ifs' of the All-Ireland semi-final the previous August, particularly when Galway went on to beat Kerry in the final.

Martin took the field with No.3 on his back, Jack in a new centre-forward role, with Gerry listed amongst the substitutes.

'It was a big deal,' says Gerry, 'particularly with Meath having lost the All-Ireland semi-final in very, very dubious circumstances the previous year. Wembley still had such a thing about it. You know, only the greats play in Wembley! No ordinary Joe Soaps.'

Jack agrees in terms of the stakes involved. 'That match between Meath and Galway was taken very serious because of the whole All-Ireland thing. It was like a Championship match. Ourselves and the Galway boys became great friends afterwards. We'd nothing but the height of respect for them. They were a fabulous team.'

This time, Meath came out on top, 1-15 to 1-12, the goal coming after a Noel Curran shot deceived Johnny Geraghty, the score on such a famous sod a piece of history in itself. Jack too can always say he scored, not once but twice, firing over two points.

'We got a little measure of revenge,' he says, describing how the game was well received by some of the locals. 'There were stewards at that match who had been at the FA Cup final the same year. They were at some other big rugby matches as well … I think it was rugby League. And they came over and said, "We've seen all types of football here but that's the greatest game we've ever seen. That's the truth."'

'Jack Quinn has found his best position at centre-forward' declared Paddy Downey in *The Irish Times*.

To crown the day, Martin, who had a stormer at full-back, was chaired from the field before climbing the famous steps to receive the trophy in front of a crowd of over 30,000. 'It was something special to be playing,' says someone not given to sentiment.

Lining out at the ancestral home of British football is a claim to fame Jack likes to remind a few local pals.

'I used to say that a few good soccer players I knew here, "Did you ever play in Wembley?

"Well I feckin' did!" People came from all over England to it.'

In keeping with the sense of entering unchartered territory, the coach driver in London got lost on the way to the post-match reception. 'He was way out of his area altogether,' explains Gerry. 'Peter McDermott got out and hired a taxi … got the coach to follow the taxi!

Martin adds, 'We went to a 'do' that night and we were lucky to get in ourselves to the place, the crowd that was in it … thousands … in some club in London.'

Flying cross-channel to play in Wembley would become a recurring theme over the next few years as Meath continued to be in the shake-up for All-Irelands.

'Great trips,' says Jack. 'We stayed in top class hotels. I think one year the four teams were in the one hotel and we had mighty craic. The matches were treated seriously. Now you might have a few jars before – it wasn't like an All-Ireland – but it was taken serious enough.'

One particular trip brings a warm smile to Jack's face. 'One of the matches we were going over to play in London in Wembley … and we were all sitting on the plane. And the plane was full. But the captain wouldn't take the plane up. It was one of old big 747s. About five times he came over the loudspeaker and said, "I've been told to take this plane up but I'm not happy with it."

'There were fellas on the plane and you could see the sweat dropping out of them … they'd never been on one before.

'Well the gas we had slagging them. And it ended up that he didn't bring the plane up and we all stayed over in the Viscount [Hotel]. We had to wait for another.

'You have to laugh.

'There were two auld lads who had never been on a plane before who were involved with Meath,' he explains. 'You know when you're up … and the plane goes like that,' stretching his arms out and bending to imitate a plane banking. '"GOOD JAYSUS" … this fella shouted. The plane's going to turn over! Dive over this side.

'So the two lads dived over the other side!'

Good times.

A first trip to Wembley though didn't do Meath a whole lot of favour in the long run in 1965. After taking the All-Ireland champions down a notch, a Leinster semi-final against Longford had a touch of formality about it.

Nobody heeded the warning signs of the opposition's ambush of a fancied Offaly in the first round, or a thoroughly deserved quarter-final victory over Laois.

A preview in *The Meath Chronicle* summed up the mood, taking the midfield pairing of Jack Quinn and Peter Moore as a case in point. 'On their day they have no equals in the country and it will be a surprise if they do not gain a clear supremacy over the opposing centrefield pair'. But it never happened, in part because Moore and Dinny Donnelly were late withdrawals due to injury, which upset the balance of the team.

Bobby Burns too gave Martin a bit of an unexpected run-around at the back and Longford deservedly won out, 2-8 to 1-7.

'Shell-shocked,' is how Jack describes the feeling afterwards, 'they were as bloody good a county team as was around at the time. There was no disgrace losing to them.'

✦✦✦✦✦

Gerry Quinn's daughter, Janet tells a story about a trip to Ardara on the west coast of Donegal. Sitting in a local pub with a friend and teammate from the Meath ladies football team, the conversation turns, naturally enough, to football and the bloodlines of the pub's visitors are uncovered.

'Let me shake your hand,' says the bartender. 'I'm delighted to meet a Quinn. 'The man who sat on the ball!'

The story of Martin's act in the Meath county final of 1965, after being ordered off by the referee, travelled the length and breadth of the country and is still remembered to this day.

A couple of years after that trip, Janet is perched in Tatler Jack's pub in Killarney, the well-known spot where one of Gerry's Meath jerseys hangs above the bar, No.15 emblazoned in gold lettering on the back. On a pub crawl as part of a good friend's hen party, the name etched underneath doesn't go unnoticed by another member of the same gang of girls Janet pals around with.

'Quinner ... there's your father's jersey,' goes the shout before the slagging starts about how they can travel from the west coast of Donegal to the west coast of Kerry, and still get caught up in the Quinn family history. Anytime Janet travels down south with her husband, Darren and the four kids, they get a warm welcome.

The full story is told later of how Martin, a Meath regular since '58 became the central character of one of the greatest club controversies when he picked up a 12-month suspension as a result of the fall-out from the county final between Kilbride and Skryne, which the referee abandoned when it was clear Martin wasn't for shifting.

Just like Paddy O'Brien, Jack's conversion to full-back came about due to a bizarre twist of fate, rather than any grand plan. With Martin ruled out, his brother was handed the No.3 shirt in his stead. Little did he realise he would wear it for nearly a full decade.

By the time Meath squeezed past Kildare in the 1966 Leinster final, he looked like he had played there all his life, his presence and high fielding invaluable assets. They chaired captain, Dave Carthy from the field in the heady aftermath, the Skryne man proudly carrying the Cup.

The All-Ireland semi-final pitted Meath against a star-studded Down team. With Martin still out of the frame due to suspension - 'I wasn't togged out at all. No jersey ... no nothing. But I was in the dug-out in Croke Park' - Jack and Gerry took up the cause, the latter banging in two second-half goals on a day of days.

'It was something like the Meath-Kerry All-Ireland semi-final [of 2001]. Meath couldn't kick the ball wide. Everything they touched went over the bar. We scored 2-16, a big score.'

And yet the first half gave little indication of what was to come. After playing with the breeze into the Canal End goal, Down led 0-6 to 0-3.

'It was an amazing turnaround at half-time,' admits Gerry. 'I think Meath had only about three points from frees. The second half transformation was unbelievable. All those famous Down players ... they were all there.'

Joe Lennon, Dan McCartan, Seán O'Neill, Paddy Doherty and company.

That was the day Jack announced himself in the position he would become famous for, turning in one of the great full-back performances at

Croke Park, so reminiscent of his hero Paddy O'Brien, the player he idolised as a youngster.

'What I do remember is that I got 'Sportstar of the Week' for that match. In the first twenty minutes it was all Down. And they were sending in the high balls, which I loved of course.

'I had a field day at full-back catching high balls. It was ding-dong for a while then. We got a few points ... they missed a few chances. And then Gerry got the two goals and it changed the whole course of the game.'

The key switch was Noel Curran going to full-forward and Gerry going to the right corner. Noel would kick five points from play, and Gerry would conjure the two killer goals.

Seven minutes into the second half, Ollie Shanley punched down a high Curran kick to the unmarked Gerry, who soloed in before burying the ball in the net. His second mirrored it three minutes later, winning the ball in behind the Down defence after a high ball in from Pat Reynolds.

By that stage, the Meath crowd knew they were bearing witness to a truly memorable display from their county team.

From there to the finish it was high-five football, all sweeping moves and sparkling points.

'After the match we were heroes,' says Gerry. 'To destroy a team like Down! The semi-final display against Down was possibly one of the greatest displays from a Meath team at Croke Park – but it was possibly too good.'

What he means is that it set Meath up for a fall against Galway in the final - just like in 2001. He draws a parallel to the grand-stand performance against Kerry in that year's semi-final and the subsequent wash-out in the final, one which would lead to a crisis in confidence for Darren Fay, a player who was already well on the way to being mentioned in the same conversation as Paddy 'Hands' O'Brien, Jack Quinn and Mick Lyons after just five years of Championship football.

'Galway coming along nice and quietly,' explains Gerry. 'Two All-Irelands. All the experience. Watching it all. Meath getting all the publicity. Exactly as happened in '01.

'This was a Down team which was one of the greatest teams of all time and we destroyed them in the All-Ireland semi-final.

'It says everything about the calibre of Jack's performance on the edge of the square that he could land that 'Sportstar of the Week' award – one of many – on an afternoon when his older brother rattled in a brace of goals. But that was Jack. Grace under pressure.

'Jack had the game of his life that day at full-back,' explains Gerry. 'Meath weren't good in the first half but Jack held the Meath square.

'Down kept putting in these high balls thinking they could beat him. In the second half Meath just seemed to explode and took Down apart. It rained points that day.'

One topic of conversation that popped up regularly in the lead-up to the All-Ireland final concerned the missing Quinn brother. Martin's 12-month suspension was due to run out on the eve of the final.

Right to this day, it remains an emotive topic for all three brothers. 'It was rumoured … yes, that it was on the cards,' recalls Martin. 'It was Father Tully in all fairness to him who said he had to go by the rulebook and the referee's report. I never touched the referee. Never touched him. But they hung me for it.'

Not being part of Meath's odyssey, especially when Jack and Gerry were there, was tough.

'It wasn't easy … it was … not … easy. When Meath beat Down in the semi-final, the big craic coming up to the final was, "Would I be playing or would I not be playing?" All this type of thing was going on.

'I was nervous about it myself for the simple reason that, even though you were kicking football, you weren't playing competitively. Fitness wasn't the thing, there was never any problem with fitness. It was just match sharpness.

'The whole country was talking about it at that time, "Will he or won't he?" Papers, pubs … particularly around Meath. No matter where I went I was damned with the same thing, "Will you be playing?"

'Are you fit?

'Are you this?

'Are you that?'

Meanwhile, Jack thought he was only keeping the jersey warm until released back out the field. Just like Paddy 'Hands' O'Brien, Mick Lyons and Darren Fay, he always preferred the open spaces of midfield before being recast as a No.3. And just like O'Brien, deputising there on the infamous League trip to Cavan when a carload of players failed to turn up, it proved to be an inspired move.

But the final against Galway wasn't the last time that Jack was needed in two places at the one time.

'The only reason that I was put in full-back was that he got the suspension and they were looking for a full-back then. I was put in in his place. Because they knew I had played full-back with the junior team. I used to love playing midfield ... always preferred it. I'd say I would have been out midfield for another few years but for his suspension.

'Martin got 12 months. So he hadn't kicked a football properly. He couldn't play challenge matches ... nothing. And his suspension was up the night before the All-Ireland. I think only for it we could have won it.'

When Kerry took on Offaly in the 1982 All-Ireland final, one of the famous stories of how the five-in-a-row went west concerned the set of replacement jerseys that had to be ordered at the last minute - after an objection by Croke Park to the county's regular strip - only arriving by special order the night before the match.

Gerry recalls a similarly themed incident as the Meath players gathered at Croke Park on Sunday, September 25, 1966.

'The build-up to it was totally wrong,' he says. 'The preparation for the match was as if the team didn't need to be coached.

'People wanted to get involved. Business people began to make presentations of football socks, and jerseys and togs. Because some of the gear wasn't ready the Thursday before the match, these people were allowed into the dressing room while the minor match was going on. The Meath team actually togged out in time for the minor match, never mind the senior match ... to see what gear suited them best.'

It's an arresting image; the players standing around in their gear, stretching the fabric to see if the fit was right, hours before throw-in. Just one giant distraction on a day when nothing went to plan.

'When the full-time whistle in the minor match went, the Meath team went straight out onto the field. Were ordered back off the field to let President de Valera back in to the stand.

'The whole attitude was wrong. Brian Smyth, who wasn't actually involved with the team ... he might have been a county official at the time ... he came into the dressing room and saw the team togged out during the minor match and was very annoyed.

'There was no plan in the dressing room. No tactics that should be there for an All-Ireland final.'

Martin has a vexed look thinking back to that day, 'I thought it was crazy. Crazy before an All-Ireland final. And then to go out on to the field and be sent straight back in off it. It was a bad day for Meath. Everything went wrong before the match.'

The mood of optimism amongst after the performance against Down filtered through to the players. 'I think that was part of the problem,' says Jack. 'Maybe we were a little over-confident after having such a display against Down. Galway started so fast and we never got going. It's hard to put your finger on it.'

A Galway team at the peak of their powers, for whom a three-in-a-row would cement their reputation among the greatest teams of all time, played as if history was theirs to write.

By half time, the damage was 1-6 to 0-1, Meath's sole score a free from Murty O'Sullivan 26 minutes in.

That's why Gerry thinks the 1964 semi-final and Jack's famous disallowed goal proved to be so pivotal: Galway now had the swagger of champions. 'They were so confident. They were a different team from the team we should have beaten in '64.

'In the '66 final, they beat us fair and square on the day. I suppose we all thought that if we had Martin it might have been different but on the day we could have no complaints.'

Galway's dominance at midfield that day through the in-form pairing of Jimmy Duggan and Pat Donnellan was crucial, compounding Jack's growing sense of frustration. 'Now we ended up being good friends but Pat Donnellan from Galway - Pat was barely 5'10" – looking at him catching high balls in the middle of the field I was thinking, "Aw, Christ." It sickened me at the time.

Sure when I was put out there it was too late.

'Even if they'd put Martin in at half time and me out … but I'd say there wasn't enough time left when the switch was made. It was ridiculous.'

A pumped up Martin was getting increasingly agitated as the match wore on and his name wasn't being called by any member of the Meath management. 'Itching to get in,' he admits. 'But unless Meath were going to get a goal or two, it was a lost cause at that stage. We were six or seven points behind against a Galway team who were playing very well.'

Only nine minutes were left on the clock before he got the nod to allow Jack firefight further out the field. 'It was Peter McDermott said it. There was a lot of chat going on. I was sitting in the dug-out and the selectors were talking in a huddle. I knew they were talking about me. I knew I was going in but I knew as well that unless we were going to get goals it was all over.'

He makes the point that it wasn't his presence at full-back that could have made the difference, rather the freeing up of Jack to go midfield where the main problems were.

'If I'd been there from the start, from the word go … yeah, it might have made a difference. When Jack was playing well out the field, Meath were nearly unbeatable. Because he kept the ball down the other end.

'It would be a free in to Galway … or whoever we'd be playing. Jack would be standing in the square with me. If it came to his side he'd get it; if it came to my side I'd get it. We had that relationship. Sometimes I'd be tired or feeling wrecked … and he'd be below on the other 21 in a blink!'

Gerry recalls sections of the Meath support calling for Martin's introduction. 'The crowd were chanting from early on in the game for Martin to come in, even though he hadn't played a game for Meath for 12 months.

'I could hear it. The Meath supporters were going mad. Because we were losing midfield; never got going as a team.

'Martin was so badly needed in the backline because he was such a dominant figure at that time. Sure he had three or four years playing great football for Kilbride after that. Unfortunately, whether politics came into it or not, he never got his place back.'

A minute after Jack's introduction, Meath scored their fifth point of the half to leave it 1-8 to 0-6, Pat Collier a defiant figure driving things on from wing-back. But Noel Tierney stood tall as a towering presence for Galway who ran down the clock to seal a remarkable three-in-a-row.

For Meath, after the high of the Down game and everything that went with it, this was the ultimate low. Gerry finished scoreless; Martin begrudged the short time on the field, his cameo pointless given the way the match panned out. Jack remained unbowed at full-back but hurting all the same.

1967 would be different he swore. And it was.

+ + + + +

The rise and rise of Kilbride would carry the Quinns through another dark winter. When the National League resumed before Christmas, Jack was still bouncing between full-back and midfield, depending on where the need was greatest and whether big brother was in the team.

By 1967, Meath were auditioning other players for some vital parts. A tall and agile youngster named Mattie Kerrigan did enough in one cameo in the Division Two final against Cavan to hold his place for the National League semi-final proper against Dublin; the prize for winning the competition outright a trip to the United States to play New York in May.

Meath and Dublin again.

Ten points down, though against the wind and a Dublin team in full flow, a recurring trend was captured by *The Irish Times*, *'The rally was launched by the switch of Jack Quinn to midfield – a move that might well have been made with greater profit much earlier. Jack's brother Martin went in at full-back and right away Meath took over control of the proceedings.'*

Despite getting to within four at one stage, Dublin powered home.

By the first round of the Championship against Louth, Jack still held the No.3 shirt, Gerry and Martin jockeying to break into the team.

Asked if it was tough to be on the sideline watching on, Martin has no hesitation in answering: 'Not really … no. Once Meath kept on winning, that was the whole thing.

'Jack had settled in to full-back. He played better that year at full-back than any other year.'

Gerry adds, 'There was a different attitude in the Meath camp. Losing an

All-Ireland buoys you up for the next one. You ain't going to lose the next one.'

In the first round of the Leinster Championship against Louth, Noel Curran proved to be the star of the show, banging in 2-5 from full-forward to seal the deal.

A double scores victory over Westmeath in the semi-final, 0-12 to 0-6, was marked by the *'fielding of Jack Quinn and tearaway interceptions of Pat Collier'* as one newspaper report put it. And a few more pieces of the jigsaw were coming together; Terry Kearns impressing in a debut at midfield alongside Peter Moore, who ran the show that afternoon.

In the Leinster final, Meath raced into a first half lead, hitting seven points to a single score by Offaly before having to fight a rearguard action after the break - Bertie Cunningham, Pat Collier, Peter Darby and Quinn lifting the siege time after time to allow Meath squeeze home by two points.

Meath reserved their best performance of the year for the All-Ireland semi-final. In a match that ebbed and flowed one way and then the other, two mistakes from Mayo full-back, Ray Prendergast were critical, the blinding sun playing a part in him spilling the ball from his grasp and over the line in the first half. When the same thing happened in the second, there was no way back, especially after Peter Moore had banged in a fine goal.

Meath's sole substitute that day was one Austin Lyons, first cousin of Mick, who came on for the injured Collier.

'Red' though would be back for the final.

Having learned a hard lesson from the carnival of the previous year, this time Meath entertained no distractions.

'The year we won the All-Ireland we had Peter McDermott, God rest him,' recalls Jack. 'There was no real coaching before he came in. There was a few times they got down army men for the fitness end of it. For some of the matches we were training three nights a week.'

And Gerry too acknowledges the contribution of two men in particular, 'Father Pat Tully and Peter McDermott … they were great men. The preparation went wrong in '66 but they didn't get it wrong in '67.'

In the squad of twenty-seven announced for the final were six Kilbride men, a remarkable achievement for such a small, rural club. Jack of course started at full-back with Pat Rooney, Pat Bruton and Murty O'Sullivan named among the substitutes, along with Martin and Gerry.

Another thing that stood this team apart was the fact that the starting fifteen all came from fifteen different clubs.

Croke Park, Sunday, September 24, 1967

Jack Quinn stands shoulder to shoulder with Con O'Sullivan as referee John Moloney, complete with peaked cap, throws up the ball. It's a day when Croke Park is bursting at the seams, a line of spectators in the crowd of 70,343 lining the perimeter of the pitch, inside the wire.

In the first minute, Pat Reynolds launches a ball in from distance, his kick very nearly bouncing over the bar. But Meath can't get a foothold.

With the breeze at their backs, Cork batter the Meath defence and slowly pick off their scores. Jack has his hands full with the burly presence of O'Sullivan and when Mick O'Loughlin hits a fourth unanswered point for Cork 25 minutes in, commentator Michael O'Hehir proclaims: 'I wonder if the historians are working out how long a team hasn't scored in an All-Ireland final?' before adding: 'I don't know what happens the Meath forwards when they get to an All-Ireland final but whatever happened them last year is happening again.'

Jack stands shoulder to shoulder beside O'Sullivan and tries not to think of history repeating itself.

'We had a terrible bad first half. For some reason the same thing happened in '66 – we had a terrible bad start. And in the All-Ireland semi-finals we seemed to be flying from the word go. Whether it was nerves or whatever ... we couldn't get things going.'

When the players troop off at half time, a left foot point from Paddy Mulvaney a full 28 minutes into the game is all they have to show.

'We all had a chat,' says Jack. 'Said to each other, "We've been here before and we've let our followers down. It's about time we gave ourselves a kick in the tail end and went out there and did something."'

Switching Mattie Kerrigan to midfield and Terry Kearns to the attack helps to spark things. Mulvaney kicks a left foot point over his shoulder on the turn to start the comeback. Noel Curran sails another one over on the breeze. With Pat Collier, Bertie Cunningham and Pat Reynolds driving it on from the half-back line, and Mick White and captain

Peter Darby rock solid alongside Jack, Meath get the defining score of the game.

Kerrigan sends in a high speculative kick as the Cork defence hesitates. What happened next brings Jack Quinn up off his seat again as he re-enacts it.

'Say the goal was here and the ball was landing out there … out of reach. Terry Kearns couldn't get to catch it … it was just too high. But he was able to do that,' and he jumps in the air showing a brilliantly improvised back-flick of the wrists. 'And he connected. Billy Morgan was coming out so it went into the empty net. So we finally got a change of luck!

'The one thing I remember is the fear in the last minute … I'll never forget it for as long as I live. Because it was ding-dong and we were just three points ahead.'

He had reason to worry. At 1-9 to 0-9 entering the final moments, it is still a one-score game. And Cork aren't about to die without their boots on.

'With time practically up, Cork got a '50' as we called it at the time. A high ball landed right under the crossbar. And I caught it. Of course, half of Cork then landed on me chest. I had Cork fellas pushing me towards the goals; Meath men pushing me out. Serious f**kin' pressure.

'I brought off a great catch and I'll never forget what happened … the referee gave a fourteen-yard free against me. I nearly went berserk … should have been a free out!

'I do have to say that John Moloney who gave the decision against me would be a very good referee. Very fair, God rest him. A lovely man and I'd never have any qualms against him. He obviously thought he was doing right.'

But the footage proves Quinn's memory right, the full-back wrestled to the ground before being blown for over-carrying.

With Cork needing a goal, Con Sullivan decides to try and play a short pass along the ground only for Moloney to blow a free against him for his teammates not being far enough away!

Bedlam ensues, the players swallowed up in the traditional pitch invasion.

'I remember getting that many belts me back was sore!' he laughs. The feeling at the final whistle? 'Sheer relief and elation. At last we've done it. After getting there after so many near misses.'

Jack is the first to pop through the cordon of gardai in front of the Hogan Stand and climb the steps, flicking the hair back as he waits for his brothers to join him.

'Magic … absolutely magic,' recalls Gerry. 'Once you're part of the panel, it's just brilliant. Just elation that it had been done at last. When you walk up the steps and

turn around and see the supporters filling the pitch, it was unbelievable.'

When Peter Darby, the longest serving member of the team, lifts the cup, the roar said it all about bridging the gap to 1954 and what it means to this bunch of players.

'It was a build-up from '64,' explains Jack. 'We still had a core group from then. There was a great bond as well between the players. We built up a great friendship with each other. We more or less decided, "Look lads, if we don't do it now we'll never do it." We'd been knocking about a few years and we didn't want to be the 'nearly' team. Thank God we got there.

'After winning Leinster, we just felt we had to do it. We met a good, strong Cork team in the final … Cork were always good footballers, big, strong men.'

One of tradition's quirks back then involved a trip to the RTE studio the following day. While the later ritual of bringing the two finalists together for a meal was discontinued, mainly to allow the beaten side to count their losses privately, the '60s saw the four teams involved – the senior and minor finalists – traipse out to Donnybrook to watch the matches back.

'It is bloody tough if you lose! You've lads sitting there delighted and the others sitting licking their wounds.

'Later on they'd bring you to a different hotel and you'd be treated to drinks and all of that.

'Then you'd assemble for the journey back to your county.'

'The thing about losing in '66, even though we were disappointed in it … we got great crowds from Clonee all the way down to Navan. I remember every one of us pledged that we'd be back in '67 and we wouldn't let them down. Little did we realise that we'd be able to keep the promise!'

No open-top bus ride home existed back then. Jack was one of the various team members who travelled on by car, and after a couple of unscheduled stops, managed to miss part of the team's reception in Trim.

Noting his absence, the high-spirited supporters who gathered started chanting his name. Little did they know he was stuck at the back of the crowd.

'There was a few of us in the car. We stopped in Clonee … stopped in lots of places.

'By the time we got to Trim the boys were coming down off the stage. The crowd were roaring for where I was!

'All of a sudden, there was a serious surge … couldn't make it to the stage. So I went back to the car and took a short cut and got over to Navan ahead of the rest of the boys. And Navan was absolutely jammed. Now I was full as a pinkeen … I'd a good few pints in me. I remember getting up on the stage in Navan and talking to the crowd for about 10 minutes before the rest of the lads arrived.

'And to this day I don't remember a word I said!'

His laugh is infectious as he remembers it all: Jack Quinn, a one-man warm-up act. And the party was only starting. 'Then it was back to the Beechmount Hotel. The county team used to always eat there after matches and training. So we were there on the Monday night for a meal.

'Of course, Jim and Paddy Fitzsimons had pubs in Navan so we ended up staying … I think there was eight or ten of us in the one room upstairs!

'The next thing we were there … sure we couldn't sleep with the traffic the next morning around half six or seven. None of us could sleep. So Paddy and Jim said, "Look lads, if you're feeling thirsty, go down and fill yourselves a drink if you want to … don't be waking us."

'So down we go. Now we paid for everything. But we were drinking pints and there was a sing-song going in the pub by eleven o'clock. There was fellas going to work and coming back as quick as they could to join in again.

'Then we go down to the Central Hotel – we were down there. Had a meal courtesy of the county board. Then there were two lads with cars who brought us in to Baggot Street in Dublin. They had money to collect. Sure we were in Baggot Street having more of a fill. And then back again. It was great craic … fantastic.

'Then, of course, afterwards we brought the Cup around to the various clubs and had some fantastic nights.'

Gerry remembers Fitzsimons' being a source of great craic. 'The first department was the grocery department … then you went through into the bar. There was a great old character called Bosco. He came in looking for autographs so the lads persuaded him to bring his horse in – they wouldn't give him the autographs unless he did it. So we made him go out and unyoke the horse and bring it in.

'There were great characters on that team; Pat Reynolds, Red Collier, Martin. On and off the field. They certainly knew how to celebrate.'

And yet, behind the revelry, the Quinns' late father, James was never too far from their thoughts. To see his three sons, All-Ireland winners all, would have given great pride, to see the interest and passion for the game he helped to instil take root and flourish in the best way imaginable.

Seven days after winning the All-Ireland, they could lay claim to the title of 'World Champions'. A new, grandly-named World Championship Cup saw the best team in Ireland take on the National League holders, who happened to be New York.

With Mattie Kerrigan leading the charge, Meath added another trophy to the cabinet.

Winning an All-Ireland opened doors the players never could have imagined. As champions, they enjoyed the privilege of taking on a touring Australian side packed with the cream of the AFL at Croke Park that October with the promise of a return trip. If there was one man who made it all happen, it was coach Peter McDermott, and that trail-blazing world tour involving five tests against different AFL selections would become the stuff of legend.

'We often do say afterwards, we were very friendly with the Galway lads.

'Every team we played against we always got on well with when the match was over,' says Jack. 'We were very friendly with the Galway lads and they used to say to us, "Holy Jaysus we're after winning three All-Irelands but you've gone one better than us: you've won one and got a trip to Australia!"

'Here we are touring the world after one!

'So I suppose we got a level of revenge!'

✦ ✦ ✦ ✦ ✦

After the high of that historic tour in which Meath won all five tests in Australia against their professional counterparts, a level of expectation attached itself to a bid for back-to-back All-Irelands.

Losing a cracking National League semi-final to Down by a Joe Lennon

'50' in the dying moments – a day when Jack endured one of his most testing afternoons at Croke Park on Seán O'Neill, the best full-forward in the country at the time – did little to dispel that perception.

And then Longford came along and gate-crashed the party at Cusack Park. 'Back to earth with a big bang. We met Longford below in Mullingar and they bet us by a point.

'If we had got over Longford, I think we would have had a smashing team to have a go at it,' says Jack. 'We just weren't ready. We needed a game under our belt again after not being long home from Australia. They were a bloody good team. They were unlucky they didn't go on and win an All-Ireland.'

Martin recalls what was his last year to be involved with the county team, Gerry too. 'I played against Down in '68 in the League. On Seán O'Neill in Navan. I held him to one point … and was dropped! Seán was scoring goals against everybody that year and Down went on to win the All-Ireland. He was unplayable that year. I had the better of him. And he didn't like one bit of it!

'They were playing Westmeath in Croke Park the following Sunday and I was dropped. Jack was brought back from midfield and I'm not sure who was brought in to midfield. That was virtually the end of my playing days.'

Gerry feels that his brother could have made a difference in a hard-fought game against Longford. 'On a tight pitch … that's the day Martin should have been playing. That was a man's game.

'It's some comedown to travel around the world, see those sights, win all our games and then come back and lose like that.

'We felt that there was a reaction in Meath to the fact that there were six Kilbride lads on the panel, that they'd have to thin it out. And that's the way it happened. Which was not surprising really.'

From beating the pick of the Australian professional sport to being dumped out in the Leinster semi-final – the result had repercussions that lasted beyond just 1968. The following year's Championship was a wash-out too, knocked out by Kildare in the first round, 2-16 to 1-11.

And Jack explains just how quickly the bubble burst. 'A chap called Mick

Campbell took over in 1970. He would have been a very inexperienced coach but he was a good lad.

'We were down to play Sligo in a League match in Kells. Football had gone so low in the county, Mick had to go down the town and look for two or three players to get a full team together. It's hard to understand it. You had fellas retiring, a few bad results … and Mick had a job to get a team together.'

That was March 1970. Kilbride's continued dominance meant that the club had the right to name their Meath captain, and Jack was a natural fit.

At the start of a new decade, there was little to suggest Meath would cut a swathe through Leinster. But that's exactly what they did. First they hammered Carlow, Mattie Kerrigan grabbing the headlines after stepping in to goals to save a penalty following an injury to Sean McCormack. Tony Brennan was the main man as Meath toughed it out against Kildare, before Offaly awaited then in the Leinster final.

A change of rule meant that Championship matches jumped from 60 minutes in duration to 80, a situation that lasted until the modern compromise of 70 minutes came into effect in 1975.

The extended duration played its own part in a Leinster final that deserves the title 'epic'. Involving seven goals and 34 points, it remains the most high scoring final ever. If finished Meath 2-22, Offaly 5-12. Truly, one of the great GAA Championship matches.

Asked about his memories of that game, Jack comes over all coy.

'I don't want to remember them!' he says rolling his eyes.

For the Quinns, the weekend had a special resonance all of its own. Around lunchtime on the Friday, just over 48 hours before the throw-in, Gerry married Maureen Toole in Ratoath Church with the reception taking place at the Marine Hotel in Sutton. And the best man? A certain Meath captain.

A photograph from the day caught the flavour of the weekend perfectly; the four lads all togged out in their wedding finest, jumping for a ball with a good crew from Kilbride gathered round.

Jack gave his speech, toasted his brother and did his best to leave the party early as the celebrations rumbled into the small hours.

Between the emotion of the day and giving his brother a proper send-off, a first Leinster final that would last 80 minutes is not what he needed come Sunday afternoon.

A clash of colours meant that Meath lined out in the jerseys they'd worn with such pride across Australia. But the way the match started, it looked like the players were still living off past exploits in a foreign land.

'It was probably my worst game I ever played for Meath,' says Jack with disarming honesty. 'Now the chap playing on me was a very good footballer, Murt Connor, a brother of Matt. You had Matt and Richie … all top footballers.'

Nevertheless, the ease with which Offaly scored made it seem as if the entire defence had been at a wedding the day before. At half-time, the scoreboard had a surreal look to it; Offaly 4-7, Meath 0-9.

What Jack must have been thinking at that stage? 'Get me outta here!' he says with that infectious laugh.

What took place from there to the finish is one reason why Meath football is celebrated for its never-say-die spirit, its capacity to chase a lost cause.

Substitute Mickey Fay, a brother of Jimmy who was also on the panel, hammered home two goals. 'It was a spectacular turnaround but at the time we were renowned for it. Even to the present day, that's the one thing Meath still have, they'll never throw in the towel.

'A fantastic game of football … it was just unbelievable. We actually went four points in front. They got a goal late in the game to bring it back to a point again.'

A rip-roaring encounter was actually level with just four minutes left. And then Tony Brennan took on the mantle of match-winning hero, rounding off a remarkable 10-point haul with a score two minutes from time.

In those two minutes, every Offaly player except goalkeeper Martin Furlong was in the Meath half. It said it all that the last scoring effort came off the right full-back and captain, Eamonn Mulligan who shot wide from long range.

Murt Connor scored 2-3 off Jack Quinn but *The Irish Press* report says Quinn, *'had a great second half and was a tower of strength in beating off Offaly's final surges.'*

And so an incredible afternoon's action ended with Quinn lifting the Cup. In *The Meath Chronicle*, the headline ran: *'The Mighty Men Of Meath'*.

Such was the contribution of both counties, the *Irish Independent* took the unusual step of according both Meath and Offaly their 'Sports Stars of the Week' award, along with Mary Peters who just happened to win her second gold medal at the Commonwealth Games in Edinburgh, adding the shot putt to the pentathlon.

They were in good company.

By now Jack had a national profile.

There's a great photo of him kicking a ball about with the prettiest face his company could roll out before the All-Ireland final, CIE rail hostess, Elaine Hughes, showing how the fame of 'fitter Jack Quinn of Inchicore railway engineering works' went far beyond the county boundary.

'Just a great footballer … easily recognisable,' explains Gerry. 'When you're playing at that standard you're recognised in every other county. It was like being with Martin in the late '50s, early '60s. Instantly recognisable.'

In the All-Ireland semi-final against Galway, the Jack Quinn-Terry Kearns axis at three and six were rock solid, Mattie Kerrigan pulling the strings up front at centre-forward.

Kerry then, in the final.

This time, Jack's own preparations came with a dose of drama. His reputation back then carried across the Atlantic where he regularly lent his support to the Monaghan cause in the New York Championship. 'I badly hurt my ankle in Gaelic Park … New York. When I came back I was getting non-stop treatment. I never trained one night in the six weeks before the final. I just barely made it for the final itself.

'On the Tuesday night before the match I tried to train hard on it and couldn't. Jack Fitzgerald, God rest him, was the Leinster delegate from Meath. And he was very friendly with Dr Stuart … he was the main doctor in the Coombe hospital at the time delivering babies. Who subsequently delivered most of my kids!

'Jack says, "I was talking to Dr Stuart and he says he'll look after you'. Now Dr Stuart was a former president of the GAA.

'He came over to me and says, "Jack Quinn, I'm going to give you a spray. It's a bloody good spray so you won't feel the slightest bit of pain. And the one good thing about it is that it's better than an injection. Because, while it will deaden everything, if you really hurt your ankle you'll feel it. If I give you an injection, you could actually break it and play away."

'It was touch and go. On the Thursday night all I could do was jog. But if I went into any kind of gallop at all the pain would go up from my ankle.'

Croke Park, Sunday, September 27, 1970.

On the day of the match, Dr Stuart makes one more appearance.

'I guarantee you this is the only time this happened at Croke Park, that a GAA president got out of his seat on All-Ireland final day, walked across Croke Park, came into the dressing room, sprayed some stuff on my ankle and bandaged it. So that's what I played with in that match.'

The former president certainly knows his stuff. Jack's ankle holds out. Meath's ambitions don't.

Two-thirds of Meath's starting line-up are survivors from the 1967 final. This time, the team is drawn from 14 different clubs, one less than before.

Being the first 80 minute All-Ireland football final adds an extra dimension. And the football was fast and furious from the off. Six times the sides are level in the first half before Kerry cut loose in the second, Mick Gleeson's goal opening up a seven-point gap. With Mickey Fay in the form of his life – he would finish with 10 points, eight from frees – Meath narrow the gap to just a goal.

Then Terry Kearns, who has switched to midfield in a swap with Vincent Lynch, races through and is pulled down on the edge of the square. Referee Paul Kelly says the foul happened outside. Tony Brennan chips it over the bar but Meath's best chance is gone.

Din Joe Crowley's goal for Kerry seals the deal.

'The thing about it … the Kerry selectors had been running up and down the sideline trying to get him off,' recalls Martin. 'The next thing the ball broke and the fecker went off on a 40-yard solo run and put it in the net.'

While the decision to disallow the goal in the 1964 semi-final is still a bone of contention, Jack is not really one for regret. 'It was a great achievement to get that far,' he says stoically of being deprived the opportunity to captain Meath to an All-Ireland, what would have been only the county's fourth.

'After the '70 final, the teams had lunch in the Intercontinental when the Meath players showed their calibre. Mick Mellett started singing, "We will not let you down" – that changed the whole mood. We always liked to have the craic with the lads from the other team.'

To reach the final, Jack feels, was an achievement in itself. History shows that a changing of the guard was on the way in Leinster.

Until Seán Boylan came along and worked the oracle, Meath wouldn't win another Leinster title until 1986.

Jack's star still burned bright.

Selected as back up on the All Stars team in 1970-71 that toured San Francisco, Gerry remembers him suffering from that ankle injury. And driving him right up to his collection point so he could make the plane.

'He went off to America where he was picked for the games in San Francisco. There was a bus going from Croke Park to Shannon where they were flying out from. I brought him in, drove him so I could park right beside the bus and he could step from the car to the bus. Because he wasn't able to take a step further! He was that bad.

'The man over Dublin, Jimmy Grey, saw Jack hopping off the bus and says, "Ah, you'll be fit for the game."

'Sure he couldn't walk!'

Maybe Jack sensed the bright lights dimming with Meath.

In terms of trophies, the next part of his career represented the wilderness years. Meath reached the Leinster final in 1973 only to be thumped 3-21 to 2-12 by Offaly.

With Kevin Heffernan fanning the flames of the Dublin revolution and Mick O'Dwyer about to unleash the greatest team the game would ever see, a new rivalry to define Gaelic football was to blossom.

And yet Meath came close to stopping Heffo's Army before it ever went on a march in 1974, being squeezed out in a hard-fought Leinster final, 1-14 to 1-9, Jack's tussle with Jimmy Keaveney one of the duels of the game.

'We were in front of them for a good while. I remember one of our backs getting caught out, there was a bit of a mistake made, and my man Jimmy

Keaveney got a goal … I was left with two of them to mark so there was not a thing I could do about it.

'They had brought him back. He used to play centre-forward for Dublin. I played, not on him, but against him. We always knew Jimmy Keaveney was a smashing footballer. He was nothing new to us when he came back. We knew he was good.'

As for Kevin Heffernan and the impact he would make with Dublin?

'I'm not saying that you'd know he was going to be such a success but you certainly knew he was a top man taking over. He had the reputation and had proved it with St Vincent's as well. You have to hand it to him … it was brilliant. And it's still going. He definitely did get the whole thing going.'

Back then, he says Heffo's Army only consisted of a single regiment of hardened foot soldiers. 'Dublin were down for a number of years. Like us, they had a bad spell for a long time. I remember going up to see Dublin play an early round of the Championship in 1974, against Offaly, and they beat Offaly by a point or two. And there was only a handful at the match.

'You talk about the great Dublin supporters of that time … there wasn't a feckin' hundred at the match!'

While the careers of Mick Lyons and Darren Fay would be defined by Dublin, Jack Quinn's time echoed Paddy O'Brien's in that it was about Leinster's other contenders just as much.

'It was more Offaly in our time. In '66 we beat Kildare in a Leinster final. Dublin weren't at the races during those years.'

But there was to be one last great hurrah for the Meath team that Quinn played on. Trust it to come against Dublin.

After an impressive National League campaign, they found themselves catapulted into a quarter-final. Pitted against Kerry, they were roundly written off. Here was a team who collected National League titles like baubles, chasing a record fifth title in-a-row. Now managed by the one and only Mick O'Dwyer. No contest then.

Except Meath, and Jack, never read the script.

At Croke Park, on an April Sunday, Meath turned the formbook upside down.

'That was the same Kerry team that won the All-Ireland. They were just getting going.

'I was marking a fella called John Bunion … he didn't make it afterwards.

'Funnily enough, on the same day there was at least four different Kerry fellas put on me, maybe five. I had one of those days that if I fell at the corner flag the ball would come into my hands. It was one of those glory days. John Egan came in on me … Pat Spillane finished up on me.'

When the *Irish Independent* named their 'Sportstar of the Week', 31 year-old Jack Quinn was selected, sharing it with Galway hurler, John Connolly.

One game later, he picked up another award, this time for a stellar display in the semi-final against Mayo, Joe Cassells making a name for himself at midfield.

And so to the National League final against Dublin.

Little did Jack or any Meath player or supporter guess that it would be the county's last big day for 11 years. That was the day Jack's pre-match ritual almost got him in a spot of bother.

When the team assembled at Barry's Hotel, he stayed for a while shooting the breeze before he set off for Croker. Off he went on his own, gear bag over shoulder. Down and round the back of the Cusack Stand where he just had to tip his hat to the regular on the gate. Took a seat to watch a bit of the minor game until a few Dublin supporters decided to start ragging at him. It was a sign of things to come later in the afternoon.

Just like the Kerry and Mayo games, a storming second half carried the day for Meath, reeling in a six-point deficit to stun the reigning All-Ireland champions.

Ollie O'Brien's accuracy from play and dead balls kept Meath in touch, and Joe Cassells and Mick Ryan powered the team on from midfield. Ken Rennicks, too, stood out and old stagers Quinn and Pat Reynolds led the defensive effort.

Sensing the game slipping, a crowd of young Dublin supporters sparked further drama by threatening an invasion.

'When it happened first, myself, Ronan Giles who was in the goals and the rest of the backs who were closest to it all, we were kinda scared. They came right in and around behind us at our end.

'They came off the Hill … we were defending Hill 16 at the time. When it all happened it was bloody scary seeing them all come flying down off it. Climbed over the palings no problem to them … didn't care if they tore their trousers.

'I knew there were a few in the stands at the time who were very worried about all of us. They were shocking worried, "Were we going to be destroyed?"

'There was teenagers, fellas in their 20s. Then they surrounded the whole pitch. I have to hand it to them at the same time, they never did anything wrong. They never touched a player. They jumped around the place, danced here and there and acted the eejit but they didn't go near any player. They were okay that day.

'Okay, they did wrong coming in … but give them their due, they didn't touch anyone. I'd never seen it happen. You'd see the supporters coming in when a team won – but not the losers.'

One match report suggested that the intention was to pressurise referee, Harry Reilly to blow it up early, thus force a replay. '*According to the timing of press reporters,*' stated *The Irish Times, 'there was still almost a minute left for play when Mr Reilly signalled full time.*'

'I don't know about that,' says Jack. 'We knew ourselves that time was almost up. You get that vibe at a match when it's just about over. We did hear the referee blow the final whistle.'

That's when the Meath supporters joined their Dublin counterparts on the pitch in a massive outpouring of emotion as the attendance of 40,853 witnessed Meath win the trophy for the first time since 1951, Ronan Giles lifting the Cup.

'The celebrations were huge. Absolutely huge. I'd say they cost us. It was the one thing we hadn't won as a bunch of players.'

That night, plenty of renditions of *'The Mighty Quinn'* were belted out in the pubs around Meath.

Jack recalls the days when he'd hear the strains of it drift from the stands. 'You'd hear it alright but you wouldn't let it bother you. Otherwise you wouldn't play football!'

It wasn't the only thing either in his honour. 'There was meant to be a horse then called after me that Mick O'Toole had, I think it won nine or 10 races on the flat, called The Mighty Quinn. I'm told that was named after me.'

When the *Irish Independent* named its 'Sports Stars of the Week', this time he shared it with tournament winning golfer John O'Leary and Eamonn Coghlan who had become the fastest Irish miler of all time. Serious company.

Just like Paddy 'Hands' O'Brien, his place in Meath folklore was already secure.

But that victory would carry a sting in the tail. Louth, typically, stole their thunder in the first round of the Leinster Championship.

'Louth shocked us in the first round. We were caught off guard after beating Dublin in the League final. If we'd got over that game we might have gone on.

'We thought we'd a right good team at the time too. The Louth defeat shook up Meath football because we were after having that great win against what turned out to be the great Kerry team. We didn't realise that at the time, how good they were going to be.

'That was the start of the great Kerry-Dublin teams. We felt we should have been up there with those boys. You'd know they were good teams but you would never think they'd go on to dominate as they did. You certainly wouldn't.

'That game was the finish of me because I fecked up my knee. I wasn't able to play in the following year's Championship.

'We were only after beating Dublin and three or four weeks later I was playing a club match here in Trim with Kilbride and I busted up my knee … destroyed it. I got a cartilage operation a couple of months later and tried to come back a couple of times, but I never got it right.'

But they wouldn't let him get out of the game easily. Still half crocked, he did tog out as a substitute against Dublin the 1976 Leinster final, when Meath pushed the eventual All-Ireland champions to the brink. 'They actually asked me would I play? They were going to put Kevin McConnell somewhere else. But I said, "don't". I told them to leave him full-back. He's only a young lad starting and he's entitled to it, and I'm nearly shagged anyhow. I'd played no football and I'd probably have made a show of myself.

'I actually asked them to do one thing which they didn't. I asked that if we were a point or two behind with 10 minutes to go, would they put me in full-forward? Because I was lucky that way ... I could play anywhere.

'But they didn't put me on.'

It ended Dublin 2-8 Meath 1-9. He'll never know if he could have made the difference and change the course of Dublin's history with Kerry which was to take on a life of its own.

'I actually played a League match or two and busted my knee again and then retired. I said enough is enough.'

His last game for Meath came against Galway when he scored a point from full-forward before tearing a ligament in training the following week.

'Farewell Jack and thanks!' ran the headline in the *Evening Press* in November 1976 when the story broke.

Kevin McConnell filled the No.3 jersey straight after him, before Quinn graduated to the senior selection committee where he lent his support to the call-up of a young Mick Lyons in 1979.

'I got to know Mick very well,' says Jack. 'He has his golf club [Rathcore] not too far from here. I got to know him going to certain matches and playing with Summerhill.

'A great full-back ... a great man for Meath football.'

Another legend in the making.

CHAPTER 5

MICK LYONS

Until Seán Boylan came along, Mick Lyons remembers life as an inter-county footballer as nothing to be especially proud about. From 1979 to 1982 the years were a wilderness, when interest seemed to be at an all-time low.

He recalls a trip to play Clare, in the National League, that summed up the sense of anything goes. Went down and stayed in Ennis on the Saturday night. Landed in to the hotel before the county board officials to find the usual set menu absent. Ordered all around them, prawn cocktails, glasses of wine, the lot. Disco, late game of cards, and to bed.

And in Kilrush the following afternoon? They won. The biggest shock of the day came when county board secretary, Liam Creavin went to settle the hotel bill.

'There were four people there from Meath … from Trim. That's the truth. There were more seagulls on the field, outside the wire, than there were Meath supporters.'

In 1981, Meath lost to Wexford in the first round in Leinster. When they fell through the same trap door in 1982, *The Meath Chronicle* famously featured a coffin on its front page with 'Meath Football Team' printed on the lid.

And then the word went around that Boylan had the gig.

A former Meath hurler?

'I would only have known Seán as a hurler,' admits Lyons. 'That was it.

Sure Seán was a masseur. No-one would touch it with a 40-foot pole! And I wouldn't blame them.'

His brother Paraic recalls hearing the news, and quizzing Mick about the new manager. 'He was announced as manager and I didn't even know who he was,' explains Paraic.

'Michael had been there for a couple of years. Seán had been in doing masseur ... a bit of rubbing and that, and Michael says, "You know the little fella that was rubbing your leg the last day ... he's the manager."

'And you thought, "Well, that's enough!" And the rest is history.'

The 'little fella' had big plans.

Mick's reaction wasn't a million miles removed from his brother's. 'Ah, this is another year. We'll have a different lad the next year.'

Which was meant to be the plan. Boylan himself only agreed to take the job on a 'caretaker' basis. 'You had Gerry McEntee there, Colm O'Rourke, I was there, Joe Cassells – all the lads who went on to win All-Irelands,' explains Mick. 'We were very lucky he came along.'

Nobody knew then it would be the start of a beautiful relationship.

'No ... let's call a spade a spade,' says Mick.

Except one of Boylan's first acts was to cut Mick Lyons loose. Dropped him without fuss or fanfare.

His first panel included a Lyons from Summerhill alright; it just happened to be Paraic. 'Seán dropped me for a couple of months,' admits Mick with a rueful smile. 'Discarded me ... !'

'I wasn't part of the panel called together. I think that was the time I was playing full-forward with the club.' The snub cut him. 'I suppose it would bother you a bit ... it would. I didn't unduly say, "Oh Jesus, that's the end of my career as a county footballer."' But it stung.

Straight away, Boylan had made it clear: he wasn't there to play politics or play the long game. If the new manager wanted to send out a message that he was an independent spirit who meant business, he couldn't have done a better job if he burned it onto the Hill Of Tara.

Boylan confirms Mick's suspicions as to his original exclusion. 'Because he was playing full-forward for Summerhill,' confirms Seán.

He recalls going to watch him as Summerhill took on O'Mahonys. 'He was like a fish out of water. The '82 Championship was on and Summerhill won the Championship. There were six selectors with me ... and Mick didn't make the cut.'

On his first meeting with the Meath players, the new manager felt like the school teacher who stumbles across the gang of smokers down the back of the bike sheds, except that the heavy gang paid him no heed. The Meath team at the time were an intimidating bunch.

'Remember I'd come in from nowhere,' continues Seán. 'We were meeting under the stand in Navan and Rourkey came in, and he had Gerry and a few more with him. He just looked around and said, just loud enough for the boys to hear, "Who are these f**kers?" I pretended not to hear.'

Boylan's first homily set the tone.

He knew he had to address a dressing room full of cliques and barely concealed club grudges. He remembers his every word. 'I told them, "I just want to say something lads. When you play with each other on Sunday, I don't care if you're from Oldcastle, from Dunboyne, Ballinabrackey, Summerhill, Bettystown ... whatever. Kick the shit out of each other on Sunday. But when you come in to me on Tuesday, you come in as Meath men."

'That was the start of it.'

As Boylan says himself, 'I never curse', but he knew he had to catch their attention. After all, he was only there on a promise.

'I took the job for three months. Until they got somebody. Because Mattie Kerrigan, Gerry Mac, Mick O'Brien ... they had all been proposed but for different reasons they couldn't do it. That's how I ended up doing it ... until they would get somebody.'

Twenty-three years later he would pass on the baton.

The fact that Paraic, and not Mick, received an invitation to that first meeting remains a source of merriment to the former. If he wants to get a rise out of his big brother, he knows which button to press.

'That's the only thing I have on him. He has his All Stars and everything else but I always tell him, "I was never dropped off the panel!"

'One of the selectors said at the time, "Sure he can't even play full-back in his own club." As if to say he wasn't good enough to play full-back for Summerhill. But the club were only trying things out. It didn't last too long.'

He didn't feel the need to offer a shoulder to cry on to Mick. 'No! There was a sort of a feeling, "They'll come to their senses in time!" We were all a bit mystified. Mattie Kerrigan was a big noise at the time, I'd say he would have a big input in relation to the selectors. I'd say it was along the lines of, "What the feck are you at?"'

November 7, 1982.

Meath versus Galway in Navan. By the third game of the National League, Mick's exile had ended.

There was no hug from Boylan or clap on the back when he landed back in. His reappearance hardly merited a collective shrug from the dressing room.

'Just business as usual,' says Mick.

Boylan remembers a club match being the turning point. 'Summerhill played Walsh Island and Mick was playing midfield. And he had an outstanding match. And I asked Mick in from there.'

And Lyons would slowly become one of his most trusted lieutenants.

'The first match I brought him on was against Galway. Meath got a penalty. Paraic was playing corner-back; Jimmy Fay was in goals. Paraic goes haring up the field to take the penalty. And Jimmy's talking to the umpire: "I can tell you now, this will be in the back of the net or the swimming pool!" Y'know … where the car park runs?'

That day, Mick had to make do with a cameo as a substitute.

'He played a few games centre-back,' says Paraic. 'He was never happy there. It just didn't fit the bill with him. He played nearly all his football for Summerhill at midfield. And I wouldn't want to be blowing his head too much but we haven't had a midfielder like him since. To this day.'

But Mick was back on board the bus. That was all that mattered.

✦✦✦✦✦

The first time he walked into a Meath senior dressing room was 1979.

His abiding memory brings a laugh out of him. 'It was cold! Down in Navan. It was different. First of all, the older lads would all be in their own seats … we saw that when we were older ourselves. A young lad would come in and we'd say, "You'll not be sitting there!" It wouldn't be that you wanted to make little of them, that's just the way it was. You have your own corner.'

It took Boylan's arrival to shake things up in the dressing room.

'We ended up being great friends, with a real sense of unity, especially when it came to what we wanted to win, but it took us a long time to learn. Back then, when you went out playing inter-county football it was everyone playing for himself.'

That May of 1979 he was handed his Championship debut. At centre-back. Against Kilkenny, in Navan. The final scoreline read, Meath 6-19 Kilkenny 0-3. The sense of farce to the fixture didn't exactly make it a memorable debut. 'No. It was nice to play for Meath I suppose, but it wouldn't have been like years later when there was such a buzz about it.'

Dessie Ferguson was team coach then, and one of his selectors just happened to be Jack Quinn. Turns out Quinn was to play some small part in unearthing a long-term successor.

As to the idea that Lyons might later be part of one of the greatest Meath teams? 'You'd never think that then!

'We played Kildare the next day in the Championship in Croke Park. I didn't last too long at centre-back that day. I wasn't going that well … I was lucky enough not to be spared the chop to the sideline. Instead I was brought back corner-back.'

Pat Mangan of Kildare handed him his first lesson in a Meath senior jersey. 'He was coming to the end of his days but he was well able for me that day … too clever for me.'

Jimmy Fay's 40 metre dash up the field, soloing out from goal to great excitement, started the move that led to Meath's late equaliser, his brother Mickey lining out in the corner the same afternoon.

'Jimmy's a great character. A fierce character. After a while it got so serious playing football. It was fun … but it wasn't fun … if you know what I mean? It took us a long time to get to that stage. After that … it was a ruthless machine.'

They drew with Kildare. For the replay, Lyons was picked where he finished, at left corner-back - Kevin McConnell was still the regular full-back at the time. Meath shipped three goals but still squeezed through - Mickey Ryan and Ken Rennicks leading the charge.

Marking the great Matt Connor in the Leinster semi-final against Offaly represented a very different sort of challenge. 'Matt was a great footballer. Sure I was the same age as Matt then. I suppose I would have been 20. Back then, he was probably like myself starting out. Just a better footballer than I was.'

Connor sneaked a couple of points off him but Lyons' performance was highlighted in *The Irish Press* match report the following day.

By the following summer, he had laid claim to the No.3 jersey, but playing Dublin in the Leinster semi-final, in Navan, turned out to be an eye-opening experience.

'Kevin Moran came on that day. What I remember about that match is that it showed you the difference between playing club football and county football. Lads would be telling you about experience and all this ... blah ... blah. When you're young you'd be saying, "yeah, whatever".

'Well Jaysus, we learned a valuable lesson that day. We were with Dublin for a good while of the match and they just upped the tempo. Blew us out of the water! In every dimension of what's involved in Gaelic football; physically, mentally, fitness wise ... everything.

'I remember Kevin Moran came on and I had an angle on him. Most of the times when I'd have an angle on a forward, I'd get him.

'But he wasn't there when I got there.

'That's the truth. I said to myself ... "Hmmm." I started thinking straight away about the work needed to get to that level.'

'He had the soccer thing going on. I'm not sure whether he was on the Manchester United team at that stage ... he was certainly on the fringes of it, but he got off free to come home. His speed was at a different level.'

It ended, Dublin 3-13 Meath 2-7, and Dublin worth every inch of their nine-point victory. 'That's why there was such great rivalry between Meath and Dublin. We left terrible marks on them, if you take the likes of 1991 and that, but you have to remember that they created the monster.

'They were so dominant. Winning All-Irelands! They only beat Meath by a point or two in the early years before they went on … and went on to win All-Irelands some of those years.

'I'd live and die to play the Dubs. You'd nearly still go out and try and play football to get to Croke Park … full house, Meath and Dublin.

'That was it.

'I'd live and die for that.

'Win, lose or draw.

'It's just we built up such a rivalry. And a healthy rivalry. There was no auld bitterness … just adrenaline all the way.

'You end up playing against them and simply say to yourself, "If we're going to compete, we've got to be better than this."'

Instead, Meath football bottomed out, losing to Wexford in the first round of the Leinster Championship in 1981, and then to Longford at the first time of asking in 1982, the latter defeat sparking the famous edition of the *Chronicle* which administered the last rites to the county team.

✦✦✦✦✦

Paraic Lyons' Championship debut just happened to dovetail with that infamous defeat in Tullamore to Longford. The whole season was a nerve-jangling experience. 'I think I made my debut in Navan in a League match … could have been against Monaghan, and I remember hoping and praying that the ball wouldn't come over my side. If it was coming down the far side, "that's grand!"'

Still, the Lyons' house was buzzing at the time to have two brothers representing Meath. Starting side by side, Mick wearing No.3, Paraic No.4. 'In our house, Monday was taken over by discussing football. Austin would come down as well. My father is still alive, he's 86 now … they'd come down, especially after Summerhill matches. You'd get it, straight up, how you played.

'If you played bad you were told you played bad. There was no such thing as, "Ah, you were in hard luck." That was it. If you passed the grade … told you were playing well, you were buzzing! Most of the time you wouldn't be. That's the way it was ... you were told the truth.'

'Mick O'Brien was over us that day. That was my first Championship match in '82; I played League in '81. At that stage the Summerhill thing was still big and you'd say, "Right, we'll go back to the club." Where if that happened in the late '80s and you got a bad beating you had a different perspective on it. If you went out in the first round of the Championship, you'd feel very different.'

Mick remembers the *Chronicle's* spin on it.

'*Meath football RIP* ... I remember it in the paper. Everyone says you don't read the papers but you would read them ... you'd like to see what lads would be saying. Now you wouldn't put huge store on it!

'Lads who say they don't read the papers don't be telling the truth. They'd be having a peek. Back then, you'd expect to be beaten ... well maybe not expect, but no-one feared you. There was no respect for Meath. You knew well you weren't going to win anything.

'You wouldn't hear a lot in the dressing room after a defeat like that. You'd be getting your bag and getting out of there quick. A badly beaten dressing room ... you don't hang around. Silence. Maybe someone says, "We'll get together Wednesday or Thursday ... we have to do something about this." But that was it.

'There was a bit of shock, but at that stage we weren't going anywhere.'

Enter Seán Boylan.

♦ ♦ ♦ ♦ ♦

Eleven victories on the bounce endeared the new manager to his players. Promotion to Division One and a National League semi-final can do that.

For the first time in his Meath career,- and one of the very few times - Lyons got the line over the course of that spring, in the final round game against Roscommon.

'We gained promotion, and the personal foul had been introduced,' explains Boylan. 'John O'Keeffe had been sent off playing in the Railway Cup in Croke Park for pulling a jersey, and the same happened Mick Lyons.

'That team gained promotion. We played Armagh in the semi-finals in '83. Mick had a marvellous game at full-back. Jim McConville scored a great goal against us; Rourkey scored a cracker for us as well.

'That was the day Fr Seán Hegarty came in to the dressing room after the match. He went to say a few words and the boys started slagging. They couldn't believe there was another manager smaller than me!'

That day, Meath discovered a ready-made heir to the No.3 shirt, someone with the broad shoulders to carry the legacy of Paddy 'Hands' O'Brien and Jack Quinn.

'He never looked back from there,' confirms Boylan.

Lyons remembers the big hits that went in that day in terrible conditions, Joe Cassells immense too for Meath at centre-back.

'Sure that's the way it was. You threw yourself in and hopefully took someone down with you!' he says, laughing. 'It's a bit like the rugby is now. If you can take your opposite number out … that's it! Legally, and within the rules, you do it.

'We were beaten by Armagh on a real wet day … the muck, and the rain. That was tough going.' Promotion softened the blow. 'There is no team that comes from Division Three or Four and wins an All-Ireland. You have to be in the first Division.'

A first trophy endeared Boylan to his troops even further. It arrived that May after an O'Byrne Cup final win over Longford in Pearse Park on a scoreline of 1-11 to 1-9. Mick Downes captained a side notable for Martin O'Connell making a first big-game appearance at centre-back.

Quickly, a month later, a two-leg first round Championship match re-ignites the whole Meath-Dublin rivalry.

For the first time, Boylan is pitting his wits against the brains trust of Kevin Heffernan and Tony Hanahoe. 'It kicked off then,' says Lyons. With Jimmy Fay gone from the scene Meath somehow hanged tough to force a draw, despite two soft goals conceded.

The last came when a Joe McNally shot is deflected in off corner-back Phil Smith's chest, a sucker punch on a day when O'Rourke hit 1-5.

For Lyons, marking Joe McNally was always a testing experience.

'Joe was alright. Joe was Joe, I suppose! I knew we were starting to creep up a little bit.'

For all the running battles he would have with the likes of McNally down the years, he baulks at the idea that he would ever try and use verbals to psyche out an opponent.

'I was never one for jawing at anyone. That wasn't my style. I didn't see any point in it. They knew what I was going to do … so…'

The way he leaves the sentence trail off is enough of a statement in itself. In that respect, he was very much old school. 'I don't think you should say anything … I think it's wrong.'

Considering how the Meath and Dublin pairing would take on almost mythical dimensions in later years, it's worth noting a crowd of only 24,383 showed for a thrilling replay which went to extra-time, Barney Rock's punched goal settling it.

'Barney was a good player,' admits Lyons, adding, 'We held no fear for any of them. Not when we got going. In fairness, Seán brought us up to a level of fitness where we could compete. That was a major thing. We already knew we could play football.

'And he broke the stranglehold of the clubs. He basically got Meath football as a club … brought the club mentality to the county. We had a fair idea then where we were. We knew that if we could beat Dublin we could win the All-Ireland.

'That was our yardstick.'

Because, by the end of that summer in '83, the same Dublin team that had scraped by Meath with the help of those fortunate goals went on to famously lift the Sam Maguire Cup, even with 12 men to Galway's 14 in the final.

Lining up to give Dublin a guard of honour in the first game of the National League that October, he didn't resent tipping the hat to the old enemy. 'I don't think we were ever like that. We took our beatings.'

It just made him more determined, picturing the scene with the boot on the other foot. 'We had a taste of the big time. To get into Croke Park with a good crowd there is just the best. Like any top sportsman, that's what you play for.'

For him, there was always something special about Dublin versus Meath.

'It has a better atmosphere than an All-Ireland. I said that to Seán Boylan. "There is no better atmosphere." It's a constant noise up and down.

'All-Ireland day is muted sometimes. You can even see it nowadays. I think the two counties involved should get all the tickets going.'

In Navan, in that National League encounter, last gasp scores from Richie Crean and John Caffrey denied Meath a famous win. But they were inching ever closer.

Boylan has the players climbing dunes and slashing into the sea at the end of each session as Bettystown became the new base camp for the Meath team. It would just be the first of his left-field training regimes.

When the rowing trips down the canal are mentioned, or the swimming pool sessions in the buoyancy suits, or the running around Fairyhouse race course, it's easy to picture Lyons – old school in the traditional sense of how he felt the game should be played – shaking his head at it all. But, it says everything about Boylan's charisma, that the Summerhill man was one of his true disciples. He could see the method in the madness.

'All those mad things. Was the allure of Meath football there when I started? No. Was it there then? Yes.'

Memories of running around the Hill of Tara in the near-dark bring a wide smile.

'Did you ever see the old films where you'd have a fella with a lantern minding sheep? It was like that.

'It was hard going. But you always knew that if you got it over with, it would stand to us. Because you had to have that level of fitness to be able to play. You knew you needed to do it. I wasn't there thinking … "Is there a handy way out of this?" Because if you got a handy way out of it, the day might come where it would come back on you.

'We had to do that so that if you got knocked down, you got straight back up and kept going.'

A snapshot of the mentality that Meath would build their kingdom on.

When the star-spangled football banner that is the Kerry team rolled into Navan for the final League game before Christmas in 1983, it was the first chance for Meath to rub shoulders with the game's greatest team.

Legendary broadcaster, Mícheál Ó Muircheartaigh tells a story about one particular exchange that day between Mick Lyons and Jack O'Shea. 'He wasn't a dirty player,' he says describing Lyons. 'A powerfully strong man, the head and chest of him. All that came from the father as well. Paddy was from Louisburgh in Mayo. I knew him as well. They were reared on the fact that that was the type of football to play.

'I remember Jack O'Shea telling me one time about the League game against Meath in Navan. And Mick was full-back. Jack, as was his usual custom, was attacking and sailed by, and scored a point.

'Coming out, Mick told him not to be coming too often or …

'Jack's answer to that was to come again.'

Lyons remembers having a cut alright, telling O'Shea that his card had been marked. 'Jacko used to be up in Leixlip working. I think I said something like that at the time … I said something to him anyway! It was one of the few occasions, I did'

The low chuckle suggests it might have been a more colourful version of same.

Back then, there were times he felt awestruck in the company of Jacko, Spillane et al. 'Ah, you would be. I know Dwyer is a great manager but I think they would have won All-Irelands themselves … Jaysus, they were some team.'

Typically, Kerry pick-pocketed the points, 1-13 to 2-9.

Paraic Lyons looked to have sneaked a point, lashing a penalty to the net two minutes from the end to equalise, only for Mikey Sheehy to float over a free to win it from all of 48 yards.

Meath though, were learning to swim in shark-infested waters. Losing to All-Ireland finalists, Galway in the League semi-final in 1984 confirmed as much.

Winning the Centenary Cup – a competition to celebrate 100 years of the GAA - represented another milestone. Jimmy Fay was back on board and lined out behind the two Lyons brothers as Meath edged out Monaghan, 0-10 to 0-8 in the final in Croke Park.

The banquet, as much as the match, would leave a lasting impression on a young Darren Fay.

For the first time in four years, Meath would go on to win a match in the Leinster Championship that same summer, Martin O'Connell 'Man of the Match' at wing-back.

'You were basically putting your foot on the bottom rung of the ladder,' says Lyons. 'At least you were starting to go in the right direction. People think Meath were a great team but they were very poor in spells.'

A run to a first Leinster final in seven years was undermined, however, when Lyons broke his thumb in a Championship match for Summerhill, ruling him out of lining out against The Dubs.

He sat in Croke Park, in his civvies, as Dublin-Meath suddenly had the attention of the football world, an attendance of 56,051 - over double the previous year's encounter.

And he watched a game of twists and turns, and an all too familiar result. Despite John Caffrey's early dismissal, the old pals' act of Barney Rock and Ciaran Duff shared 2-8 to carry Dublin through on their backs.

If Paraic Lyons likes to slag Mick about being omitted from Boylan's first squad, big brother has an easy one to fire way: 'What about the penalty in the 1984 Leinster final, Paraic?' Meath's corner-back jogged the length of the field to take a fifth minute penalty, only to thump it wide.

'We reckon that if the poor lads in the wheelchairs were out there … he would have killed them!' quips Mick.

Robbie O'Malley was the spare man at the back against 14-man Dublin in the final, but Heffo had the street smarts to play around him.

Another defeat.

And the year would end on a further sour note when Mick got knocked unconscious playing for Ireland in the opening minutes of the first Compromise Rules test against Australia in Cork.

Another year gone.

✦ ✦ ✦ ✦

As they walked together into the ground in Tullamore, to play Laois in a Leinster semi-final the following summer, Mick Lyons made a quick observation to Liam Hayes.

'If you can't play football on a pitch like that … with a new O'Neill's football … you will never play football.'

Between the thumb injury and the concussion against Australia, 1984 was a write off. This summer, the summer of '85, was going to be different. Wishful thinking.

'It gets worse … WORSE! Laois gave us an awful beating in '85. We were trounced in Tullamore. They destroyed us … took us to the cleaners. That was a very good Laois team … had serious talent up front.

'That was very low. That was when you'd be starting to question yourself again … maybe we thought we were a better team than we were?'

Such was the fall-out from the sad summer of 1985, that Paul Kenny even opposed Seán Boylan for the manager's position, but the man in situ got the vote of confidence from board delegates and officials, a double-edged sword all of its own.

After changing the sprawling seven-man selection committee system and bringing in Pat Reynolds and Tony Brennan, two of the heroes from Meath's last team to win an All-Ireland in '67, it was win or bust for Boylan.

And not just the manager. Lyons felt another year of failure would likely have ended his own career, along with the other greybeards on the team such as Joe Cassells, Gerry McEntee and O'Rourke.

'Seán was lucky to survive that year … barely made it. We were all lucky, players included, to get a second run at it. If a new manager had have come in, I'd say he would have had to get rid of us. I was 27, 28 at that stage. Colm O'Rourke something similar.

'I didn't win my first Leinster 'til I was 28. That's a long time from starting off your career at 19, 20. It took too long to get to the top.'

+++++

Boylan was still auditioning for parts, and found a few more characters with lead potential.

Liam Harnan, Terry Ferguson, Brian Stafford and PJ Gillick all made the cut.

Meath lost again to Dublin in a League quarter-final early in 1986, this time by the narrowest of margins, but a 2-8 to 1-10 defeat came with plenty of positives. Liam Hayes and Joe Cassells bossed the midfield and there was a sense of a team coming together. Ratoath's Stan Gibney was one those vying for a jersey at full-forward, before Stafford made the transition from corner to edge of the square.

That was a day notable too for Mick Lyons getting what he thinks is his only ever score in League or Championship for Meath, kicking over a point after drifting up the field in the final minutes.

The Lyons clan don't care much for mementos of the years gone by. For Mick and Paraic, the past is a foreign country, in little need of a return visit.

Neither keep tapes or DVD's of their exploits with the county around the house. 'Horror movies I call them,' laughs Mick, explaining how the kids he coaches on the Summerhill teams often pull him up for the way the matches stayed true to the spirit of catch and kick rather than the possession game of today.

But Paraic has a soft spot for one day, one match.

July 27, 1986.

Leinster final day.

Meath and Dublin.

It's the one DVD his daughter, Linda likes to pull out and throw on, and occasionally, Paraic will pull up a chair and watch the action unfold.

This was 'The Breakthrough'.

Year Zero of the modern era. The day Meath football added a new chapter to the story.

This was the match Meath had been building towards over the course of Seán Boylan's four seasons in charge.

In the build-up, Boylan turned to a familiar old face for a note of inspiration, inviting one of the stars of the '49ers', Frankie Byrne in to say a few words to the players. He was the perfect choice, a garrulous, charismatic presence who offered a living, breathing link with the county's proud past.

'For the likes of us to breakthrough and win the All-Ireland for the first time ever … there are thousands and thousands of old people who think we walk on water,' explains Byrne. 'I said to them, "It's time to write your own history."'

And boy, did they!

Lyons' memories of that day remain vivid, even now. 'A gruelling match. I wouldn't say it was nice to watch from outside.

'Do you know what happened that day? Tommy Carr was named full-forward and he was going to bring me out the field. So we put Joe Cassells to follow Tommy out the field. And that happened, exactly as we wanted it to. I stayed in around the square and Joe went out around the middle where he was a natural midfielder.'

On a day when the rain bucketed down, Barney Rock broke his collar-bone in a jarring tackle from Liam Harnan before half time.

'They knew what Liam was like. Even Barney, I'd say, wouldn't call it a dirty tackle. He just ran into him. Hit him hard ... you run into Liam Harnan, and that's it.'

At a later date, Meath would trade on that bone-crunching reputation. Boylan offered a friendly face to the world but was smart enough to play to the strengths of the group of players at his disposal. And so a video of 'Meath's Greatest Hits' was played one evening at a squad meeting, a collection of tackles that left an array of opposition players knocked into next week. All to the tune of Queen's *'Another One Bites the Dust'*.

Lyons plays down the idea that he was the hard man of the team.

'Liam Harnan put in some hits. He was terrible strong ... awesome, strength wise. Without even wanting to be. He was by far the strongest in the 20 years we were playing. Some people are just built strong. He's what, 6'3"? And built accordingly. He'd look a bit thin looking ... but he wouldn't be thin!'

He points to the hit on Barney Rock as a prime example. 'People think that was a dirty tackle. There was nothing dirty about that. That was down to pure strength. Far stronger than I'd be. No comparison.

'They thought Liam Harnan wasn't a footballer. It took lads a long time to realise he was a serious footballer. A great man to lay off a ball. He'd put that ball into a forward's track.'

David Beggy announced himself as a rare talent early in the match, slaloming past a host of different defenders to kick a cracking point. It was tough and tight all the way from there, the scores level five different times.

Down the home straight, Meath slowly turned the screw. Finian Murtagh edged Meath in front. Then, with the clock counting down, a big punch from Liam Hayes found O'Rourke who put two in it. On a day of hard yards, it was enough.

For the first time since Jack Quinn lifted the Cup in 1970, Meath were Leinster champions.

For the first time since Martin, Jack and Gerry Quinn played their part on an emotional day in 1964, Meath had beaten Dublin in a Leinster final.

Lyons says he didn't feel weighed down by the sense of history or Meath's losing record against Dublin. 'No … if you kept thinking about them things, you'd never win anything. You'd probably see it in the papers and people might say it to you.

'That was a milestone,' he concedes. 'To beat Dublin … Croke Park … full of people! We knew we had arrived.'

Meath celebrated, but with Kerry on the horizon in an All-Ireland semi-final the players quickly reined it in, says Lyons. 'We did enjoy it. But we didn't go mad.'

Boylan was busy figuring out a plan to thwart the Munster champions bid for an eighth All-Ireland under Mick O'Dwyer, a three-in-a-row to go with the four-in-a-row of 1978-81.

'At that stage we had videos, clips of all the players. Seán had Eamon O'Farrell, who used to do the video, dissect all the pieces out that were needed. It wasn't just cobbled together.

It was done the right way.'

And yet, he admits, 'I don't know if we were ready for Kerry. They were on the way down in '86 … it was the last kick of that team.'

Naming long-time midfielder Joe Cassells at corner-back worked like a dream in the Leinster final when Tommy Carr took off out the field, but it backfired badly against Kerry's standard attacking formation.

'We fell into the trap then the next day of leaving Joe corner-back. And it didn't work out. We should have played an orthodox corner-back on Ger Power.'

Lyons felt nervous going up against the all-singing, all-dancing Kerry forward line. His direct opponent Eoin 'Bomber' Liston was the prototype full-forward; an aerial threat, a ball-winner, a goal-scorer, a towering player with no little grace on the ball.

Adding a touch of the exotic to the whole occasion, they lined out in their provincial colours; Meath in Leinster green, Kerry in Munster blue.

'You would be worried because Kerry could destroy you in one fell swoop. They could have two goals in ... like that! In five minutes of football they could beat you.

'I remember the Tyrone final, in 1986, when they were well up against Kerry. Next thing, back of the net ... BANG! You could see the life draining out of the Tyrone lads.

'If you could just call a time out. Get lads off the field ... get them together again. Because it was all going the wrong way.'

But Meath, and Lyons, adapted quickly to the big stage in their first All-Ireland semi-final of the 80s, powering into a 0-4 to 0-2 lead.

'The first half of that match was great football. Fast, furious stuff. It was the fastest football we had played up to that stage ... ever.

'I remember thinking "This is great!" It was up and down the field. Tommy Doyle got a little cut on his knee. It looked like they were saying "stay down". It looked as if they wanted the break in play.

'We nearly had them broke. Their experience beat us that day ... our inexperience beat us.' That inexperience was all too evident in one the most famous incidents from any All-Ireland semi-final.

'The Collision', as Darren Fay calls it.

A ball is sent in from Kerry's Denis 'Ogie' Moran.
Ger Power is running on to it with Joe Cassells chasing him back.
Mick Lyons too is flying back to cover as goalkeeper Mickey McQuillan also converges under the dropping ball.
McQuillan jumps to punch the ball.
He clobbers Lyons instead.

Cassells goes tumbling too.

Ger Power nearly has enough time to draw chalk outlines around the bodies on the ground. Instead, he strokes the ball into an empty net.

'It was a stupid collision. It shouldn't have happened at that level of football. All I remember … and this is the truth … I don't remember hitting the ground. All I remember is looking up like that and your man f**kin' on his own, tipping the ball into the net. I thought, "Aw good Jesus!"'

As to the 'ins' and 'outs' of whose fault it was, or who called for the ball, he replies, 'Sure you wouldn't hear in Croke Park. You know when you'd be telling young lads, "Shout when you go up for a ball." In Croke Park you don't hear a thing … you live on instinct.

'Did I think it looked bad for us? No. I thought we were well in the match.'

Lyons and Cassells shared a close enough bond on and off the field to get plenty of mileage out of it afterwards.

'I'd be great friends with Joe. Sure we slagged him for months and years because of it. He even agreed himself that he shouldn't have been in there. He was an out-and-out midfielder.

When we beat Dublin, they should have gone with a natural corner-back and put Joe out midfield or where he was suited. Because Joe was a hell of a footballer.'

Paraic, the only member of the full-back line not to be fingered at the scene of the crime admits, 'It was just a disaster … to give Kerry such a golden opportunity like that. If they had have nailed Ger Power, at least he might have been gone for the rest of the game. But he slipped out and put it in the net … and that was the end of that.'

And yet Meath regrouped.

Regrouped and surged into a 0-7 to 1-2 lead coming up to half time. A loss of concentration allowed Kerry to ping over four answered points before the break, and the Munster champions always had Meath at arm's length in the second half – Liam Harnan's dismissal and a Willie Maher goal signalling game over.

'The biggest thing we learned that day,' says Mick, 'I remember Kerry were four or five points up, and we looking around at the clock. And there was still 10 minutes to go.

'If that happened a couple of years later we'd be thinking, "plenty of time left here".

'Inexperience probably beat us that day.'

And other things.

'Sure Martin O'Connell was playing full-forward!'

When the 'Team of the Millennium' was named, only one Meath man made the cut. Despite being honoured at full-back on the GAA's official 'Team of the Century' in 1984, Paddy 'Hands' O'Brien lost favour with a new generation of judges.

The county still had a representative though to celebrate on this choice selection of champions. At left half-back, it was the self-same Martin O'Connell, who looked about as comfortable at full-forward against Kerry as Lyons did in his brief experiment there with Summerhill, but whose natural talent couldn't be ignored.

Lyons' running battle with 'The Bomber' was worth a good portion of the price of the ticket.

Before he limped off with a hamstring injury, the most well-known bearded full-forward in Gaelic football history had three points to his name, even as Lyons' reputation remained undimmed.

'We had a fair battle but I'd say he won it by the finish. Lads would ask you, "Who is the best player you ever played on?" It's a bit like anything ... whether it's Gaelic football or rugby ... if you're on the back foot, anyone will beat you. If your midfield is losing and the ball is coming in every which way, you can stand wherever you like ... and you won't get it.'

For all that, the feeling lingers that Eoin Liston might just top the list. As if to answer the charge, Lyons adds, 'You could kick it in high, any way at all, and he could still get it. He wasn't afraid to go for it. When he came on the scene first ... sure, he terrorised half the country! A serious footballer.'

Nothing that Lyons had experienced before on a football field up to then prepared him for the intensity of that contest. It had a different dimension to the rough-hewn battle of wills with Dublin - the border rivalry framed Championship matches in a certain way.

'That game was a proper game of Championship football. Meath and

Dublin was a different type of football. That's the way it had to be. That's the way it was right 'til the bitter end.'

When a depleted Kerry travelled to Kells for a routine National League encounter, late in '86, having wrapped up an eighth All-Ireland on Mick O'Dwyer's watch, adding to the mythology of their story by storming back from seven down against Tyrone in the final to win by eight, alarm bells hardly started ringing in The Kingdom after Meath turned the tables.

Pore over the fine print of the 1-12 to 0-4 scoreline in Kells that afternoon, however, and there was a sense of a changing of the guard.

'I thought that Kerry team were finished … on the way down.' says Lyons unequivocally. But another year would have to pass before the truth of that statement became clear.

✦ ✦ ✦ ✦

With Summerhill winning the Meath county Championship later in the year, Boylan had one man in mind for the 1987 assault on Leinster and a first All-Ireland in 20 years – Mick Lyons.

One night at training, the manager pulled him aside and let him know. 'It was an honour but it wasn't a huge thing to me. If Seán had have come to me and said he wanted Colm [O'Rourke] or Gerry [McEntee] to be captain instead, I wouldn't have said, "No Seán, you can't do that."

'It was about the group. Because if you don't have that, you don't have anything. At that stage we weren't happy with winning Leinsters … we wanted the All-Ireland.

'We went to Australia in '86 with Kevin Heffernan. When we came back from that, I knew we had a fair chance of winning the All-Ireland. Because I knew the way Kevin Heffernan worked with his teams. When I saw what he did with the Ireland team out there, I could imagine what he did with a Dublin team at home.'

And then, out of the blue, Seán Boylan resigned in March, a curveball nobody saw coming.

Mick recalls the players being nonplussed more than anything else. The manager's black mood felt like a squall that would blow itself out. And so it proved.

'We're close but I wouldn't have discussed that much with Seán. I don't think Seán was ever going to go properly. I'd say he was making a point.'

An approach from the players and he was back again in a matter of days.

As the summer went on, when it came to Meath training, it was like trying to keep the lid on a saucepan of boiling point.

July threw up another flashpoint; Boylan throwing the whistle at Liam Hayes' feet and telling him to take the session if that's the way he wanted it. The midfielder ended up tailing after him with a whistle, and an apology in hand.

Laois and Kildare acted as a pair of stage rehearsals to another Leinster final against Dublin.

Hot and heavy from the start of the final, Kevin Foley and Charlie Redmond were fingered for the line as a big punch-up broke out. It disrupted Meath's rhythm, after Mattie McCabe's earlier goal had put them in the driving seat.

Dublin led 0-9 to 1-5 at the break.

By now, though, Meath had acquired a ruthless edge. McEntee and Hayes held sway at midfield, and with Brian Stafford, Finian Murtagh and McCabe in form up front, the end result was a clinical 1-13 to 0-12 victory.

'We had the upper hand at that stage,' says Lyons. 'Even though we didn't win by much, you just knew it.'

This time, Derry awaited in the All-Ireland semi-final. Lyons had the considerable talent of Dermot McNicholl to get his head around. 'Very fast … he was only a young player then. A super, little athlete. A huge spring … very strong. Good footballer.'

A hamstring injury didn't help the Derry player's case, or that of his team, and Meath coasted to a perfunctory 0-15 to 0-8 victory.

Now Lyons truly was following in the footsteps of another great Meath full-back, ready to lead his county out on All-Ireland final day for the first time since Jack Quinn in 1970.

Once more, the opposition consisted of the Munster champions. It took

Brian Smyth leads Meath on the parade before the 1949 All-Ireland final victory over Cavan in Croke Park. Full-back Paddy O'Brien is at the back of the Meath line that includes (from right): B Smyth, Micheál O'Brien, Paddy Dixon, Kevin McConnell, Paddy Connell, Peter McDermott, Frankie Byrne, Matty McDonnell, Kevin Smyth, Jim Kearney, Seamus Heery, Bill Halpenny, Paddy Meegan, Christo Hand and Paddy O'Brien.

Meath attack the Cavan goal in '49 (from left): Bill Halpenny (M), S McCabe (C), PJ Duke (C), Peter McDermott (M), Mattie McDonnell (M), Brian Smyth (M), and referee Dan Ryan from Kerry.

Paddy O'Brien (third from left) and his Meath colleagues listen to instructions from team trainer, Fr Patrick Tully PP Duleek.

Paddy O'Brian relaxes (front of photo) with the Meath team and officials at Butlins in 1949.

Peter McDermott, Paddy Connell, Pat Carolan and Frankie Byrne relax with some tennis while training in Gibbstown before the '49 final.

Brian Smyth celebrates with the Sam Maguire Cup and jubilant Meath supporters after the '49 victory. Frankie Byrne is on Brian's right, and William Eggleston, Meath Co Board secretary is on his left.

Paddy O'Brien (front, with football) with the Meath team before the 1954 Leinster final victory over Offaly.

Meath and Galway teams leave New York for Cobh aboard the New Amsterdam in 1951.

Meath and Galway welcomed to New York on the steps of City Hall.

Most Rev Dr J Kyne, Bishop of Meath, throws in the ball at the start of the 1954 All-Ireland final between Meath and Kerry.

Brian Smyth wins possession in the 1954 All-Ireland final surrounded by S Murphy (K), M Palmer (K), N Roche (K), Michael Grace (M), Tom Moriarty (M), Paddy Connell (M) and Peter McDermott (M).

Jack Quinn (third from left) steps it out behind Meath captain Davy Carty in 1966.

Jack Quinn fields magnificently in the 1966 All-Ireland final versus Galway.

Jack Quinn celebrates in the foreground on the steps of the Hogan Stand as Peter Darby lifts the Sam Maguire Cup after defeating Cork.

The Meath team that defeated Cork in the 1967 All-Ireland final.

Jack Quinn (centre) and Australian captain Ron Barassi await the toss of the coin to begin the first match in the 1968 Australian tour.

The 'Red' Collier in action for Meath during the Australian tour in 1968.

The Meath team and officials set off for their historic tour of Australia in 1968.

Taking in the sights at Sydney Opera House (left) and looking the part on the team's touchdown in Hawaii, even though Jack Quinn didn't make the reception.

*Mick Lyons
punches the ball
clear in the hectic
finale to Meath's
breakthrough
Leinster final
victory over
Dublin in 1986.*

*Meath manager, Sean
Boylan and Meath County
Board secretary, Liam
Creavin celebrate after the
1986 Leinster final victory.*

The Meath team that defeated Cork in the 1987 All-Ireland final.

Mick Lyons makes a magnificent block on Jimmy Kerrigan to 'save the day' in the first-half of the '87 All-Ireland final as Meath struggled five points adrift.

Mick Lyons (top photo) is tackled by Australia's Scott Salisbury during the International Rules series in 1987. Mick outfields Joe McNally (above) in the 1988 Leinster final and breaks out with the ball.

The iconic figure of one of the most respected full-backs in the history of the game.

Mick Lyons blocks Vinny Murphy in the third replay in the 'four game' Leinster Championship series with Dublin that gripped the country in 1991.

The Meath team that defeated Mayo in the 1996 All-Ireland final replay.

Darren Fay parades before the 1998 Leinster final against Dublin, with Donal Curtis and Mark O'Reilly.

Darren Fay emerges from the dressing room before the 1999 All-Ireland final against Cork.

Darren Fay celebrates with Kildare's Anthony Rainbow after defeating Australia in the second International Rules test in Football Park, Adelaide in 2001.

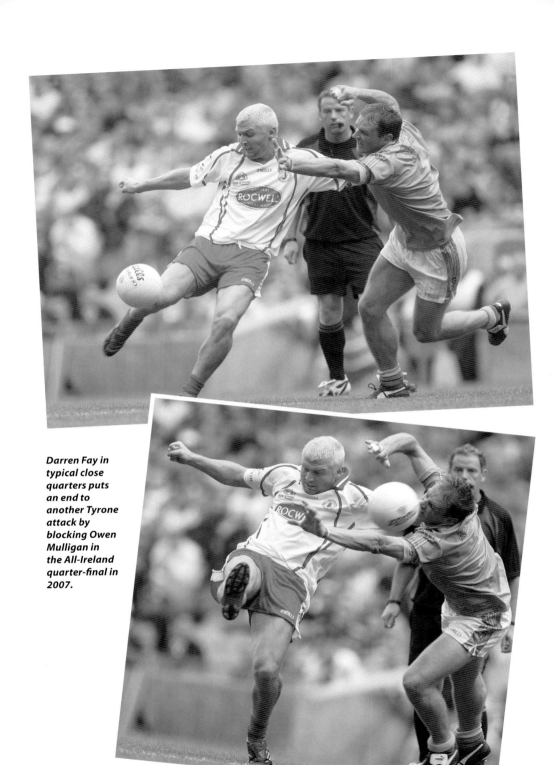

Darren Fay in typical close quarters puts an end to another Tyrone attack by blocking Owen Mulligan in the All-Ireland quarter-final in 2007.

a replay, but Cork added the final full-stop to the Golden Years era for Kerry on Sunday, August 2, 1987 when they knocked out the defending champions – and ended any Kerry dreams of another four-in-a-row.

Billy Morgan, goalkeeper in the 1967 All-Ireland final when Terry Kearns scored the clinching goal with a flick to the net, was now in charge as manager of Cork.

The links with the past were impossible to ignore. Pat Reynolds and Tony Brennan, two more stars from Meath's team of '67 were Boylan's two trusted lieutenants on the line. For the first time since the final 20 years before, Meath and Cork were meeting in a Championship match.

Martin and Gerry Quinn too were involved on the fringes, providing match-day feedback from the stands to the dressing room and their old friend Reynolds on match days. In fact, Martin was instrumental in getting Noel Keating and Kepak involved after supplying him with cattle long before he took over as Meath sponsor and literally carried the first supply of flat pack steaks down to team training one evening.

Lyons remembers thinking how far he had come in the build up to his first All-Ireland final.

'The crowds at training … there was bigger crowds at training than we had at some matches down the years! You look back from the four people below in Clare … to hundreds of people, maybe even 500 or 600, turning up for training at Dalgan Park. That's some change.'

Captains come in many different guises. Natural speech-makers, men who can push the right buttons in the dressing room. Lyons wasn't a talker; he was a doer. He led rather than said. There were no oratorical flights of fancy, no 'Any Given Sunday' style sermons from the mount in the mould of Al Pacino in that famous movie. Quiet, calm and measured; that was Mick's way.

A steely resolve that reflected the mood of the team; fearless, unbending, driven.

'He wasn't big into talking,' admits Paraic. 'He'd never want to talk. He'd have something to say at a team meeting alright but it would be short and sweet.

Boylan describes him in glowing terms as a 'most uncomplicated man'.

"What do you want done?" Mick would say to me. 'Even to the day of the final … going over what was going to happen on the morning of the match out in Malahide. Everything was clear.'

Lyons kept the focus purely on football.

Nothing mattered outside the white lines.

Croke Park, Sunday, September 20, 1987

Boylan rarely feels the need to whip the players up into a frenzy on the big day. This September Sunday is no different. 'Seán wouldn't be a banger of tables. Or he wouldn't curse. There would be no craw-thumping.'

In the dressing room, Lyons keeps his few words simple. When he says he didn't feel any added pressure as captain, twenty years after Peter Darby led out the last Meath team to lift the Sam Maguire Cup, it's not an affectation.

'At that stage, we knew we were very near the end of our line. But we had the belief. That no matter what time was left you could get out of it. There's always going to be a spell in any match that the opposing team is going to get on top of you. Like Cork were five points up at one stage early on. It wasn't looking good!

'You'd be starting to question things a little bit but you can't really afford to think of them things when you're playing. If you start thinking of something else … the head's gone.'

Not looking good is an understatement. Even with Liam Hayes pulling down balls from the clouds at midfield, Meath aren't functioning as a unit. It's Cork instead who are going through the gears. Lyons and Cork's burly full-forward Christy Ryan are having a ding-dong battle and when Ryan wins a ball and points, Cork lead 0-5 to 0-1 midway through the half.

Then, the moment that arguably defined Mick Lyons' career …

The Block.

The photo that hangs in his house captures the split-second nature of it all. Jimmy Kerrigan, galloping through on the overlap; Lyons, trying to cover his man while covering the goal. Then, just as the Cork man makes his mind up to shoot for goal and in all likelihood kill off the game, Lyons springs across and dives full-length at his boot. Meath go up the field and Colm O'Rourke points.

Seán Boylan makes no bones about the importance of that dramatic intervention. 'The defining moment in that '87 match was the block. It changed the course of history. I can still see Jimmy Kerrigan coming down … and coming down the field. The timing was absolutely impeccable. But throughout his career, his hallmark was timing.'

O'Rourke's cleverly improvised goal, punching to the net after Bernard Flynn's original effort is saved, helps Meath into a 1-6 to 0-8 lead.

In the second half, Meath have heroes all over the field, Robbie O'Malley sweeping brilliantly at the back, Hayes putting in the performance of his career at midfield, and Beggy punching holes through the Cork defence.

Gerry McEntee and Billy Morgan almost come to blows, the Cork manager grabbing a fistful of the Meath's player's shirt as Kerrigan lies on the ground needing attention.

A few other late tackles set the scene for bad blood the following year.

By this stage, Lyons has Christy Ryan spooked, and the Cork forward cuts a frustrated figure as he is substituted. In the final quarter, the Meath full-back has a field day as Cork pepper the Meath full-back line.

'That's easy meat for Mick Lyons, absolutely enjoying himself down there at the moment,' says Ger Canning in the RTE commentary box. 'A player who evokes twin emotions in many people. Some see him as the iron man, hard man of the defence; others see him as just a gentle giant.'

In those closing moments, Lyons is immense.

On comes Paraic in place of Martin O'Connell to add a further footnote to the family history.

A long and painful rehab meant that he had struggled all year to break into the team.

Injured in the 1986 county final when he captained Summerhill to a famous victory, the injury carried over to the Australia trip with Ireland soon after, before he aggravated it further one night in training with Meath.

'I tore the ligaments in my knee that night out of pure thickness,' admits Paraic. 'I tried to kick Bernie Flynn out over a f**kin forest of trees … and paid the ultimate penalty. I nearly didn't want to go on for the five minutes because I thought, "What's the point?" But in hindsight, I could always say I played in the 1987 All-Ireland final.'

He was actually close to declining the offer to go on. 'Seán would have called me over. I said "Seán, it's okay… it's okay." It wasn't out of stubbornness or anything. Just, "I'm fine. Really, it's okay." But he said "c'mon" … and I went on.'

Boylan's instincts, as usual, were right; Paraic is glad now he had his moment. 'I'd an hour's energy to pack into five minutes,' he smiles.

At the end, he gets rid of his substitute's jersey and swops it for Cork forward, Colm

O'Neill's instead. The same player's fate would intertwine with the Lyons family in a very different way when the same teams met in the final three years' later.

Just like in 1967, it took time for all the players to thread a path through the delirium.

Biding his time at the podium where the Sam Maguire Cup is ready to be presented, Lyons decides to rest his feet. Plonks down in the seat beside Charlie Haughey.

'The seat was open there. The fella does a lot of talking before he hands the cup over so I just sat down. I was chatting away to him.

'My grandfather wouldn't have liked that. My mother's father was a Fine Gael TD. There was a bit of craic about that.'

Only one thing is left to do. The thing about it, he has no speech prepared. In the build-up, he rebuffed an attempt from the Meath county secretary to make things easy for him.

'I would be embarrassed to say I don't speak Irish. Liam Creavin handed me a speech and I said, "Liam, I won't be reading that out." It was the usual stuff to start off with. So I said, "Liam, we mightn't even be up there. I'll deal with it when it comes."'

When the moment arrives, he takes it in his stride.

'I'd rather have been down the front rather than get up there. That's the way I'd be. I just spoke off the cuff.'

Short, sweet, and to the point, he makes sure to thank his club for the part played in leading him to this point.

'Again, I wouldn't be lifting it for myself. And I'd be very proud of my club Summerhill.

'Because it was still in me. When you're living there all your life, they're the people you socialise with, are closest to.'

Typical of Lyons, after the presentation, he makes a quick get-away. One person he distinctly remembers meeting afterwards is Mattie Kerrigan, another All-Ireland winner from '67 and an iconic figure in Summerhill growing up.

'I didn't go out on the field after the match. I went up the steps and down the back way. Down the tunnel ... met Mattie there. When I started playing football, Mattie would have been the creator of Summerhill football, of that team. I owe a lot to Mattie.'

The banquet in the Grand Hotel in Malahide is a blast. 'We socialised, had great *craic, but we didn't go loopers. We didn't go crazy.'*

The homecoming too stays with him. He gets a special kick out of the Dublin leg of the journey.

'The bus going out. After the Burlington, going out through your arch enemy!

'Then out to Kepak and meeting all of your own. Lord have mercy on Noel Keating [Kepak's MD]. Seán was very friendly with him. He was very good to the Meath team before it ever turned about.

'And then to Summerhill ... and all the faces from the club.'

Brian Smyth in 1949.

Peter McDermott in 1954.

Peter Darby in 1967.

Now Lyons is part of an elite club of Meath All-Ireland winning captains. And he wants more. 'You get used to it ... not used to it, but it's an adrenaline thing ... you get hooked on it. When you know what's there ... when the stakes are that high.

' It's like a drug.'

✦ ✦ ✦ ✦ ✦

Meath barrelled through the 1987-88 season like a team making up for lost time. Rather than any hangover from the All-Ireland, the confidence that came with winning carried Boylan's men right through to the National League final.

Opponents? The 'arch enemy'.

Just to set the scene for the summer, Meath met Dublin in Croke Park in mid-April in a rugged encounter that finished level, Meath 0-11 Dublin 1-8 - Joe McNally for once winning the ball out in front of Lyons and pointing in the final seconds.

Timing suddenly became an issue. Meath were scheduled to go on the All Stars tour of the United States, meaning a replay would be squeezed in after they came home three weeks later.

'We went to America. Socialised, but also trained hard out there. Boston. San Francisco. We'd great craic - and then beat Dublin when we came back. When you're fit, a few drinks here and there won't make any difference.'

To Boylan, the whole tone of the trip was set by his captain.

'I suppose the classic example was after we'd won the All-Ireland,' remembers Boylan. 'We'd drawn with Dublin in the National League, and were going out to the All Stars trip to Boston and San Francisco. Because it was a drawn match I said to Mick, "Look, we're going to have to do a bit of work out here."

'Now the All Stars teams had never trained ... it was a first in the history of the All Stars. Fr Seán Hegarty was managing the All Stars and they trained as well. And an extra game was put on in San Francisco mid-week ... about 5,000 people at it, it was massive.'

'He said, "Do you mind if I talk to the lads?"

'"Mick, I'd be delighted."

'"Lads," he said. "We had our holidays in January. This is an All Stars trip. We're representing our county, we're representing our country. If Seánie wants us to train every day we'll train every day. We'll have good times as well. But we had our holiday in January."

'And that was that.'

When Lyons spoke, he had the full command of the dressing room. 'It was a word here and a word there. A terrific man to give advice. But he was in control of that area there. His patch. As a matter of fact, Mick would say, some fellas think I'm a fool. "But leave them thinking that way".

'Another time he said to me, "I'm getting worried now Seán ... they're beginning to like us!"'

Mixing with a number of the Dublin lads on tour had the awkwardness of a first date, or a date where both sides know a break-up is imminent.

'One of the matches ... it was a bit harder than it should have been, the playing of it,' recalls Lyons, particularly when the teams took to knocking a few lumps out of each other in the National League final replay on their return.

A big melee early on in the League final offered a chance to settle a few old grudges and create plenty of new ones. Kevin Foley ended up being red-carded again against Dublin, but Vinny Murphy suffered under a 'bad-cop, bad-cop' routine from Lyons and his first cousin, Liam Harnan.

'I don't think it was too bad,' protests the former, but then, it mightn't have felt too bad from his point of view. Murphy and a few more might beg to differ.

Goals from Liam Hayes and Brendan Reilly, the latter playing like a veteran despite lining out in his first big game at just 18, set Meath on their way. Despite playing with 14 men from the 12th minute, their supporters are singing 'easy, easy' by the end. It finishes Meath 2-13, Dublin 0-11.

Putting a National League back-to-back with an All-Ireland put the team on another level.

To add a third national title would copper-fasten Meath's legacy. Lyons knew it. All the players knew it. Roll on the Championship.

+ + + + +

A trip to Drogheda in the first round in Leinster, in 1988 posed few problems, Louth whipped to the tune of 3-13 to 0-9.

What happened in the semi-final against Offaly showed how far the team had come since looking up at the clock and panicking in the 1986 All-Ireland semi-final against Kerry. At half-time Offaly led 0-8 to 0-4, confidence buffeted by the wind at their backs.

Meath though, were only waiting to shift up the gears. In the end it was a procession, the full-forward line of O'Rourke, Stafford and Flynn going to town and contributing all but three points of Meath's final total in a 0-19 to 0-10 victory.

Another Leinster final then against Dublin.

Another chance to settle scores.

A day when any friendships were not only set aside but threatened to be sundered. Bernard Flynn happened to be working with Dublin's Dave Synnott at the time, both on the sales team for Tennants. Good friends.

But the occasion demanded a different mindset, especially seeing as they were marking each other. A wired Synnott landed one on Flynn in the second half – who responded by throwing an elbow back and breaking Synnott's nose. With Flynn down, the Dublin player was sent off.

Tennants actually had the pair down to do promotional work together in Meaghers of Ballybough after the match, and they would settle their differences before the night was out. Firm friends and work colleagues again.

Goals from PJ Gillic and Mattie McCabe gave Meath a barely deserved 2-1 to 0-6 lead at half time and it was backs to the wall stuff when Vinny Murphy was grounded right at the death. Charlie Redmond stepped up to the penalty, his team two behind. Redmond took two steps up to the ball, and fired over.

'It was close,' admits Lyons. 'We could have been gone.'

By rights, Joe Cassells should have walked up the steps to collect the Cup. Navan O'Mahonys were county champions and Boylan selected another one of the old guard to lead the team. There was just one problem; Cassells had been dropped. In his place, Lyons continued to captain the team.

On the steps of the Hogan Stand then, Mick pleaded with his good buddy to come up and lift the cup and say a few words. Not wanting to try and take the limelight after not playing, Cassells refused.

Boylan laughs as he recalls the scene. 'In the Leinster final, Joe came on for a few minutes. Mick wanted Joe to go up and lift the Cup but Joe wouldn't do it. So we were left with what was probably the shortest speech of all time.

'Jack Boothman was chairman of the Leinster Council. When Joe wouldn't come up, Mick just put his two hands out to me. Not waiting for Jack, he lifts the Cup and says, "Meath and Dublin know what it takes to win Leinster f**kin' finals … three cheers for Dublin." That's exactly what he said, exactly what happened!'

Bernard Flynn has no doubt about his influence as captain. 'Mick was straight-up. Honest. And the way he led … it was only football. Mick didn't care about anything else whatsoever. It was all about what happened on the field of play. He had no regard for anything else off it, the trimmings, the side-shows, whatever you were or weren't entitled to get.

'Mick was inspirational. Even to this day, I'd look up to him. Like Gerry McEntee or O'Rourke, you hold these guys in such esteem. Mick was one of the guys who changed Meath football.'

Despite the best efforts of Liam McHale, Meath shook off the challenge of Mayo in the 1988 All-Ireland semi-final, a nine-point haul from Stafford key to the outcome, along with the aerial supremacy of Lyons and the covering of Bobby O'Malley and Paraic alongside him.

Cork, harbouring their own set of grudges from the previous year, awaited.

Croke Park, Sunday, September 18, 1988.

Remember how the second-half played out in the 1987 final? The flashpoint between Billy Morgan and Gerry McEntee. Tompkins hitting Robbie O'Malley a late blow in the back. The verbals flying back and forward between various players.

After losing the previous year, Cork decide that to beat Meath, they will fight fire with fire. Get their retaliation in first.

Not long in, Dinny Allen catches Lyons with a blow that leaves him in a state of semi-concussion. 'They were upping the stakes. I got well knocked around early on that day.'

There is a photograph of him from that day, lying flat out on the ground.

Even though Cork are clearly intent on settling a few grudges, Lyons doesn't blame them.

'When you lose, you have to change; you have to do something different.

'We had it hard to get out by Dublin, Cork had it hard to get out by Kerry, and then the two of us meet – if one of us were weaker, the other would have won another couple of All Irelands. Cork were a good side.'

Like a bull that had been baited for 70 minutes, only for the toreador to fail to finish off the kill, Cork have one big problem at the final whistle: Meath are still standing. David Beggy cuts through and earns a hotly contested free at the finish and so an attritional affair ends.

Meath 0-12, Cork 1-9.

Lyons and Brian Stafford are amongst the casualties in a Meath dressing room of hard knocks. The players don't need to say it publicly that they won't be bullied around Croke Park in the replay, not with three weeks to nurse their grievances.

Between the drawn match and replay, the Meath training camp resembled a war zone.

'Training was hard,' says Lyons, giving a sharp insight into the squad's psyche. 'Because we were gone a bit soft. I'd say we thought we could win the All-Ireland without playing the way we normally play ... just be nice. And you win nothing that way ... absolutely nothing. Maybe we started believing what we were reading in the papers, unbeknownst to ourselves.

'At the end, you could see the demise of the Meath team in training.

Because it wasn't physical. The training wasn't as hard as it used to be. Not even hard … we couldn't just do it. Time was up.'

As the headline on a famous piece Colm O'Rourke penned for the *Sunday Tribune* read; *'Nice Guys Finish Last'*. Meath were happy to play the part of villain of the piece.

Nobody was going to accuse Meath of being too 'nice' second time around.

But there was drama unfolding behind the scenes in Meath. Boylan and his management team agonised over the team selection for the replay. Two of the hardest decisions in the 23 years he managed Meath concerned the Lyons brothers.

Never afraid to make the hard decisions, the management felt the team needed re-configuring. In the ensuing reshuffle Paraic was dropped and Joe Cassells was recalled.

The bottom line?

Mick's brother left out – and the captaincy taken from him.

The GAA is littered with fall-outs and bust-ups over team selections and captaincy issues. Knowing that the reaction to those decisions could determine Meath's chances, Boylan hit the road for Summerhill to speak to Mick.

'Very difficult,' he says of the decision taken. 'I went down to the house. There was no problem with Mick; none whatsoever.

'I'll tell you exactly what he said. He said, "Seán, that's your decision. It's your decision to pick the team; it's my decision to play. I'm not saying I agree with you. But that's your job."'

Boylan lets out a deep breath as he speaks, recalling how important that was in terms of Meath's preparations, how Lyons' reaction would set the mood for the replay.

'The calibre of the man,' he says, his voice catching, emotional even now thinking back to that conversation. 'The calibre … just an incredible man.'

Because things could have gone very differently if Lyons had decided to take either decision personally.

Captaining Meath to back-to-back All-Irelands could have set his name in stone. But that's never what the game was about to him.

'I suppose if I'd dug my heels in the ground I could have been.

'You could lose the All-Ireland over it. If that got out in the papers, that there were two lads fighting over wanting to be captain, sure the whole lot would fall asunder.

'It wouldn't bother me, being captain or not being captain. If I decided I was going to hand it over, that would be it. It was done in harmony. There was no sense of maybe I should ... or maybe I shouldn't.'

No ego.

Still, it was a big gesture. Here was a chance to be the first man to captain Meath to two All-Irelands. To captain back-to-back titles would have put him in an elite bracket again. And then there was the further history attached to the fact that he could have been the last man to lift the old Sam Maguire Cup and the first man to lift its newly remodelled version.

'There would have been people who said it to me afterwards,' he admits. 'But it's not about that – it's about Meath winning the All-Ireland. I don't care who is captain.

'Joe was an absolutely fantastic servant to Meath football. He was playing for a long time before I joined up. A long, long time. If any man was entitled to captain Meath, he would be.'

If that wasn't enough though, Mick had to live with seeing his brother dropped too for what should have been his proudest day.

It takes a big man to live with all that and hold counsel.

Boylan understood the shared bond and how hard it would be. 'Probably the most difficult thing was that Paraic wasn't picked for the replay. That was incredibly difficult.

'But that's the sort of men we're talking about.'

Mick felt for his younger brother. 'Paraic was a very, very good footballer ... probably didn't get the recognition. He always kinda got the hard end of the stick. It is hard when your brother is dropped.'

At no stage did the idea of going out in sympathy ever enter the equation. 'Ah no. I wouldn't say Paraic would ever have wanted me to do that. And I wouldn't have. Bar something very bad.

'We'd have chatted alright. It's very hard when you're nearly there but not there … and you should be there. He was after playing a lot of football for Meath. It's not nice then when you get to the very end … not to be in. Sure we'd be going into training together, we were working together a long time.

'Himself and Kevin Foley were dropped for the replay in '88. And it wouldn't have mattered who played in the replay, we would have won it. Paraic kept us in the game in the first half of the drawn final.'

Bernard Flynn explains how tight the brothers have always been. 'Mick and Paraic are incredibly close. People didn't realise that. And they are to this day. The bond they have is immense.

'That was a very tough time for Paraic Lyons. It nearly broke his heart into pieces. To this day, I'm not sure if he is over it.

'For a number of years before that, Paraic was the best corner-back in Leinster. For him to be dropped … yet we still didn't expect Mick to react any other way. Deep down, he might have had other issues or feelings. But not one per cent of him entertained holding a grudge or deflected him from the cause at hand, which was to help Meath win an All-Ireland.'

Paraic didn't expect his brother to react in any other way. He knew him well enough not to expect a diplomatic incident.

'He would never have let it get to that. Them things wouldn't be very important to Michael … not important, but that there is no way he'd kick up a fuss about who got to lift the Cup. He'd be clever enough to know that it would look very silly to have a row over something and Cork go off with the Cup. It wouldn't have entered his head. It would have been a case of, "Let's win the game – they are just little incidentals along the way."'

Yet, it's no little thing to be captain of back-to-back All-Ireland winners.

'A grand thing to look back on in history. But he wouldn't have looked on it that way at the time,'continues Paraic.

'A bigger one I'd say, at the time, was I was dropped for the replay. Three of us. Myself, Kevin Foley and Mattie McCabe. That would have bothered him more than lifting the Cup.'

Brothers in arms.

Croke Park, Sunday, October 9, 1988.

Less than 10 seconds in and the first player is fouled, what is to be a recurring theme of the afternoon. Shea Fahy launches in a high ball only for Lyons to rise above Dave Barry to make a great catch. The confrontational tone is set as players already start squaring up to each other.

Just six minutes in and Meath are rocked.

PJ Gillick jumps to catch but the ball spills. Niall Cahalane goes down on it. Is tackled as he tries to burrow a way clear. Gerry McEntee bumps him and then throws a left hook to the jaw. Referee Tommy Sugrue flashes the red card as the Cork defender gets the magic sponge treatment from the St John's ambulance crew.

The last time Meath played in a replayed final, the National League final, they were also reduced to 14 players when Kevin Foley was sent off after 10 minutes. On that occasion they came good. Could they beat the odds again?

Point for point it goes, Brian Stafford's gilded place-kicking keeping Meath ticking over. And the hits keep on coming. Colm O'Rourke knocks Cahalane on his arse with a shoulder, tackles and forces a free for over-carrying, a statement in itself.

Then, midway through the half, a moment to illustrate the hard edge to Lyons.

A ball breaks in the Meath square, Robbie O'Malley is tackled over-zealously by Michael McCarthy and fouled. Lyons comes in blindside and hits him a punch in the ribcage. Puts his arm around him at same time as if nursing the Cork player as he collapses to the ground. To anyone who turned to see what happened, including the live television cameras, it looks as if he is helping an injured man. And he is. Except he has also inflicted the damage!

On this occasion, Lyons makes no apologies. 'I don't know what it was about but he shouldn't have been in where he was. He was in on top of Mickey McQuillan and then throwing his weight around.'

So Lyons decided to remind him whose turf he was treading on. 'Meath and Cork were rough matches. Sometimes you'd do something and you'd think, "Oh I shouldn't have done that." That happens every now and again. You just react … and then you think, "Oh good Jaysus."'

With 14 men, Meath are playing like men possessed. 'Sometimes I think you're better off. It's not like rugby where you keep possession the whole time and make it pay.'

O'Rourke, immense all afternoon, shakes his fist as he kicks Meath into a 0-13 to 0-9 lead with five minutes to go. Cork lay siege from there in but time runs out as they look for an equaliser, Robbie O'Malley and Martin O'Connell stand-out figures in defence.

At the final whistle, Lyons wraps O'Rourke in a bear-hug before they cut a path to the Hogan Stand.

As a stern faced president, John Dowling goes to hand over the trophy, Joe Cassells picks it up, leaving the former waving his hands at empty space where the trophy was resting.

Cassells looks to Heaven as he lifts it. Set to turn 34 the next day, birthday presents don't come any sweeter.

Lyons has no truck with sentiment or hubris but it clearly matters to him what Meath achieved that day.

'Once you put titles back-to-back, to me that was a big thing. To win back-to-back … you were being mentioned then with other teams. You were getting there all the time.

'You're thinking then, "Can we do another one?"

'It's just so satisfying. Though as Con Houlihan wrote, a fella going on a voyage … you don't know the pitfalls. It's very true. I thought he was a great writer. But on your second and third time, you know the things that can go wrong. The longer you go on … getting older, playing sport … you know all the pitfalls.'

Turns out he's a huge admirer of Houlihan's unique prose. 'Aw Jaysus, he was brilliant. I think one time he said, "The ball was irrelevant for 10 minutes!" And it wouldn't have been far removed from that in the early days! You'd be sent to jail now, some of the stuff that went on.'

For Paraic though, there isn't even a five-minute cameo to soften the blow of missing out. 'In '88, the time there was three of us dropped, I'll be honest. I remember sitting with Mattie McCabe and Kevin Foley in the hotel after winning the All Ireland but we had mixed emotions. There was a little bit of "it's great, but …"'

The public fall-out from a fractious, ill-tempered final left a bitter aftertaste. John Dowling won few friends in Meath when he came out and denounced some of the scenes, which led to Liam Harnan and Gerry McEntee refusing to accept their medals from the GAA president at the official presentation at Warrenstown College.

'I suppose there was wrong on both sides,' says Lyons. 'I'm not going to be naming who at this stage.'

As captain, did he know the lads were going to make a personal protest?

'I'd a fair idea. I know he's dead now the poor man but what John Dowling said wasn't right. I don't think that was appropriate. A lot worse things happened in All-Ireland finals before that. I met him afterwards and didn't pass any remarks.'

It never entered his head to follow suit and refuse his medal?

'Not really. I got my knee done that year. I was on crutches in Warrenstown. There was no grand plan. It was more a case of whoever wanted to go up … go up.'

+ + + + +

Three-in-a-row?

1989 offered a chance to join the pantheon of great county teams who managed to climb the summit and pitch camp there. A third title in succession would put the team in a special bracket in GAA history.

'It would be floating in the background,' admits Lyons, thinking back. 'But it wasn't a huge, big thing around the county. I'm sure the supporters were thinking about it alright.'

Not that the early season signs were auspicious. Six consecutive League defeats hinted at a deeper malaise than merely the carry-over from back-to-back All-Ireland wins. The team was ageing together and the miles were taking their toll. Victory in the final round game against Down couldn't stave off relegation.

It's around this time that Paraic Lyons was cutting an ever-more frustrated figure as he could not break back into the full-back line.

A challenge match against Kerry broke him.

'We flew down to Farranfore to play Kerry for the opening of a pitch. I had the boots and everything on me when I picked up the jersey. That's when I saw all the numbers on the back of it … I knew straight away that there was a number too many on it!'

Mick watched him as he started to unlace his boots, and put his clothes back on.

'He just got the jersey, looked at it, and left it down beside him. I think I was on crutches that day, after getting my knee done. I knew if he wasn't going to be picked that day, he wasn't going to be playing in the Championship. If you weren't in the shake-up then, you were in trouble. It wouldn't have been good that day.'

With the team flying down though, Paraic had no escape plan. 'I remember out watching the match,' he says, sheepishly. 'Sure I'd nowhere else to go ... just stood with the rest of the crowd watching it.

'I didn't go back in to training for a while ... maybe a week and a half? Then, of course, you've to swallow your pride because there is only one loser and that's you. The county is going to go on ... so, do you want to be a part of it? So I went back in.'

Time heals.

In the early rounds of Leinster, Meath struggled past Louth before hitting their stride in the semi-final against Offaly, a scoreline of 3-13 to 0-9 keeping the three in-a-row dream alive.

So for the fourth year in succession, it was Meath and Dublin to slug it out in a Leinster final. There was just one difference; Lyons wasn't fit to make the starting 15. Injury meant that Robbie O'Malley deputised on the edge of the square in the semi-final, with Harnan posted there to handle the threat of Joe McNally against Dublin.

Lyons does not have happy memories of the day watching on.

Mattie McCabe's late goal – his third goal in three successive provincial finals – looked like earning a replay before Dublin responded in kind, Vinny Murphy's shot taking a deflection and deceiving Mickey McQuillan. The three in-a-row was dead. Only the inquest remained.

'I was in the dug-out for the Leinster final. Togged out and all. Some people say I should have been brought on ... some people say I shouldn't. I say, "I wasn't fit." I'd played absolutely no football up to that stage.'

Asked if he was itching to get on, given that he lived for playing The Dubs in Croke Park on the big days, he says it's not quite that simple. 'I don't know if I was to be honest. I was cycling bikes, doing a bit of jogging but going out in a Leinster final … you need to have the work done. You do feel powerless.'

✦✦✦✦✦

A new decade brought a clutch of new faces as Seán Boylan found a way of re-energising things. The Meath team that burned a trail into the National League semi-final against Cork featured Donal Smyth in goals, Brendan Reilly at right half-back, and Colm Brady alongside Liam Hayes at midfield.

Another encounter, full of needle, saw Niall Cahalance sent off and Meath tough it out once more.

The final against Down was a far more free-flowing affair, Mickey Linden giving Lyons a chastening opening quarter before he settled to his task. A goal from David Beggy and a penalty from Brian Stafford settled the issue.

A second League title in three years confirms Meath's status. And buoys the team for another tilt at Leinster.

An average winning margin of 16 points against Longford and Laois set the team up for yet another border battle with the old enemy.

A matter of seconds into the Leinster final, and a Brady high ball was not dealt with by the Dublin defence. O'Rourke pounced to find the net.

Coasting at half-time, 1-7 to 0-5, it looked over as a contest when the gap stretched to eight points. And then, in keeping with the Dublin-Meath encounters, the game took on a life of its own. With six minutes left, it was a one-point game. Into the Championship fray came Gerry McEntee to help guide Meath over the finishing line.

By this stage, Dublin must have been developing a complex about Boylan's teams. The proof of that theory would come, perhaps, in 1991.

Winning while playing badly is often deemed a distinguishing feature of the top teams in any sport but the warning signs were there in Meath's All-Ireland semi-final display against Donegal. And yet the team's indomitable spirit also told.

Trailing by a point 10 minutes from time, Brian Stafford and the irrepressible Bernard Flynn showed all their class with goals.

There was one difference about the Cork team that Meath had inflicted consecutive All-Ireland final defeats upon – and the Cork team they would meet in the final in 1990. Billy Morgan's men were no longer bet down; with Meath out of the equation in 1989, they took the opportunity to bag the Sam Maguire Cup for the first time since a shaven-headed Jimmy Barry-Murphy announced himself in the 1973 final against Galway with a brace of goals.

Cork, not Meath, wore the mantle of champions.

Any faint-hearted supporters could look away now.

Once more into the breach.

Croke Park, Sunday, September 16, 1990.

Cork's Colm O'Neill stands 6'2".

Weighs in at 14 stone, 7 lbs.

From the start, he's a handful for Lyons. Eight minutes in, he races through and thumps a left foot shot that smashes the underside of the crossbar and somehow rebounds out.

For every ball he wins out front, Meath's full-back is finding a way to limit his influence and three minutes before the break, with Cork leading 0-6 to 0-4, both players go full-blooded for another 50-50 ball. When it spills loose, O'Neill is penalised for picking it up off the ground.

But he doesn't give up the ball. Takes one solo, then another as Lyons goes over to take it off him. The Meath player brushes into him and O'Neill, out of the blue, hits him with a left-handed rabbit punch. Lyons just starts rubbing his jaw, then slowly walks away as referee, Paddy Russell points to the line.

'He caught me a bit here,' he says, showing the point on his jaw where the blow landed. 'Now it wasn't a hard punch, just a little thing.

'They were absolutely destroying us, the whole way down the field. We had to get tighter ... and tighter and tighter, if we were going to survive. I suppose he got frustrated. He got in ... in the first few minutes and nearly broke the crossbar.'

'That really is senseless,' declares RTE commentator, Ger Canning, himself a Cork man. 'There really is no excuse. Just a rush of blood to the head I'm afraid. Very untypical of the man.'

O'Neill takes an age to leave the field. Just looks shell-shocked, the full enormity of what he has done just sinking in.

While the Cork management huddle to discuss their options, Lyons' mind is racing. As he watches O'Neill shuffle to the sideline, shoulders bowed, alarm bells are ringing in his own head.

'Disaster … disaster!

'I hate seeing an opposing team losing a player. Because the whole thing turns around. The referee goes with them … I don't care what anyone says … they'll get the 50-50 decisions. I'd nearly have been better off hitting him back, and going off with him.'

And then he throws out a line that really grabs the attention, 'I did ask the referee that day not to send him off!'

What the replays of the incident don't show is Lyons having a word with Russell. Few, if any GAA players, have shown such sportsmanship with the stakes so high.

'I'd prefer to go to battle … to go to war!'

Referee, Paddy Russell ignores his entreaties. 'I played as a sweeper and it didn't go that well. Other games … you remember how you were going, how other lads were going … that game just seemed to go by.

'That's a bad sign. It usually means the whole team isn't tuned in or you're not tuned in … or something is just not right.'

Bernard Flynn thinks it might be a first in the history of the game. 'That's another indication of Mick Lyons. He never flinched; never went down. To actually go and try and help Colm O'Neill in those circumstances … I've got goose-pimples speaking about it.

'Even though the game is an awful lot better now, can you imagine a player doing something like that in today's game?

'It was nearly like Mick knew Colm made a mistake. He hit him … BANG! To go over to the referee then, that's a sign of his true character.

'Unbelievable.'

Given Lyons' persona, and the way he was driven by the one-on-one duel, maybe Meath would have profited from someone else sweeping behind. Just like Meath in 1988 when McEntee walked early, every Cork player lifted his game.

The story of the match is easily told. 'We ended up beaten by two points. Cork were a very good side. A good footballing side and they had Shea Fahy and Larry Tompkins. Sure Shea Fahy scored four points from midfield that day.

'Cork beat us in '90 and they deserved it. They were there four years in finals. They

got two out of it, no more than ourselves. Why didn't we win that match?

'We weren't ruthless enough.'

Seán Boylan remembers the irony of Lyons offering an apology afterwards, for not losing his head and striking back at O'Neill. 'He said to me in the dressing room after the match, "I'm really sorry, Seán. I probably should have started a row. It might have woken us up." And that was heartfelt.'

Lyons never claimed to be a saint.

O'Neill and himself were involved in a set-to early on which could have put both in trouble with the referee. And a photograph in the next day's Irish Independent shows him at another stage with a good, hard grasp of O'Neill's jersey. But that act of sportsmanship in approaching Russell over the sending off is a testament to his character.

'He would be that way anyway,' says Paraic. 'At the end of the day, O'Neill didn't hit him that hard. It's not like he knocked a couple of teeth out of his head. He threw a punch at him … it was no haymaker. It backfired on us, as a lot of those things can do.'

+ + + + +

Lyons spent the winter mulling over retirement. And he reveals that he was very nearly gone.

'I was … absolutely. Sure I was 32 at that stage. After playing in three different decades!'

The game, he felt, had given him everything he ever dreamed of. 'I suppose I consider myself awfully, awfully lucky to have played in an All-Ireland final, not alone to win an All-Ireland. When you start off playing, that's the ultimate.

'There is nowhere else you can go after that … only down! And most teams go down, bar Kerry who seem to have a chance of winning six or seven. Most teams get a chance to win one or two.

'And down you go. And rightly so. Because it's bad for football when a team keeps winning. Sure Kerry nearly destroyed football. They destroyed many a good team in Croke Park … the Roscommons, all of them teams … wrote them off. Put football out of their head!'

Good buddy Joe Cassells quietly exited stage left, giving him further reason to question his motives. In the end, it came down to one thing.

'I suppose the fact that it felt like unfinished business. Back then we used to get through Leinster reasonably easy.'

Little did he know what would unfold in 1991. Easy? No other preliminary round game in the history of the GAA spawned a documentary all of its own.

Houses dotted all over Meath still contain a copy of *'The Royal Battle: Meath v Dublin 1991 – The Epic 4 Game Saga'*. This production by Sideline contained interviews with some of the principle characters from the drama; respective managers Seán Boylan and Paddy Cullen, referee Tommy Howard, Meath stars Liam Hayes, Bernard Flynn and Kevin Foley and Dublin's Tommy Carr, Vinny Murphy, Charlie Redmond and Jack Sheedy.

It's no exaggeration to say that this saga ushered in a new era for the GAA. By the end, 237,383 supporters had paid through the gates.

And put the GAA front and centre once again after being overshadowed by Ireland's participation in the 1990 World Cup.

Boylan too describes how it changed the game, how the pairing brought a special dimension to any Championship contest. 'All the players involved, their names will be etched in stone because of what they did for Gaelic football. I think they just brought it to a new level.

'You felt that you weren't worthy Leinster champions if you hadn't played Dublin. And it meant more to a lot of the players even than actually winning the All-Irelands or being involved in the All-Irelands. Because it was their supporters and our supporters. When you reach the final you have people from everywhere there. But this was local.'

Here, Lyons adds his own take. Rather than adding to the mythology, he's happy to strip it back.

'Jaysus it's poor football … poor stuff. And Dublin were a far better team. We were like a boxer on the ropes, ready to be knocked out … ready to be knocked out!

'They had us by the neck. And you'd know it, because that's the way we'd be with other teams. Things were starting to turn.'

In an attempt to keep Meath guessing, National League champions Dublin decided to pull a few rabbits from the hat in terms of team selection for Game One.

Once again, Mick Lyons' reputation preceded him. Vinny Murphy was the scoring sensation of the spring. An uncut diamond; raw and unpolished. Rather than throwing him in on Lyons and seeing all the development possibly undercut, Cullen and his heavyweight think-tank of Pat O'Neill, Jim Brogan and Fran Ryder opted to put old midfield warhorse Dave Foran in on the edge of the square.

'I got a couple of points in the first game but my confidence was sort of drained,' revealed Murphy in the documentary.

With both sides afraid of exiting the Championship so early, on the Bank Holiday weekend, it was a fraught, nerve-ridden affair. Con Houlihan put it best. *'The few who attempted to play football were like poets struggling to express themselves in a barbaric language.'*

And the game finished in the sort of 'did that just happen?' fashion that characterised an incredible series of games. Even with Hayes' fielding around the middle doing enough to earn the 'Man of the Match' award, Meath trailed by a point with the clock counting down. PJ Gillic thumped a ball goalwards from out on the right and John O'Leary jumped in traffic to try and punch it clear. Except he never connected. Instead, over 51,000 drew their breath in a collective gasp as the 'O'Neills' cleared the goalkeeper, bounced, and somehow cleared the empty net to go over the bar.

Game Two would end in similar dramatic fashion.

At the time, there was no system of changing referees for replays so Tommy Howard from Kildare took charge a second time.

On this occasion, Meath were the better team for long periods, but just couldn't close out the deal.

And Lyons, despite his rugged reputation, was red-carded for one of the few times in his Meath career. The sight of Vinny Murphy pole-axed on the ground left the Dublin fans howling for justice. As he tried to sit up, he looked like he was literally seeing stars, shaking his head to try and figure out exactly where he was. All that was missing were the cartoon birds fluttering around

Murphy's head.

Television replays showed Lyons caught, 'bang to rights', throwing a short arm back at Murphy as they were both running goalwards. For the one and only time in the four-match series, Tommy Howard reached for his red card not long before the end of normal time.

'I deserved to be sent off in '91 alright,' admits Lyons. 'Had to go that day. Even though there was nothing wrong with him.'

It said everything about his presence that Meath conceded two clear goal chances in the short time he was missing. A simple high ball found both Murphy and Paul Clarke in space only for the pair to crash into each other and cough up the chance.

A second high ball in then carried echoes of Seamus Darby's famous goal to deprive Kerry the five-in-a-row in 1982. Murphy jumped from behind Martin O'Connell, and bumped him as he rose to pull the ball down from the clouds.

With the scores level, Murphy turned and instinctively let fly. In one swing of his boot, he could stick it to the absent Lyons, to Meath, to the Dublin management team who treated him like a character actor rather than handing him the lead role. Mickey McQuillan spread himself superbly and made the save.

'He should have scored,' says Lyons, knowing that Meath's season could very well have ended with him being fingered as the villain of the piece. 'Over the bar even.'

In extra-time, Meath brought Liam Harnan on to man the edge of the square. David Beggy, with a sidestep to justify his nickname, 'Jinxy', danced past Ciaran Walsh and hit the top corner of the net. Dublin had hung in there through the exquisite free-taking of recalled legend, Barney Rock and when one effort dropped short, Jack Sheedy – in only his second Championship start but playing like he was born for this stage – rose and fisted the ball to the net.

'When Mick was sent off for the incident with Vinny Murphy, normally you'd go straight off,' recalls Boylan. 'But what did Mick do? Well the sneering and the jeering as he walked around in front of the Dublin supporters…

'It came to the draw and we could bring on the extra player. We took off Harnan who wasn't playing well. I said, "Listen, will you go back in full-back."

He didn't want to.

"Don't bother your f**kin' arse then … stay where you are." That's what I said. And I never curse!

"'If you want me I'm available…'"

'Everyone talking then about the great game that Harnan had in extra time on Vinny Murphy. They covered every blade of grass but I don't think either touched the ball.'

Neither team could add to their tally in the second period of extra time, the stalemate guaranteeing a third match.

By now, the Dublin-Meath roadshow was a national event. This was football gone viral. The players were only too conscious that they were part of something special.

'You were,' says Lyons. 'But you wanted to get it over too. Because you knew the longer it went on, the harder it was going to be in the long run.'

Once more, Con Houlihan captured the essence of the encounter, one with *'a kind of wild magnificence'*.

As it became a national story, Tommy Howard's postal route began to take ever longer as everyone looked for an angle, television cameras even following his steps.

Hard as it is to believe now, in an era when Dublin's football brand is judged in terms of millions of euro, the sky blue jerseys started out that summer unadorned. Just think of it. No sponsor.

It was Game Three before 'Arnotts' first appeared across the front of the players' jerseys. That very same game, 'Kepak' first appeared on a Meath jersey, replacing 'O'Reilly Transport'.

Everyone wanted a piece of the action. Dublin-Meath was the only act in town.

Front page of the programme for the second replay showed Mick Lyons and Vinny Murphy in a tussle for possession, each with one hand across the other, leveraging position. *'To find a comparison I have to evoke Leo Tolstoy's War and Peace,'* wrote Lyons' favourite writer Houlihan. *'It is a novel of daunting length. I wouldn't call it a great book but there are great things in it.'*

By now, the players had entered a 'Twilight Zone' as Dublin captain Tommy Carr so colourfully put it. Particularly when Dublin played Meath off the park, broke five clear in the second half and looked home and hosed. The bravery of Bernard Flynn, all 5'8" of him, rising to beat John O'Leary to the punch late on, summed up Meath's indomitable spirit.

Extra-time threw up goals, first from Colm Coyle, and then Paul Clarke after brilliant approach play by Jack Sheedy, and when the final whistle blew, it was to a rare mix of shock and inevitability.

Meath 2-11, Dublin 1-14.

A fourth date beckoned.

When Lyons says 'the whole 91 saga has entered into folklore,' Game Four deserves a special place all of its own.

Meath's trip out of the country, to a hotel in Drymen in Scotland, a village on the shores of Loch Lomond famous for being the home of Billy Connolly, added to it all; Boylan approaching county chairman Fintan Ginnity and getting the board's blessing for the trip, even going so far as to fly over there with team sponsor, Noel Keating and reconnoitre the place. The Friday morning after the third drawn game, players, wives and girlfriends flew out together.

Living inside a goldfish bowl for Sunday after Sunday, the break was intended to provide some vital R&R for the group, with the football mixed in.

'We went over there and we drank hard ... and trained hard,' says Lyons. 'The training sessions were brutal. On a small, hard pitch. We socialised hard right til three or four o'clock in the morning ... then got up and trained at ten o'clock in the morning for a good long time.

'It was different. You enjoyed yourself.'

Meath returned home ready for the defining contest.

Before a ball had been kicked, Game Four had broken the mould for the GAA.

'That was the first Saturday match,' recalls Lyons. 'They were saying at the time ... "Meath people won't go to it", that they'll be farming, milking ... or whatever. But there was a massive crowd at it.

'But the standard of football was terribly poor. If you look back at it, you'd be coaching young lads now and you'd be telling them ... "Don't give away the ball!" and they'd be saying back to you ... "I was looking at you on the television the other night!"

'"All right … all right!"

'Things were different then.'

If the football over the four games was often 'rugged and vigorous' as RTE commentator Ger Canning colourfully captured it, the fact that the fourth episode of the drama was played out in glorious sunshine only added to the sense of occasion.

A knee injury in training the day before meant that Tommy Dowd was a late call-up for Seán Kelly. And when Terry Ferguson pulled a muscle in his back in the dressing room getting changed, suddenly Paraic Lyons found himself lining out beside his brother in the full-back line.

When Keith Barr thundered into Colm O'Rourke early on, laying him out as he went to catch a handpass, it looked like Meath had suffered a mortal blow. Even Paddy Cullen cringed at the hit, before thinking, as O'Rourke needed two bodies to help him stagger from the field, 'My second thought was that if he was dead … that maybe we had a chance.'

That's how important O'Rourke was to Meath.

Plenty of Dublin supporters thought they were seeing a ghost when, barely five minutes later, O'Rourke jogged back onto the field, still rubbing his jaw gingerly. Yet even he could do little to halt Dublin who cut loose after half time. By the 50th minute, it was double scores, 0-12 to 0-6.

'I literally thought we were home and dry,' admitted Pat O'Neill later. Meath engineered a goal via Brian Stafford but then Declan Sheehan was hauled down … penalty! Keith Barr's record from the spot was as good as anyone's in training so he went up the field to take it.

What happened next added to the Lyons' legend. There are Dublin supporters for whom he will forever remain Public Enemy Number One after a moment that is framed in Box 686 in Croke Park.

As Keith Barr ran forward to strike the ball, something went off inside Lyons' head. And he took off alongside him. Shadowed Barr all the way until he struck the ball hard and clean and low with his right boot. Matched him stride for stride.

It happened so fast, it took the television replays to confirm what a disbelieving crowd just witnessed. As he sits back on the couch, in his back room at home in Summerhill, he tries to explain his thought processes at that very moment.

And he wants to make one thing clear, 'I never said anything to him. I never touched him … I never made contact with him.'

But why did he take off?

'I don't know,' he says shaking his head in bemusement, 'Why I was running along, I don't know? It wouldn't have been planned or anything.

'I told Keith later, "I thought he was faster!"'

'Just instinct. I just decided to go. I know I was too quick but you'd always try and be first in after the ball. Big matches like that … penalties are hard scored. If you can get in and get the rebound … get the ball away.

'I knew that if he scored it was all over. I think they would have gone a long way at that stage.'

Deep down, there was probably a realisation that if Barr scored, it was all over. All for nothing. His career too, because he had pretty much decided that it was his last year.

In the commentary box, Ger Canning captured the penalty strike in breathless gasps, "It's a goal… no, it's outside! He's missed it!"

Barr's low drilled shot rattled past Mickey McQuillan's right hand side and wide.

When television replays showed Lyons close enough to play tag with Barr, even Tommy Howard admitted that technically, it should have been retaken. For a split second, the Meath full-back took a deep breath and listened out for the whistle, knowing that he could now be responsible for a re-take. It never came.

'You'd be looking and waiting alright. Sure it should have been taken again.

'You take the chance. You wouldn't think that starting … I just ran. When you play sport, sometimes you think, "Oh Jesus Christ, what did I do that for?" But you just do.'

Crucially, Tommy Carr had shipped a knock and had been helped from the field distraught. Like O'Rourke, the Dublin captain represented the heart and soul of the team, its will to win.

'It's okay. We have them,' shouted Dave Foran to buck him up as he makes it to the sideline.

In the dramatic end-game, could his presence have altered what happened? We'll never know.

Meath still trailed by three points entering stoppage time. Cue the sequence that resulted in one of the greatest goals ever scored at Croke Park. When RTE held a poll for the 'Top 20 GAA Moments' nearly 25 years later, it checked in at number six.

Martin O'Connell fetches a ball rolling out along his own end line. Handpasses to Mick Lyons who shrugs off a hefty shoulder from Vinny Murphy and arrows a nerveless kick pass down the right sideline, to Mattie McCabe, who slips the ball to Liam Harnan.

His attempted pass is half intercepted by Dublin only for the ball to break to O'Rourke who is fouled. His quick free out to the left sideline is picked up by David Beggy who switches the play. It goes from Kevin Foley to PJ Gillick to Tommy Dowd, who plays a one-two with Colm O'Rourke before handpassing the ball across to Foley who has carried on his run upfield to score his only goal ever in a Meath jersey. The whole stadium draws breath to try and process what has just happened.

'The goal we got was a goal we used to do in training,' says Lyons. 'That's the truth.

'We did an exercise in training ... not just that year but from years and years before. Seán would have 20 footballs in ... back in the early days we might only train with two. But he had loads.

'And there was one drill where a group of six lads would start at one end of the field and work all the way down to the other end. The aim was to get a goal. Maybe four tacklers. Whoever lost it then would have to defend.

'So it wasn't unusual to see someone up the field. Now it was pure luck as well that you get a chance to score a goal. Like if Dublin had kicked the ball out of play the game was over.

'The Dublin team of latter years would have pulled the player down to allow bodies get behind the ball. Kerry were caught in 2011 the time Dublin won the All-Ireland. That was very naïve on Kerry's part. They don't normally get caught like that.

'That's the difference then between the time we played Kerry in '86. The match was all but over. But we still didn't get the ball and just kick it up in the air. We worked it down the field.'

On a bone hard pitch in Drymen, they had practiced the same drill. Over and over.

Lyons' part in the move for the goal is interesting in itself. He had the strength to take the hit from Vinny Murphy and not cough up possession. The wherewithal not to simply thump it downfield under the severest of pressure. And the football ability to pick out a punt pass to Mattie McCabe that was instinctive and had no margin for error down the right sideline.

'When you play midfield, as I did with the club, you don't just get the ball and kick it up in the air,' he explains. 'You've got to work out where to play a pass.'

To cap it all, McCabe won the kick out. He handpassed the ball to Liam Hayes. Hayes found Gillic with a cross-field pass, and Gillic off-loaded to David Beggy, who kicked the winning point to break Dublin hearts in an epic finish to crown an epic four-game saga.

'And to do it to your arch enemies!' proclaims Lyons. 'Not trying to rub it in! To get the winning point then … when they were by far the better team.'

A civic reception at the Mansion House to honour both teams seemed like a bright idea at the time but the players were too shattered to care.

Tommy Carr made a long and impassioned speech that caught the despair of the losers and the enduring respect between the fiercest of rivals. Lyons felt for the Dublin captain, and all his team. 'Ah you do … you'd have to. You never want to rub anyone's nose in it. Fine, the end of the season, when the Championship is over, you can say we're going to honour Meath.'

In the next edition of the *Evening Press*, Houlihan again eulogised one Meath player. *'Dublin had another obvious flaw: they lacked a Lyons tamer. In this generation the goalkeepers got their Magna Carta: now they cannot be challenged inside the small box. There is no law which says that Mick Lyons cannot be challenged inside a certain area, but it seems that way.'*

The educated guess amongst his own in Summerhill is that he marked eight different full-forwards and conceded just a single point to the roll call of heavyweight opponents.

After such an emotionally and physically draining experience, it nearly counted for nothing, the delayed schedule meaning Meath had to line out in the first round proper against Wicklow the following Sunday. Incredibly, it ended in another draw, Kevin O'Brien showcasing the full extent of his talents for Wicklow.

'We struggled. Bernie Flynn kicked the ball over the bar that day and the referee blew when the ball was in flight. The winner … so that should have been over.'

By the time Meath won the replay, beat Offaly in the semi-final, and Laois in the Leinster final, it had taken eight games to be crowned champions, another record.

'It was very enjoyable because we did no hard training. It was just games … games. You see the lads playing soccer in England, games every week. That's all players want to do.'

The All-Ireland semi-final represented another struggle against Roscommon but they squeezed through. Facing Down, it seemed like their name had to be on the cup.

Didn't it?

Croke Park, Sunday, September 15, 1991.

Colm O'Rourke's health is of greatest concern to Meath in the days before the match. Laid low with pneumonia, he is in no fit state to play.

Lyons played in three different decades for Meath. If there is one man he puts on a pedestal with the county, it's the Skryne man. 'Colm was a huge player for Meath; Colm nearly was Meath. Colm was some footballer. Any team you'd pick in the last 100 years, he'd be on it every time.'

Still, for all the doubts that surrounded their forward talisman, Meath felt they could take Down, especially after beating them in the 1990 National League final. Confidence is high. Compared to Down who were making a first All-Ireland final appearance since 1968, Meath have all the experience.

Whether it is an accumulation of the whole summer – tired legs, tired minds – the trend of Meath giving teams a head-start continues.

'We just didn't get it right on the day. They were fast and aggressive. Every time I looked up, the ball was going over the bar! I says, "Aw good Jaysus."'

Lyons is marking Peter Withnell and more than holding his own. The damage is being done further out the field.

At half time, the gap is four points, Down 0-8 Meath 0-4. Adding to Meath's woes is the fact that Lyons is hobbling badly.

'If I was to do it again, I wouldn't have come out after half time. Because I twisted my knee before half time going for a ball.

'I remember a ball came in along the endline and I went to step off it and it wouldn't go … wouldn't move. I says, "Out of here." That's when I went off. Midway through the second half.

'Withnell was there to do a job. Mickey Linden was the same. If you take the likes of Ross Carr as well … they had good players.

'We had great battles with Down all through the years. Ambrose Rogers, Lord rest him, I had great battles with him. He wasn't starting on the All-Ireland team that won but he came on.'

With James McCartan unmarkable, Down power ahead, Barry Breen's fisted goal added to a lead that stretches to 11 points at the 50 minute mark.

With Lyons soon to lead the fray injured, Martin O'Connell switches to full-back. And O'Rourke inspires yet another remarkable comeback after being introduced, Bernard Flynn producing the game of his life outside him.

The four matches proved that Meath wouldn't give it up until the bitter end. The character of the team, the sense of spirit that Boylan had instilled, is remarkable.

When Flynn skims the crossbar with his sixth point of the day three minutes from time, there's only two points between the sides. Down are like a panicked sailor, hanging on to the life raft for dear life.

And then time runs out.

Meath's incredible odyssey ends in tears.

Not a man given to exaggeration, Lyons states baldly, 'It would have been the greatest All-Ireland of all time. But that's sport. Down came up and, by Jaysus they did their homework.

'Down could appear, could land out of nowhere and win an All-Ireland. Back when we were learning our trade, if you wanted a good challenge, you headed up to Down. They've changed now. In my time Down played good, fast football. Aggressive.

You wouldn't mow them out of it.

'Ah we were beaten in a lot of places that day.'

Asked if he has any regrets, he remains stoic about it. 'No. If we were good enough, we would have won it. We weren't good enough.'

✦ ✦ ✦ ✦ ✦

Very few players get out at the top. Walk back down the steps of the Hogan Stand with the Sam Maguire in tow and off into the sunset.

If the All-Ireland final had gone to script, Lyons would have retired, Meath's legend complete after the 'greatest All Ireland of all time'.

Instead, losing convinced him to give it one more year.

As the Championship approached, Boylan clearly felt the team needed a shake-up and gambled by leaving out enough big names to shake a stick at. And so the bench for the first round of the Leinster Championship against Laois in Navan is weighted by All Ireland medallists and All Stars, the likes of Liam Hayes, Robbie O'Malley and Colm Coyle.

Lyons escaped the cull. It hardly mattered. John McDermott started for the first time in the Championship only to be knocked unconscious in the first quarter – a sign of how things went from bad to worse on the day.

In the dressing room in Páirc Tailteann afterwards, Lyons pulled off the jersey for one last time.

'That was the final nail,' he admits. By close of business that evening, he was an ex-Meath footballer. 'I went for a drink with Colm O'Rourke that evening. A pub in Navan ... could have been the Railway Bar. Think it was just the two of us. I said to him that was it. I'd a fair idea I was going.'

Did anyone try and change his mind?

'No.'

He was full sure in his own mind his time was up. 'Well up. It was nearly up in '91. That's why I can't understand why players don't know when to go. I can't understand it!'

Playing the role of impact substitute or grizzled veteran to guide the younger players just didn't appeal to him.

'My kids were getting older at that stage. I'd enough of it, especially the hard training in the winter time. It's all fine when you're looking at Croker in sunshine thinking, "this is lovely". But Jaysus … you think of what went into it beforehand.'

Full-back too was not a position where it was possible to grow old gracefully. In conversation with Liam Hayes late one night, he described the position as being like a gunslinger with a price on his back in the Wild West, 'always being one bullet away' from taking a fall.

'You make decisions and you live and die by them,' is what he says now.

'I always reckoned that team will always be held up. Because it played the way older people liked to see Gaelic football being played. A bit of everything in it … anything could happen! Things modernise, things change, things roll on. And it will change again. But we did grab the attention of people outside our county that they'd follow Meath because of the way we played football then. I still have people coming in to play golf in Rathcore and you can tell, that's what attracted them.'

From being the subject of national criticism at times, that team became hugely admired and respected for their achievements.

'We did things the way we wanted to,' he adds. 'We did a lot of things that we weren't supposed to do. People were saying we were "dirty" which I thought was way over the top. I really did. If you go back to any of the teams that won All-Irelands, there's always five or six lads who'll ask the question.

'Go back to the good Kerry team. Lord have mercy, Páidí Ó Sé, Tim Kennelly … those boys didn't stand around on ceremony. But they never got that sort of a reputation.'

But it never got under his skin.

'No. You can look in any of the papers, I never said, "I'm disappointed about this" or anything like that.'

Even when people wanted to paint him as a dirty footballer?

'They did. But it didn't bother me. Now if a lad came in to me now and said something along those lines I'd say, "You're wrong. I played it physical."'

Sometimes, the odd brave soul would have a cut at him. 'They would. After a while … and maybe they've had a few drinks. People that would know football would know differently. But genuinely, it never bothered me.

'I played football all my life at midfield with my club. So I could play ball.

I just wasn't good enough to play midfield for the county.

'You'd use it as if "everyone's against us". You know the way a manager turns around and says, "We're playing against everyone now lads!" It drives the thing on to another level.'

As for the reputation that came with being the hard man, did he play up to it?

'You have to earn that first. And you have to be able to carry it out! And I didn't mean do anything wrong. Like ... take Mickey Linden playing for Down. No matter how hard you go for that ball, Mickey will still land there beside you. The reputation didn't bother me. People can let it bother them.'

If other people saw a trail of psyched out full-forwards, then so be it.

'I can't say what's in their heads! I'd only be trying to keep my own head right. I got plenty of roastings. I got plenty of knocks too. You get them ... and give them ... and move on.'

His disciplinary record too stands up to scrutiny. Over the course of 13 years with Meath, he was rightly sent off after catching Vinny Murphy in 1991 and wrongly, he says, back in a National League game in 1983.

'They were after bringing out new rules and I actually missed out on an All Star that year. I pulled a lad's jersey twice ... and I was off. There were new rules and I was off ... just like that.

'At that time, if you were sent off you couldn't win an All Star.'

An All Star in 1984 and '86, he reckons that incident cost him a third.

'I'd say it would have. I'd say it came down to that.'

Right to this day, his name and reputation carries a resonance that endures. They still come to the golf club in Rathcore to talk about one thing - 'it's all football' – looking for nuggets and stories about the good old days and everything that went with it. Even when he's out and about, the unmistakable cut of him draws football fans over.

The game had given him everything he had ever dreamed.

So no regrets, none?

'Before ... fellas would laugh at you playing for Meath. We went from the point of people laughing at us ... to people looking up to us.

'That was it.'

That was everything.

CHAPTER 6

DARREN FAY

To Darren Fay growing up, Mick Lyons was many things. His father's buddy. The player he idolised. The reason he stencilled No.3 on the back of his jersey at his first and only summer camp.

And Lyons would play a part in finding a natural heir to his jersey, someone to mention in the same breath as Paddy O'Brien, Jack Quinn and himself - someone to continue the county's remarkable tradition of producing fabled No. 3's.

It's funny how their lives intersected.

Leinster final day 1988.

Meath and Dublin, Croke Park.

In the dressing room at the interval, Lyons, the captain, isn't happy. Nobody is. Out of sync, out of sorts, the team barely deserve to be up by the narrowest of margins.

Outside on the pitch, Darren Fay is having the time of his life. Part of a Meath under-12 selection to feature in the half time match, here he is living out his dreams, lining out on the same sod as his heroes.

Dad, Jimmy had another reason to be proud. Looking down from the stand, it's not hard to spot Darren. In goals. Goalkeeping gloves on. Safe hands and a booming kick already identified as assets. Like father, like son.

Six years later, he would be back at Croke Park, lining out at centre-back on a Meath minor team in a Leinster final, a rising star who suddenly popped up like a bright light on the radar of Seán Boylan and his management team.

By this stage, Lyons and his old pal Joe Cassells – a twin pair of All-Ireland winning captains – have been cajoled into filling the gap left by retirement, by joining Boylan as selectors.

Fay tells the tale of his senior call-up with good humour and heart-on-sleeve honesty about his own ability.

'It's a funny story. It's amazing the way the chance came along. Growing up, I would never have been an exceptional footballer. Decent enough club footballer; never, even to this day, would I have been the best footballer in my club … never. I would have been up in the top three, but there would always have been someone there better.

'Mick was a selector with Seán in 1994-95. Seán was away on holidays and Meath had to open the pitch in Nobber. So Mick was left to manage the team.

'He was walking along Trim one day, a couple of days before the game, and he was stuck for numbers because it was off season. He met my father on the street and says, "Howya Jimmy … blah blah blah." He says, "I've to f**kin' organise this game. Boylan's away on holidays. Would Darren be interested in coming along, or would you let him come along?" Because I was only 18 at the time.

'Mick had seen me playing. I had started playing senior football with Trim and I actually played against Mick earlier that year. He was playing full-forward for Summerhill and I was midfield for Trim.

'Mick just asked my father, "Is it alright if he comes along. I know he's young but I'll stick him in corner-forward … out of the way. I mightn't even play him if I've enough players." My father says, "Yeah, throw him in … he'll be grand."

'So Mick brought me along to that game. It was against Dublin up in Nobber. I'll never forget walking into the dressing room and basically had the 1987, '88 team looking back at me – the likes of Colm O'Rourke, Brian Stafford. You're going in as a young lad, still in school. I had actually just started doing my Leaving Cert year that September.

'There were only 16 or 17 players. He played me corner-forward and just said, "Come out midfield. Just stay out of trouble. Your father will kill me if you go back and you're injured!"

'So I played that game pretty much as a third midfielder.

'Even at 18 years of age I kinda felt, "I'm getting a chance here." And I played very well coming out around the middle, got on an awful lot of ball.

'I was marking Keith Barr for a good bit. That was huge because he was such a figure for Dublin. Tommy Carr was playing that time as well.'

For Dublin, this wasn't just an aimless kick-about, rather a tune-up for the All-Ireland. No wonder Fay came off the field buzzing. His new manager too.

'Mick was delighted. He said, "I can't believe how well you got on ... this is great." So when Boylan came back from holidays, Mick told him about what was after happening and Seán says, "grand". I knew Seán from my father's time playing. Now I hadn't spoken to him in years but he would have known exactly who I was.

'So the following week we played Armagh in another challenge, up in Armagh, and Seán started me wing-forward. And I was absolutely useless in the first half. And he put me back at wing-back in the second half and I played very well. It all started then from there.'

Fay is right when he says Boylan knew exactly who he was. If you walked, talked and kicked a ball with any sort of promise, the Meath manager had your number. Like a one-man scouting agency.

With his encyclopaedic knowledge of all things GAA, he can tell you without hesitation the first time he spotted Fay.

'The first time I met him was when Meath won the Centenary Cup. I can still see the blondie head of him. We played Louth then in the grounds of Slane Castle where they play the concerts. A Meath selection and a Louth selection dressed in the garb of 100 years earlier. And Darren was there ... his dad was playing of course. And to think 10 years down the road, he'd be in there himself.

'My first time to see Darren play anything of significance was the All-Ireland minor final of '93. That day in Croke Park they were beaten. They had Paddy Reynolds, Mark O'Reilly, Ollie Murphy – Barry Callaghan was injured – there was half a dozen off that squad.

'Darren was the first schoolboy brought in. When he came in first … very committed, but the hand would be on the back, or he'd be fouling.

'You might say, "Why did you bring him in so young?" I didn't want him to develop bad habits. That was nothing to do with the club or anything else, just it can happen to a young player defeated in an All-Ireland minor.'

With the old guard and his old team breaking up, Boylan was in the process of building a new team – 1993 ended in an early Championship exit against Dublin and Fay, still at school in St Michael's Christian Brothers in Trim, was drafted in properly for the National League campaign of 1994-95.

In light of the battles to come down the road, it was somehow fitting that it was Dublin again who he first showed his mettle against in serious competition.

'It was a surreal experience but because I was so young, I just didn't care. It was a privilege to mark Jack Sheedy. It's gas … I was still at an age where I was thinking "Jesus, he's a guard!"

'You'd be more afraid of him for that, than because of who he was. That's how young I was.

'He was playing No.12 and I was playing five.

'It went great. I even had a shot at goal. It went about 20 yards wide but I didn't care! Vinny Murphy came on to me then and all I knew about Vinny was that he would have had a bit of a reputation.

'He came on for Jack Sheedy at wing-forward with about 10 minutes to go and stood in front of me. All I can remember is that he had this big scar on the back of his head – his head was shaved – and I just thought, "Jesus Christ almighty!"

'I was nearly at that age where you were nearly checking out how hairy lads' legs were … I was that young!

'Mick put his arm around me after that game and says, "Right … listen! You're on to a very good thing here now, just make sure your feet stay on the ground." I'll never forget coming out of the old dressing room in the Hogan Stand … the old dressing room in the corner and him putting his arm around me and having a word. I knew I wouldn't – but I'm glad he said it to me.'

Lyons had a simple reason for the quiet word. 'Because young lads can take their eyes off the ball. If you can keep right, it's so important. Because with county football, you're always waiting for the next roasting.'

Typically, he plays down his own role in Fay's fast-track development. 'Darren Fay was always going to be a class footballer. If I didn't bring him in, somebody else would have. At that stage, he was being well talked about. Sure he was centre-back for the Meath minors. He was well able to play. Strong … and a good tackler.'

For Fay, having Lyons around the set-up eased the step-up to the big leagues.

'There is so much of a massive link there. Between him giving me my first start with Meath, from him being around the place growing up and being drawn to this iconic figure.

'Mick Lyons gave me my chance with Meath. Without Mick Lyons giving me that chance, I might never have made it. It all started from there. I was doing my Leaving Cert that year and I started every League game. Wing-back for the first few. Cormac Murphy got injured then – I think he broke his wrist – and I was put in centre-back then for the rest of the League games. You're marking fellas like Tony Boyle … Seamus Downey. These lads have won All-Ireland medals and you're just kinda in awe of them. But you're so excited too because you want to test yourself. If you got any ball on them you'd be delighted. It wasn't like in later years where if they got one ball you'd be disappointed.

'I'd go into training then and the likes of Colm O'Rourke would be there and I'd say nothing. Even when I was 30 I said nothing! But I was going in with my school uniform still on me.

'Boylan says to me, "You're the first and only fella who ever came in to me with the school uniform on him." And a school uniform without the tie! I'd go home and just throw that in the corner.

'The likes of Evan Kelly was in there, Trevor [Giles], who I knew from minor … Graham [Geraghty]. Because they were younger you got to know them quicker. Then you had the likes of Colm O'Rourke, Bernard Flynn, PJ Gillick, Robbie O'Malley, Mickey McQuillan, Donal Smyth, Colm Coyle … still the guts of the team of 1987, '88.'

At times, the learning curve was steep and not without its sharp edges.

When he watched James McCartan take over as Down senior football manager and guide his county back to an All-Ireland final in 2010 for the first time since playing a starring role himself on the 1991 and 1994 winning teams, he wasn't surprised.

'Wee James' was the sort of driven, hard-nosed competitor that Fay could appreciate, cut in the same mould of Lyons and company. His first lesson in a senior football jersey came at the hands of the pint-sized Down veteran.

'In my third ever match with Meath back in '94,' recalls Fay. 'We played Down who were All-Ireland champions at the time. I was wing-back and marking James McCartan. This was the be-all and end-all for me.

'We were going for a ball but it didn't come. And I slipped. As soon as I slipped and was on the ground, he just turned around and gave me a clip on the ear. And ran off.

'You knew how clever it was. Once he saw me on the ground and could get away, he made sure I stayed on the ground. I'll never forget it. The difference in the cleverness and the cuteness … I was so raw.

'You could see that he was so streetwise. It probably came from years of playing against lads who were going to hit him first. It's alright being able to run as quick as him, kick the ball the same as him, but you have to be as streetwise as well. You only gain that from experience.

'I would have been much bigger than him but I was only 18. He went to try and get the ball then. And then he was in acres of space when the ball came.'

Fay played in every minute of every League game but an untimely leg injury picked up in a club match with Trim, not to mention his tender years, stood against him come the Leinster Championship.

Meath dispatched Offaly, Longford and Wicklow in the sort of crushing, ruthless manner that suggested they were credible contenders for the big prize in September.

'I remember on the sideline, Mick coming to me after the Longford game and saying, "Don't constantly keep looking at us, looking for your game." Because I was there looking at them thinking "Why aren't they bringing me on?"

'But I had no Championship experience … they were never going to bring me on.

'He just says, "Don't be worrying about it … you'll get your chance."'

The Leinster champions would be crowned All-Ireland champions later that year. Except the winners wore sky blue jerseys.

Being floored by Dublin to the tune of 10 points in the 1995 Leinster final, 1-18 to 1-8, shocked everyone involved.

Nobody saw it coming. In fact, on the 50th minute mark, Meath were actually a point up. Only then did the floodgates open, Paul Clarke's leap and brilliantly improvised back flick to the net summing up a rampant Dublin. Never one to paint over the cracks, whether in his own game or others, Fay believes the cracks of a team in transition were there to see.

'Meath were playing as a novelty act,' he says without sentiment. 'Going into the Dublin match, Meath were still trading on their past.'

As selector, nothing pained Lyons more than to see the old enemy running riot on Leinster final day, the day he coveted. As a player, he had never lined out on a team that lost to Dublin in a provincial decider.

He recalls those last 10 minutes with the same easy manner that characterises the conversation. 'The whole thing just went… whooish! Just like that. It happened very quick.

'That's the way it goes.'

No changes from the line were going to turn the tide, he believes. 'It was like patching up a ship that was already well water-holed. It happened so quick and there were so many things going wrong in those last few minutes.'

Fay remembers the wreckage of the dressing room and the immediate aftermath. Three years of successive defeats to Dublin, culminating in this wipe-out, meant that this looked for all the world like Meath's Waterloo.

Mick Lyons and Joe Cassells would step down. And Fay reveals how Boylan too was actually on the verge of following suit. Arguably, a conversation at the County Club just outside Dunshaughlin where the players were gathered afterwards changed the course of history.

'Seán would have said a few words in the dressing room. First and foremost, I remember him saying he had to go back and that maybe his time had run.

'We all went back to the County Club and had a meal. Martin O'Connell came up to myself and Ollie Murphy and said, "Seán is going to go. What do you think of that?"

'Seán had put his hands on the table and said, "I'm gone." Because he had basically made his decision that he was finished.

'Now Seán was an iconic figure to us. We didn't care that we were after losing by 10 points to Dublin – it made no difference to our perception of him. Myself and Ollie Murphy just said, "We'd prefer if Seán stayed. We want Seán to manage us."

'So after talking to the young players, Martin went back and said to Seán, "You can't go. All the young lads want you to stay."

'And Seán stayed because of that reason.'

That intervention would help Meath rewrite the history books. Boylan would come back with a new team, a new backroom team also, and do the unthinkable – win the All-Ireland the following year. And then add another in 1999.

Could Fay imagine it happening without him in charge?

'It wouldn't have happened,' he says without hesitation.

The 1995 Leinster final would prove to be the unlikeliest of turning points. Lyons' own mind was certainly made up. And he wasn't for turning. Looking back now, he believes getting involved so soon after playing was a mistake, even with his old sparring partner, friend and confidante, Joe Cassells in tow.

'Seán would have asked us. He could have asked a few people mind you … I wouldn't say it was just us two! We went in together.

'Why? That's a six marker question. I suppose I couldn't get away from football. It's hard to just leave it all behind. Looking back, it wasn't the right thing to do. You're after playing with all the players for seven or eight absolutely fantastic years, then you come along and have to be on the selection and management committee that maybe has to drop them? That's a very hard part of it.'

Dealing with the players he had soldiered with in the trenches for so long, it felt awkward at times running through selection meetings. 'It's nearly talking behind their backs. Even though it's not, it feels like that. Like myself and Joe having to discuss Colm O'Rourke … and he nearly a better footballer than the two of us put together?

'I did under-10s, 12s, 14s, 16s, minors, under-21s with Summerhill, as coach and manager. Yet I would have found after a year of doing selector with Meath that it wasn't the right fit at the time.

'Turns out, myself and Joe finished. Both of us had young families. I was after spending 20 years involved in football. I just found it too much.'

Even though he stepped away, the seeds that he planted would take root in time.

Fay remembers one particular conversation his father had with Lyons.

'Mick used to take the lads from south Meath on a Saturday for a training session. Seán used to take the lads in the east, the likes of Dunboyne. It was handier for lads to do that.

'Because I wasn't driving at the time, my dad used to drop me there. Myself and Conor Martin, Tom Hanley from Athboy, there was only five or six of us kicking a ball around. My father stayed because he was to give me a lift back. And Mick was training … who he hadn't seen in a while. So they were gabbing on the sideline and that day Mick says to my father, "Y'know what? I think Darren would make a great full-back."

'That was it. My father just told me that on the way home in the car. But I'd never played full-back.'

In truth, Boylan was thinking just the same thing.

For the first round of the National League against Laois that October, Fay pulled the No.3 shirt over his head for the first time. A red letter day in its own right.

'I was marking Damien Delaney … very skilful footballer. Would have been Laois's main man, along with Hugh Emerson. I completely marked him out of it. It just went like a dream. Everywhere I went the ball went.

'Going through that League, I was marking fellas like Delaney, Tony Boyle, Seamus Downey.

'Most of the full-forwards at that time were the main scorers. So every game I went out, I was the underdog.

'I let myself go. No pressure.'

He kept Delaney scoreless and continued in the same vein over the course of the winter and spring.

'Without a shadow of a doubt, Tony Boyle was the hardest fella I marked those first few years. I remember the first match I played at full-back in Navan against Donegal during the '95-96 campaign and for the full hour we just swung completely out of each other.

'I remember the battles with him, real tough encounters. The ball was kicked in and whoever was the best man would win it. There was no handpassing then around the place. It was get it in to the full-forward as quickly as possible.

'I never marked Joe Brolly because he was always in the corner. I used to think, "I hope he never comes in full-forward." Because he was so good. And yet he looked so awkward swinging the left foot with the socks up. As a back, there is always an element of trying to "get" a forward … and get away with it. And Joe Brolly, with the blowing kisses to the crowd, would have been one of them.

'Leading in to the '96 Championship we had qualified for the quarter-final of the League. Now Mayo beat us down in Roscommon and everybody was giving out. But we knew that day that we were going places. Mayo wanted that game more than us, which was fine. But we knew exactly what was in our tank.

'I had 13 full League games under my belt before I played Championship. Two full seasons.' Yet in the build-up to the first round of Leinster against Carlow, the mood outside the squad was very different.

'Seán comes with an approach that you just trust him. Our pre-season in '95-'96 was playing basketball in training, throwing 'O'Neills' and trying to get baskets over in Gormanston College.

'There were two women training us, two girls that worked with Seán up in the herbal place.

'All the craic from the past players who had just gone, the like O'Rourke and Harnan, was … "I hear the f**kin' Meath team is being trained by a bunch of women now!"

'It was great. There were actually fights on the basketball court. Because lads were so close to each other and we didn't really know how to play the game. We didn't really get the concept that you couldn't touch each other. So we were milling into each other. And there were rows … which is good. Once that's happening, it gets everyone on edge.'

Only Martin O'Connell, Colm Coyle and Tommy Dowd were left from the old guard when the Meath team was unveiled to a collective shaking of heads around the county.

'I remember when we were sitting picking the team with Frank Foley and Eamonn O'Brien for the first round of the Leinster,' explains Boylan. 'Marty was to be full-back, Darren in the corner. "No ..." I said. "Darren full-back ... Marty will mind him."

'That's how it ended up. Talk about not fouling then ... he never fouled. You could not distract him.'

That show of confidence gave Meath's new full-back a pep in his step making his Championship debut. Marked Colm Hayden. Kept him scoreless as Meath blitzed Carlow 0-24 to 0-6. In the semi-final against Laois, Fay went toe-to-toe with Damien Delaney and again didn't concede an inch, Graham Geraghty the star performer on the day.

All the time, Fay is waiting, watching, learning. Dublin, All-Ireland champions, were finding life under new manager Mickey Whelan hard. For their own Leinster semi-final against Louth, Jason Sherlock, the brightest young thing to hit Gaelic games in 1995, didn't start, a sign of the turbulence within the camp as Dublin struggled through.

Dublin-Meath then in the Leinster final.

Same as it ever was.

The moment Fay had waited for all his life.

The stage that his hero Mick Lyons coveted above any other.

'The Dubs were the be-all and end-all. Growing up in Meath, it was all about Dublin..

'It was exactly where you wanted to be. If you wanted to be in a Leinster final, you wanted to be in one against Dublin.' And Dublin gave him something to think about right from the start with their team selection.

'I went to the Dublin-Louth game in Navan in '96. Joe McNally was full-forward. Sherlock actually came on that day ... I don't know why he wasn't starting.

'Joe was full-forward, another iconic figure. Joe was burly and I was looking forward to marking him. And then all of a sudden Sherlock comes out. Which was grand at the time. Especially when you're that young, you don't worry about who you're playing. Two more different footballers though you couldn't have come across.'

From the charismatic, bullish presence of McNally, Fay had to adapt to marking someone half his size, an impish presence who was full of movement. A completely different puzzle to solve. But he felt bulletproof, in part because of the confidence Boylan instilled.

'Myself and Mark O'Reilly and Martin O'Connell were there. Seán basically said to me, "You go for absolutely everything that drops in the full-back line. And don't worry. Mark or Martin will pick up anything that breaks."

'I would have rathered marking Sherlock than McNally. Because I knew the ball would be coming in front of Sherlock and I had perfected a way of getting my fist in on the ball. The reason why I perfected that was I was so afraid of lads getting the ball and going one-on-one.'

In truth, Fay was a very modern full-back: a mobile ball-player who could run with the bulls when needed. Watching Dublin take home the Sam Maguire Cup gave him even more of a reason to try and make his mark.

On a day when the rains turned it into a battle of wills, Meath's young guns came of age.

With a hand in here, a fist away there, Fay frustrated Dublin's full-forward to the extent he failed to register a score.

Hill 16 stayed quiet that day, deprived of the opportunity to bang out the title track to the All-Ireland winning summer of the previous year, *'Boom, boom, let me hear you say Jayo!'*

John McDermott's power-play at midfield kept Meath in it, but the team still trailed by two with just 10 minutes left. And then Brendan Reilly and the inimitable Trevor Giles levelled it, before Barry Callaghan and Tommy Dowd add the grace notes.

'It was great to win and we celebrated it after. And it was big at the time. Because there was no back door. Dublin lost and were out of the Championship.

'Leinsters were huge.

'I remember a team meeting on the Tuesday night after. Tommy Dowd was captain at the time and he stood up and said, "Right lads, you might never get another chance to be in this position again. You might never win another Leinster. We can't wait another few years just because we're young and it's the first time since '91 and we think this a platform for next year. Take our chance now."

'At the time we had no fear.'

No knowledge either, as Lyons quotes Con Houlihan, of *'all the pitfalls'* that might lie ahead.

Fay tells a story of Boylan's influence in the build-up to the semi-final, of his guiding influence and uncanny knack of getting inside players' heads. Even now, he breaks into a wide smile telling it.

'For a couple of weeks previous to it Seán was talking to us about the noise that's going to be in Croke Park and the deafening silence. We were there, "deafening silence" … that's just a cliché. He kept saying it.

'And I'll never forget it … it was the only time it happened to me. When Seán said a "deafening silence" that's exactly what I experienced when Tyrone ran out … because we were out on the pitch first. It was basically like, you couldn't hear anything yet the sound seemed to be in a bubble around you.

'We're there about to play an All-Ireland semi-final, and it packed out in Croke Park … and I'm there in the middle of the pitch doing a bit of stretching thinking, "So that's what he means!"

'It just completely relaxed me. I just thought, "I'm ready for this now." Because I'd get nervous before games.' Tactically, Tyrone threw a curveball at the Meath defence just to try and unsettle them from the start. 'Peter Canavan was picked full-forward and I was really geared up for this. Then Canavan came in and actually walked over to Mark O'Reilly in the corner. We never switched. If another team wanted to go that way … then away with them. Canavan went to kick the ball over the bar with his first ball – it was actually some point – and John McDermott came in… very early.'

The last bit of the sentence is said with a straight face and perfect comic timing before he comes clean. 'John hit him late. In this day and age you'd get a straight red. He took him out … and that set the tone.

'Ciaran McBride came in on me. I thought "f**k it". I was hoping to mark him. I was that young and I wanted to test myself against the best. McBride was trying to bring me out. It was nothing new.'

By the break, there was enough incident and accident to prompt a Liveline special on RTE radio. In scrambling for a ball, Martin O'Connell accidentally caught Brian Dooher on the head with his studs and Dooher ended up with what McDermott described as a 'turban' on his head. Ciaran McBride and Peter Canavan were also injured in separate incidents.

'Tyrone coming down probably thought, "This is a bunch of kids – we can throw our weight around." Dublin were after robbing them of the All-Ireland before. They were a serious outfit.

'Here were this young Meath team, after butchering Canavan ... butchering McBride. And as for Dooher, the medical doctor or whoever put that bandage on should be ashamed of themselves. It must have been one of the selectors! It looked like we bullied them around the field.'

Outmuscled and outfought, Tyrone were ultimately played off the field, Graham Geraghty's palmed goal – a lob over the goalkeeper's head – a touch of sheer genius.

As for Fay's reaction when he heard the Liveline furore? 'We were delighted to be on the radio! I presume the likes of Colm Coyle ... Martin O'Connell weren't happy, but we were that young, we didn't pass any remarks.'

He is in no doubt that Meath were suffering from the sins of their fathers.

'Even though it was a completely different team, people where harking back to 1987, '88 and saying they are this and that. We were called thugs. When people talk about Meath football and start on about thuggery it's always '87, '88 and that team. In general, with that team, no matter where you kicked the ball there was someone capable of cleaning you out! It wasn't like that in 1996, '99.'

The parameters of the game had changed in terms of discipline but Boylan's message never changed. 'It was about playing on the line. Seán always said to us, "If there is anybody in trouble out there off the ball, make sure there are bodies around him. He never, ever said to hit anybody or do anything like that ... just make sure there are bodies there in support. And that's what we did.

Even for someone in his rookie Championship season appearing in an

All-Ireland final, there was little danger of losing the run of himself in the build-up to the final.

'You had too much respect for Seán and the team that you weren't going to let big-headedness or arrogance take over.'

Croke Park, Sunday, September 15, 1996.

Connacht champions Mayo had cut a path through to the final and the imprint of army man John Maughan was all over them; tightly drilled, well organised, superbly fit and well able to play ball. With the press restoring Meath to the status of Public Enemy Number One, Mayo were primed to meet the Meath challenge head on.

On the morning of the final, Fay's big-match rituals begin with a breakfast of a different kind.

'Every Championship match that year I had a steak. It was a gesture from Kepak where we were all given steaks every Thursday night. As a young lad I used to love it.

'I used to eat a steak every morning,' he explains laughing, 'because Mick Lyons used to eat a steak every morning!'

'So I used eat a steak about half nine in the morning – and then go to the County Club! There'd be a bite there but I never needed it!

That's what I had for breakfast on the morning of the All-Ireland final.'

At Croke Park then, he'll need every bit of pre-match comfort to draw on. For long periods of a drawn All-Ireland, Mayo push Meath around Croke Park.

It takes all Meath's trademark reserves of character and nerve to come storming back, Colm Coyle's last-gasp equalising point worth over a million pounds to the GAA, bouncing over the bar in the most dramatic fashion after being booted in from distance.

Meath know they have been dominated physically, as well as in football terms, for long periods, Liam McHale running the show at midfield. One incident where Barry Callaghan is left isolated rankles.

'I remember that incident. There was a scuffle down in our half-forward line involving Barry Callaghan. Mayo seemed to be really eager for the dust up. They certainly had more lads around. And it was definitely said afterwards ... it was what Seán always said, "Do not overstep the mark but make sure there are bodies around a player in trouble."

'After being six points down and Mayo really putting it to us, and clawing our way back as Meath do, definitely at the team meetings on the Tuesday and Thursday night *it was a case of … "If Mayo think that's what's going to happen, then. … we'll make sure of it."*

Croke Park, Sunday, September 29, 1996.

 Both teams take to the field pumped.

 This time Meath aren't going to be dictated to.

 Just over five minutes in, the most famous fight in All-Ireland history kicks off.

 It starts innocuously enough with Fay winning a ball around the square.

 'John McDermott was on the goal line as he always would be and I was marking my man.

 'John went up, missed the catch and palmed it down in front. So I went in and got the ball.

 'But Anthony Finnerty came in … not quite clotheslined me, but caught me up on the chest and halted me. Now it was a free.

 'With the team meetings and lads saying, "Don't let Mayo bully us", I think lads over-reacted.

 'Because it wasn't a bad challenge on me.

 'All of a sudden all hell broke loose in front of me. I just dropped the ball and ran in. I didn't know what I was running in for! I just tried to get at somebody … but sure I couldn't because there was that many bodies.

 'Then I looked up and I saw McHale flying in from about 30 yards. He was going for McDermott but he bumped into me, and I was able to divert him.

 'Pat McEnaney was referee. All of a sudden he calls over Liam McHale and Colm Coyle … and sent them both off.'

 He doesn't remember being thrown out of kilter by the row or stressing over the dismissals. For all his nervous energy before any big game, he became immersed in it all when the ball was thrown in; the outside world might as well have ceased to exist.

 'I was still in the mind-set of being focused,' he says.

 'I just completely blanked the fella I was marking. If he wanted to shake hands I'd shake hands but I'd never put my hand out first. It was just one of those things. Anyone that's focused enough shouldn't be talking. So there was very little jawing either.'

 His marker, John Casey had run riot in the semi-final against Kerry, putting the family hardware store in Charlestown where he worked firmly on the map. At the time, *various top flight soccer players were sporting the latest fad: nose stickers. An up-for-anything character, Mayo's full-forward decided to bring it to a whole new audience.*

'He was the first fella I came across to wear the sticker across his nose,' recalls Fay, smiling.

By the end of his double date with Meath's full-back, there was little fear of Casey's look catching on.

Mayo adapt to the loss of talisman McHale and just like the drawn game, bound six clear, PJ Loftus finding the net after being brought on to counter Martin O'Connell's dominance.

But Meath fight back again.

'I think the winning of the game was the quick thinking of Graham [Geraghty] and Tommy [Dowd] in the second half. Mayo were six points up again.

'We always knew with any team that we could pull them back more often than not. So we weren't worried about the six points. But when Graham was fouled around the 21 yard line, he got up straight away and played it in to Tommy Dowd.'

Dowd, pulled down as he solos around goalkeeper John Madden, somehow manages to swing a boot at the ball on the ground and scores.

James Horan replies for Mayo with his fifth point from play in a remarkable display of scoring from the wing-forward, leaving it level.

Then, in injury time, Trevor Giles shows incredible timing to tackle Colm McManamon and take the ball off him as he tries to solo upfield, before playing a slide rule pass down the sideline to Brendan Reilly. The converted defender beats his man before curling over the sweetest of left-foot points from the right-hand side of the field.

'People don't give Brendan Reilly enough credit for that point. It was an exceptional score.'

When Pat McEnaney's whistle blew, a familiar face came flying across the turf towards Fay.

'The feeling at the final whistle … I'll never forget it. My mother was the first one over to me. How she got there I'll never know. She ran over and just gave me a hug. When my mother gets excited you don't know what she's saying because it's all a constant scream. She must have been on the sideline ready to come in but we only won it in the last minute, so I don't know where she came from!'

Angela Fay and her All-Ireland winning son soon became swallowed up in the pitch invasion. 'Just a sea of people. We finally made it to the steps of the Hogan

Stand. It's like what you see on the television. There was a garda there and suddenly there's a cordon. It's an amazing experience to be there and be inside that cordon looking out at the sea of people.

'You know you've won the All-Ireland but it still doesn't sink in. The best way to describe it would be ... you know you've won the All-Ireland on paper but you don't feel qualified enough.'

Fay is fast becoming a fans' favourite and following the lead of his father's good buddy, Mick Lyons. En route to his first All-Ireland in his debut Championship season he conceded a miserly 0-2 from play to his direct opponents over six games. Over the course of the drawn game and replay, he conceded a single point to Casey.

In keeping with the madness of what happened on the field, there is drama when the Meath team head for their post-match meal on the Monday. 'Because it was a replay, the Burlington wasn't booked for the banquet the next day – it had been pre-booked. So it was up in the bar in the Cusack Stand.

'Tommy couldn't get in with the Cup. It was actually on the RTE news that night. He was carrying the Cup – but he'd no ticket. And the security guy wouldn't let him in. Tommy was laughing at it all. Whoever it was in the GAA had to come down and let him in.

'The row was after happening and there was an awful lot of bitterness. I was talking to John Casey in the toilets ... there was no problem with John. He was talking about the game, how disappointed he was. He congratulated me and all ... we must have been in there 10 minutes.'

Mayo's full-forward had the good grace to bravely take the defeat on the chin, but the fall-out from the fight and the final result had left many of his teammates harbouring a grudge.

After picking out their leader and midfield general, McHale for a straight dismissal, Mayo felt aggrieved that the Meath equivalent in John McDermott wasn't picked out as well. Turns out that McEnaney was going to until the intervention of an umpire fingered Coyle.

Fay recalls the ugly mood even as the Meath team celebrated in low-key fashion.

'We were having a few drinks after winning. But you're conscious of not over-celebrating because Mayo were there. You have to respect that as well.

'The Burlington room the day after the All-Ireland is usually full. There's business people, different people everywhere. For that … for the replay, it was just the two teams and their wives. That was it. It was very intense. There was nothing really separating us.

'John McDermott went over to Liam McHale and stuck his hand out as Liam was having his meal and said, "No hard feelings about yesterday."

'Liam McHale stood up and said, "Yes, there is hard feelings" and the rest of the Mayo team at that table said the same and stood up.

'Seán saw all of this and came over and basically got us all out of there. It would have been very embarrassing for the GAA if that kicked off … and it was very close to kicking off.

'I didn't know how serious it was until afterwards.

'There was an edge there. You could feel that. It was only when we got on the bus and went to the County Club that people were talking of how serious it could have got.

'It would have been embarrassing for Meath as well. At that time, there was a big thing about the row that was after happening. It would have been very bad for Meath football and anyone involved if there was a row at the banquet afterwards.'

Imagine.

The homecoming party was everything he imagined it to be.

'Just complete madness. Brought the Cup around that night. Ended up in Navan. That was the first realisation of what we were after doing.

'We met in Páirc Tailteann and got an open-top bus down to the Fair Green. And it was just a sea of people again. At that moment I thought, "This is a bit more than I ever realised." We all went on stage and lifted the Cup. I'd say I was under the influence at that stage! We had a meal then in the Ardboyne and all went home then.

'I was going out with my wife, Rhona at the time. We just came home about one or two o'clock. I think she just wanted to get me out of there before it was all a bit much.

'Tommy called and we spent the next few days calling around to the schools. We did Trim and Navan the following day.'

Taking part in the GOAL charity match was a tradition for the All-Ireland champions and so Meath togged out, some of the players still feeling the effects of the celebration. 'The GOAL match was on the Wednesday night so we played that against a Rest of Ireland selection. And then went on the beer after that. I don't think we stopped 'til the Friday or Saturday.

'I was okay for the match. It's strange but I was treating it like a normal match. I remember Tommy coming into the dressing room before it and it seemed like he was half cut – and that wouldn't be like Tommy because he wouldn't be a drinker. So the fellas who were drinkers were trying to keep themselves sober and the fellas who weren't usually drinking were half drunk.'

While a sense of anger and loss simmered in Mayo, it says something of John Casey's free and independent spirit that he turned up for the exhibition match to effectively honour the champions. A big-hearted gesture.

'I was marking John. I found it strange. To travel half way around the country to play in this match. We had a bit of a chat. He's a nice fella.

'He said to me one thing. "I probably took you for granted the first day. And the reason I did that was I was told by other people that you were roasted in an under-21 match. I shouldn't have listened to them."'

By virtue of Meath's run to September, the club Championship needed to be played off. On the following Saturday, Fay lined out against Skryne. At midfield … marking John McDermott. The timing of it meant his mind was elsewhere. 'The two of us had absolutely no interest in the middle of the field. Trevor was centre-back for Skryne and scored his customary load of points. Skryne beat us well.'

All three would be named All Stars soon afterwards. In total, five Meath men were honoured, Martin O'Connell and Tommy Dowd the others.

Boylan had done it again. What was all the more remarkable was that he had guided Meath to the Sam Maguire Cup with a new team, a different set of players.

+ + + + +

Darren Fay is the first to tell you he's the shy and retiring type generally when it comes to a crowd. The all-singing, karaoke king David Beggy, he is not.

It says something of the tight bond that Boylan engendered in his team, the family environment, that he came out of his shell on the team holiday to Lanzarote.

That's when he put on his best Liam Gallagher drawl and, *'Wonderwall'* became his party piece. A terrible beauty was born.

'I was never into singing but it was the only song when I had a few drinks on me that I could remember. My brother, Aaron taught it to me because he played the guitar.

'When we were on holidays in '96, we were at a function. And it was just us … the players, the wives, the official party. They had a band booked for the function. Everyone was sitting down and it was early evening and nobody was doing anything.

'Mocky Regan says, "Sure we need someone to sing a song here." I'd a good few drinks on me at that stage so I said, "Do you know what … feck it." So I got up. It was the first time I ever sang in public. And it actually went well.

'And the night kicked off from there. So any time I was at a function or where there was a bit of karaoke, I'd be singing *'Wonderwall'*.

'In that instance Mocky Regan played the guitar. We were up on stage. The band hardly played after that because everyone was up then singing songs. It was a great old night …

'In the yacht club in Lanzarote.

'That's my only party piece.'

An All Star and All-Ireland winner in his first Championship season, he is unfailingly honest in admitting he milked the celebrations for all their worth. Still only 20, surrounded by young friends and faces he had played up the ranks with, sure why not? The world was their oyster.

A Q&A back then offers an illustration of how all is good with the world.

Desert island necessities?

A keg of Guinness and Anna Kournikova – she can leave her racket behind!

What's your party piece?

Singing all of 'Wonderwall'. And I don't need a party – just any room with more than 10 people will set me off.

Worst job you ever had?

When I was in school, I worked on a milk-round from 1am to 8am every Monday morning and had to go straight into school an hour later. That was killing.

Thinking back, he wishes he had maturity that comes with age. Instead, Friday and Saturday nights out on the town, he wore his achievements like a badge of honour.

'It's hard to handle when you're young and looking back now, I could actually have lost the run of myself a lot more. Because I wasn't the only one. We all did. Especially with the holiday in the middle of the year.

'We went to Lanzarote in January ... it was in the middle of the League. Most of us had been suspended because of the All-Ireland final. And I remember being delighted with that. I remember [chairman] Fintan Ginnity ringing me up at work and saying, "Darren, you've got three months." I said, "Oh right."

He says, "I'm sorry for you."

'I got off the phone and I was delighted. Three months drinking. I don't have to play any League games. Most of the lads felt the same.

'I suppose that was down to a bit of immaturity and the fact that when you win an All-Ireland it takes so much out of you mentally. It's very hard to get back into the swing of things. All you want to do is party because you're after putting your life on hold.

'All through 1997 it was pretty much the same. I put on a stone and a half and I was never able to lose it. Even though I was fit with the stone and a half, I wasn't as fit as I could have been.

'We played the games against Kildare in the '97 Championship but I was never up to full fitness. I was struggling with Martin Lynch in all the games.'

Given his single-minded purpose of the previous year, it's something he regrets. 'Of course. You put it down as a wiped out year, that you didn't get the best out of yourself ... '98 was a bit the same. What made you who you were in '96 was the effort you put in. And the focus.

'I can only speak for myself but most of the team were probably doing the same. I was going training, living off, "Oh there's Darren Fay. He won an All Star and an All-Ireland in 96."'

And yet, from the outside looking in, his game looked in seriously good shape.

He is his own harshest critic; always has been.

In 1997, a blossoming Meath team added to its reputation. Just like 1991, the draw pitted the two superpowers of Leinster together in the quarter-final.

Pore through the fine print of the match and Fay gets a more-than-honourable mention, keeping Mick Galvin scoreless. In keeping with the modern tradition of games, it was played at breakneck speed; a raw, passionate encounter that ebbed and flowed, Dublin racing into a 0-3 to 0-1 lead before John McDermott and Jimmy McGuinness took over at midfield, kicking a point each as Meath cut loose. Goal poacher supreme Ollie Murphy palmed the ball past John O'Leary, and with Trevor Giles pulling the strings from centre-forward and Graham Geraghty causing trouble, Meath raced six clear.

Dublin then threw off the shackles, led by the blue-chip half-back line of Paul Curran, Keith Barr and Eamonn Heery – Barr driving forward to crash home a goal. Giles arrowed a penalty wide early in the second half and the game would come down to another dead-ball kick. Heading into injury time, Meath clung to a 1-13 to 1-10 lead. Mick Galvin won possession and shot for goal only for Fay to throw himself in the way and smother the effort. Referee, Brian White though spotted the foot-block.

Penalty! This time, Paul Bealin rather than Barr, ran up and blasted it, the ball cannoning off the underside of the crossbar and out. For Dublin, it was the cruellest of cuts.

If elements of the match mirrored the epic saga of the 1991 series, Meath's three-game semi-final against Kildare deserves its own documentary. And the All-Ireland champions embellished their reputation as the best team in the country in a tight game when the stakes are highest.

Barely a minute in and the towering figure of Martin Lynch, a midfielder reinvented as a full-forward by manager Mick O'Dwyer, in his second coming with Kildare, pilfered a goal. It says everything about Fay's refusal to flinch, his resolve, that his marker didn't get another score for the rest of the entire game. Geraghty, Dowd and the sublime Giles kept Meath in touch right through and it needed a nerveless late point from Giles to force a replay.

In terms of drama, the replay was right up there with the fourth game of the 1991 series. A game that had everything. Five goals and 37 points scored. Graham Geraghty sent off. Referee Pat O'Toole forced off himself with cramp, replaced by John Bannon. Meath, the Harry Houdini of inter-county football, pulling off another great escape.

On the way to a staggering personal haul of 2-8, Trevor Giles again was a central figure in the drama, missing a penalty at the end of normal time but then popping up to palm a goal.

Extra time.

When Kildare surge six clear in the first half of extra-time, it looks done and dusted. In the history of famous Meath comebacks, Jody Devine has his own special place. A loyal servant to the cause, the substitute suddenly finds the form of his career, hitting four points from play in a supreme show of scoring. It sparks a run of seven unanswered points that elevated the game to epic status. Paul McCormack's fisted equaliser for Kildare completes one of the great Croke Park encounters.

By the third game, familiarly had bred a level of contempt. The wet conditions contributed to a tense, fractious affair when four players were sent off and six booked. Fay was one of the four, fingered for lashing out at Lynch off the ball. A first in his Meath career, he was distraught, even as Ollie Murphy's heroics paved a passage to a Leinster final with two points to spare, 1-12 to 1-10.

Fay doesn't spare himself in his analysis. 'The year before when we had trained so hard it would never enter your head to give a fella a box because it would have cost you so much. But, because you're not putting in the same effort in training, to turn around and give a lad a box is much easier. You lose your discipline. Now he fell down a little bit easily but, how and ever. The referee didn't see it … came down and talked to his umpire … and sent me off. I remember walking off the field and thinking, "Oh Jesus!"

'Ollie Murphy got a goal and we won and it dawned on me that I'd miss the Leinster final. And that was devastating. At 21 years of age, it was devastating.

'Seán said to me, "The [disciplinary] meeting is on Tuesday and you're probably going to miss the Leinster final but be ready for the All-Ireland semi-final. I just thought to myself, "yeah whatever". I was so devastated.

'I felt I'd let myself down. We used to play A versus B games. The following

Saturday I was on the B team because I wasn't going to be available for the Leinster final and that was devastating again. Because you put so much work into trying to be the best you can be and then end up, because of your own stupidity and your own indiscipline, to be playing on the B side.'

For Meath, the three game series had taken a serious toll.

'Mark O'Reilly suspended. Martin O'Connell was injured as well. So the whole full-back line was gone. And Graham was suspended from the second game.

'Seán had only 17 or 18 players togged out that day and one of them was Cormac Sullivan the goalkeeper because you could tog him out as an outfield player.' In the build-up to the Leinster final, Offaly manager Tommy Lyons had a dream that involved his side winning. Not only that, the margin brokered no doubt: seven points.

His side won by eight.

In the absence of Mark O'Reilly, Darren Fay and Martin O'Connell, the Offaly full-forward line made hay, hitting 3-9 of a 3-17 tally. Fay watched, with a heavy heart, No. 14 Roy Malone slalom through for two goals.

'You're watching the final and you feel like you've let everybody down. Offaly were destroying us, Roy Malone was walking through. You're sitting there amongst the crowd … because you're not allowed sit in the dug-out, and you just think, "This isn't where I should be."'

Fay feels that his working life wasn't doing him any favours at the time.

'Looking at my own circumstances, I was probably in a job I didn't want to be in … wasn't putting the effort in. I was selling beds. My boss just loved football. He didn't care. It ended up that I was working one day a week.

'I was always of the mindset that if I was happy outside of football, I'd always be happy inside of football. It was strange listening to Oisín McConville saying how one of his best years with Armagh was one of his worst off it. I could never do that. If I was happy off the pitch I was always happy on it.'

Boylan sensed that Fay's focus was slipping a bit and had a quiet word. In his own unique way.

'Seán always tells you things where you have to read between the lines. I remember Seán bringing me to one side at the start of 1998 and saying, "If you go running at seven o'clock in the morning it's worth double what you do in the evenings."

'I says, "grand" and he says, "I'll leave that with you."

'I thought to myself then, "What is he on about? I'm fecked if I'm getting up at seven o'clock to go for a run."

'I said it to Barry Callaghan then coming home from training the next night. Barry thought about it and said, "I'd say it's the weight you have on you. I'd say he wants you to run it off."

'That might be it, I thought.

'Seán is very cautious about what he says to players. Another manager might have said, "You've a lot of weight on you – get it f**kin' off or you won't be part of my team." Seán handles players an awful lot different than that. That's why he commands such respect.'

So 1998 offered a source of redemption.

From the moment Meath were drawn against Offaly in the first round of the Leinster Championship, the motivation was to wipe the slate clean.

'It was a chance to exorcise a ghost. It was a bit of a nervous game for us because people were saying, "We'll beat them this time because the full-back line was missing the last day. And you weren't on Roy Malone." And he ran riot.

'So I was under an awful lot of pressure. Horrid pressure. It was one of the first games that I felt that. So you have fear. But fear is a good thing at times. It keeps you on your toes.'

With Fay marshalling a superb defensive effort, Meath restricted Offaly to a meagre seven points. Bar one inspired Roy Malone point, the full-back line performed a shut-out on the much-vaunted Offaly full-forward line.

Meanwhile Graham Geraghty produced a tour de force at the other end, having a hand in all three Meath second half goals in a 3-10 to 0-7 victory.

Struggling past Louth in the semi-final set off some warning lights though. Fay, concussed in the first half, wasn't fit to make it out after the interval and the team were clinging to a one-point lead when the final whistle went.

For the decider, Kildare came to Croke Park with history in their sights and a first Leinster title since 1956. And they landed it, Brian Murphy's late goal strike prompting scenes of delirium among Lilywhite supporters who stayed on the field long afterwards as captain, Glenn Ryan made a victory speech of record length.

'We were a young team. We should have won more,' says Fay.

Being selected on the Ireland team for the freshly resurrected International Rules series against Australia at home, later that year, gave him a new sense of focus.

'We won the International Rules which was massive. I felt a huge sense of pride and said to myself, "I have to cop myself on now."

'I went back in with Meath then because the League was still on before Christmas. There was fellas missing through injury and whatever, so Seán made me captain because I was the most senior player coming back. I felt a real sense of pride about that.'

Boylan's show of faith drew the Trim player further out of his shell. 'I didn't really talk to people before that in the dressing room. So being able to do that gave me a spur. The League games before Christmas went very well. We played against Monaghan and I was flying around the place at full-back and I knew then I was on the right track.'

Boylan had seen how Lyons didn't need to say a whole lot to inspire his team as captain. Fay too wasn't a natural speech-maker but he blossomed in the role. 'It helped me at that time. It's not something I was ever comfortable with over a prolonged period. I was so proud though after the International Rules. I was able to deliver great speeches before matches. And actually found it comfortable to do so.

'I knew in my own self that I was happy in my own self as a footballer, that I was qualified to speak in the dressing room. Because I was putting everything into it. At that particular time, it was exactly what I needed. The responsibility. It was only a stop-gap until Graham took it over.'

By that stage, he had his own manic training routine to get himself in peak condition. 'I started training on my own before Christmas. I used to run around Dunderry on the way home from work. We were living in Trim at the time and I'd go home then to where I had an exercise bike. An auld yoke ... how I didn't kill myself on it I'll never know!

'It was done by a rope, not a chain. Pedalling against a rope! I was that dedicated I used to run up and down the stairs of the house in Trim. I used to do that for half an hour after running around the pitch in Dunderry. That's what started it off in '99.'

Rhona was used to her husband shutting down before the big matches, moody and mono-syllabic, mind weighted with the match and all its possible scenarios. Running up and down the stairs though, this was new.

In terms of the captaincy, he says Boylan's instincts were on the button once more.

'Seán did a great thing in '99 by making Graham captain. He was that kind of a fella where the pressure didn't get to him. He's the sort of guy who doesn't realise the pressure it should bring. But everyone else would.

'It was completely from left-field. Because there was talk at the time ... "They're thinking of making Graham captain – that's a strange one."

'From Seán giving him the captaincy, he developed the discipline. One led to the other.

'It was a massive call. He was probably looking around thinking, "Who is this least likely to affect?"

'He was very good in the role. A great captain.

'For inter-county, you don't need someone to get you up for a game. If you're not up for it at that level you may go home. You just need someone to say the things that you need to be reminded of, pure and simple ... and then out the door.'

From the All-Ireland winning team of 1996, the likes of Martin O'Connell, Colm Coyle and Brendan Reilly had slipped away. But the core of the team remained hungry for more.

'Everyone, as a collective decided, "We've gone long enough here acting the bollocks. We've nothing to show for the last three years." Everyone just knuckled down.

'I'd say Seán got a bit fed up with it. It was a huge thing for him in '96. He had gone through a number of years of really bad times, bad games, to a stage where he'd quit. So it needed to happen in '99.'

When the Meath team burst out of the tunnel for the quarter-final of the Leinster Championship against Wicklow, supporters had to do a double-take when it came to their full-back.

The idea of dying his hair blond seemed like a great one at the time. He tells the story with a line of self-deprecating humour that would work well on stage.

'Rhona just said, "Why don't you get highlights in your hair?"

'My auntie's a hairdresser. She did it.

'I wouldn't do it in normal working hours. I got her to close the shop at six o'clock and did it in the evening time. She put a plastic bag on my head and starting popping out hairs with a pliars or whatever she had and then bleaching the head.

'I went into training that Saturday … the game was on the Sunday against Wicklow. John McDermott said to me, "Have you highlights in your hair?"

I says, "yeah" and sure I started laughing. And with a bit of a thick head on him he says, "Jesus Christ, I never thought you'd be into that s**t." I thought it didn't look that bad. But when I saw the picture in the paper it looked all blond … it was only meant to be a couple of streaks.

'My hair was long when I was getting it done. Once I got it cut a week later it didn't look half as bad. It just looked like you were out in the sun abroad and it had lightened.'

In that respect, himself and Mick Lyons certainly differed. Thinking of the slagging he'd get in the Meath dressing room didn't faze him.

'Sure I was only 23. I did it as a bit of a laugh. At that age you don't care too much. I guess it's not the done thing to do.' On a Meath team that still traded on a fearsome reputation, he drew quizzical looks.

'Enda McManus was another who said, "Holy God, what's going on?"

'It wasn't something I'd normally do. It was just a moment of madness. But you always knew you could cut it out of your hair. It wasn't as if it was going to be a permanent thing. Certainly you wouldn't have seen Mick Lyons going around with highlights!'

Now there's an image.

That day against Wicklow was significant for more important reasons. 'Going into the Championship, you're still wondering if you have it.

'That told us we did.'

Another rematch with Offaly came next. Once again, Fay's tussle with Roy Malone encapsulated the match; the Offaly full-forward fought hard, battled gamely but couldn't find the space to get his elusive running game going. By the end, Malone cut a frustrated figure, unable to step out of his marker's shadow.

'He started off very well … won a good few balls. But I was always there with him. I felt comfortable the first half. 'He was a very dangerous forward. If you were on your game on the day, you always felt you had the better of him. But if you weren't on your game on the day, he could easily score 1-1 and more.'

Routine is rarely a word used for Meath-Dublin clashes but the semi-final was just that. Ian Robertson showed well at full-forward for Dublin yet finished without brackets beside his name.

Self-critical to a fault, Fay's own performance still rankles.

'I was actually lucky that day. Wherever I was, he was always in a better place. But he didn't get the breaks. He was palming the ball down but his teammates weren't picking it up. The team were comfortable that day … but I wasn't.

'Rhona had booked a holiday for the Monday to go away for a week. It was the best thing that ever happened in the long run. Maybe up to that point I was a bit jaded. Playing the International Rules and then not getting a break, maybe that was it.

'We were supposed to go away on the Monday. I hadn't told Seán beforehand because we were busy training and there was a four-week gap between Championship matches.

'We went to The Canaries. It was a first holiday for myself and Rhona. I was actually in a bar over there, getting a drink, and a fella came up to me and said, 'You're Darren Fay. What the f**k are you doing here? Weren't you playing the Leinster there a few days ago?' He couldn't get over it. I felt a bit guilty then.

'I came back the following Sunday. Trained that same evening. And I felt a changed man. So fresh. I only missed two training sessions and I had done a bit of a training over there on my own.'

He felt refreshed and energised for the challenge of Armagh, riding a wave of emotion after clinching a first Ulster title in 17 years. 'Jarlath Burns, Kieran McGeeney, Oisín McConville, Diarmuid Marsden … they were a super bunch of footballers.'

Come match day, Fay went through his usual routine and walked over to his usual spot on the edge of the square when the last strains of Amhrán na bhFiann rang out. He was still standing alone when the ball was thrown up.

'I remember standing in full-back … referee blew the whistle. And there was no full-forward to mark. John McEntee stayed out in the middle. And it upset us. Because I had to go out then.

'They scored two goals then in the first 20 minutes, were completely on top.

'It was a strange one. Usually the forward comes in and then goes out. But he never went near me.

'I wasn't too upset about it but everyone else seemed to be. I used to love playing out around the middle. The hardest thing for a full-back is to keep a full-forward scoreless. And he ain't going to kick too many balls over from 70 yards.

'I actually had a wide in the first 10 minutes. I was down in the full-forward line having a go.'

But when the ball came in, the defence was in sixes and sevens.

'I went back on Oisín McConville then and everything seemed to settle down. We chipped away and chipped away.'

By the time Armagh full-back, Gerard Reid was sent off for a second bookable offence, Meath had the foot to the floor. 'The second half then was a fantastic performance. John Donaldson was actually playing for Armagh at the time … he'd switched from Louth. He was running up the sideline and McDermott hit him a shoulder. That set the tone for the second half.

'I remember talking to McGeeney after the game because I'd known him from the International Rules. And he was just absolutely devastated.

'I know I'd be devastated after matches but he was much worse. It gave me an inkling of what he's about. I'd say he was more devastated about it because he put in more than anyone else.

'I walked away that day thinking it was a little bit over the top. Because he basically couldn't talk. That's no exaggeration. But looking back now, you can see that this is what made him what he is. Other times, he's very engaging. Nice fella. But that day he was speechless. He was obsessive.'

Second time around, the All-Ireland final experience felt different. Even if the opposition was all too familiar.

Cork again.

Same as 1967, 1987, 1988 and 1990.

Enough of a back story to add another dimension to the game.

'It was a bit different because you know the pitfalls. In '96, it was just like any other game. But '99, even though Seán was trying to play it that way with the same routine, we knew deep down it wasn't.'

Just as Mick Lyons felt as he got older.

'Cork were saying all the right things, saying we were favourites ... which we were. Don Davis was in the paper saying, "Darren Fay doesn't have to turn up. He has his All Star already."

'When you're looking it, you're thinking, "I don't believe that... but I f**kin' kinda do and I hate myself for it!" Everything like that just takes the edge off you.'

Croke Park, Sunday, September 26, 1999.

When the ball is thrown in, Cork try to solve the Meath puzzle by taking Fay out of the equation.

'Don Davis came in on me and then went out. He was lost in traffic in the middle. There was a sea of people and it was a wet day. So I decided to hang back most times.'

And with 20 minutes gone, Cork's attack has only two points on the board. In the television coverage, Marty Morrissey, sideline reporter on the day, talks about a possible change up front for Cork as 'Don Davis does a tour of Croke Park.'

Then Fay wins a great ball on his man to set in motion the move that ends with Geraghty breaking the ball down to Ollie Murphy, who slides it to the net.

It takes Joe Kavanagh's slaloming run and cracking goal 10 minutes into the second half to fire the Cork challenge. But Meath slowly turn the screw. Paddy Reynolds is hoovering up ball at wing-back, and John McDermott is untouchable around the middle.

'In the second half, we went man-to-man. It ended up that I was out near the sideline most of the game and it by-passed me.'

Davis had little impact on the game but if the ploy was to reduce Fay's influence, it worked to a point. Like Lyons on the big days, he wanted the thrill of the chase, not the soft option. 'You're disappointed when you get to an All-Ireland final and you don't have an impact,' he says.

'We were comfortable. Joe Kavanagh scored a goal but they were always playing catch-up. Graham had a fantastic second half. Scored three or four points from play.'

And yet his marker, a very young looking Seán Óg Ó hAilpín, is also playing out of his skin at full-back for Cork.

Whatever about his own critical view, Fay has an impact. Even for Cork's very last attempt at an equalising goal, he makes a key intervention, winning the tussle with Joe Kavanagh from a sideline ball, laying it off to Paddy Reynolds who off-loads to Giles, who boots the ball downfield as the final whistle blows.

That September, the GAA decided to dispense with the traditional Cup presentation on the steps of the Hogan Stand. Standing on a make-shift podium in the middle of the field is not one of the highlights of Fay's career.

'It was surreal after '99 because it was the first year that the Cup was lifted in the middle of the field ... and it was crap.

'The Cup was presented and it was just us ... the Cork players were there somewhere. And then we went around the field with it. It just didn't feel right. Especially compared to '96 when you had everyone running onto the field. It was a really strange experience with no-one allowed on to the field.

'I don't know what it was about '99. I wasn't someone who felt, "Oh I have to go out and I have to play well every day." But I have to contribute every day. Whether that was a block or a hand in or a tackle.

'I didn't enjoy the final as much because I felt I didn't contribute as much. I was delighted we won ... delighted I can always say I've two All-Ireland medals. But on a personal level, '96 felt special.'

Still, there is a special sense of history attached to Meath's seventh All-Ireland. On September 25, 1949, Brian Smyth became the county's first captain to lift the Sam Maguire Cup. Now, almost exactly 50 years later, Graham Geraghty lifts the trophy. At the subsequent victory banquet is Peter McDermott, the 1954 captain and compatriot of Paddy O'Brien.

Boylan ensured that the players always had a sense of that history and tradition.

'When we had our meals in Dalgan after training, Seán was always inviting members of the old Meath teams in so we were a bit aware of it. Just didn't really dwell on it.'

Fay's concession rate since his Championship debut in 1996 is up there with any of the game's legendary full-backs, averaging out at less than a single point a game. Truly remarkable.

To have two All-Ireland medals puts him in an elite bracket of Meath footballers, an esteemed list that included Paddy 'Hands' O'Brien and Mick Lyons.

'The significance certainly isn't lost on him. 'It's definitely important to have two. One can be beginner's luck or whatever you want to call it. To have two spaced apart is nearly better than two-in-a-row. Because it shows that you're consistent. That's all I wanted to be; consistent rather than brilliant.

'Consistency is a strength in itself.

'Anyone can go along and do something once. But to constantly do it … that's what I wanted to achieve.'

Meath's seven All Stars dovetailed sweetly with the county's seven All-Irelands. Mark O'Reilly, Darren Fay, Paddy Reynolds, John McDermott, Trevor Giles, Graham Geraghty and Ollie Murphy. A roll call of shining stars. Further confirmation that Meath had no rivals during the 1999 season.

Ireland called once more for the International Rules and the 1999 tour to Australia down under would have a distinctly Meath flavour to it, with Colm O'Rourke as manager and John McDermott captain.

After returning home with the spoils of victory, Boylan decided that Fay would be a permanent fixture as team captain for the 2000 season after having long since dispensed with the practice of the captain being foisted upon him by virtue of the county champions.

'Seán asked me, "Would I be interested in being captain?" I was delighted. Absolutely delighted. And yet it never sat well with me. You know the way some people are able to be captains and others aren't? I had to be so focused on my game I often felt it was a distraction, even though the captaincy is only as much as you let it affect you.'

Twenty three years old. Already a two-time All-Ireland winner and double All Star. With his new-found status as captain of the reigning champions, little wonder people wanted a piece of him.

Anything seemed possible. 'The most amazing game we have ever been involved in,' claimed Boylan after seeing his team hit 4-11 past Kerry in a famous League semi-final, stealing the win late on after trailing by seven points with just 20 minutes left, before losing the final to Derry after a replay in Clones.

At times, Darren Fay was a bit naïve in his dealings. As a first round Championship date with Offaly loomed on the horizon, he took up the offer of a personal sponsorship deal with Flooring Excellence in Navan.

'The sponsorship was done with Kerr Reilly, he's deceased now. He was part of Flooring Excellence. Mad into sport … a big Irish soccer fan, went to every game across the continent. A huge sports fan in general.

'Basically he said, "I'll give you a bit of money for sponsorship and you do a few openings of shops" because he had a couple of shops in Dublin and things like that." I said, "Yeah, grand."

'He wanted to pay me a cheque there and then. So I went over to the shop and took a picture and it was all grand.'

Not for a second did he think he would be viewed as a test case for one of the cornerstones of the GAA, the amateur ideal, after the *Evening Herald* made a nice splash of the story and photo.

'I remember being in the house … we were living in Avondale in Trim at the time. The phone rang just as I was actually due to go training on the Tuesday. I did this on the Friday, but it appeared in the paper on the Monday.

'So the phone rang and it was, "Darren … Seán here. I couldn't believe when I picked up the paper. What's the story with this sponsorship deal? Do you know I've Croke Park in my ear now about players not being able to be paid?"

"Croke Park are looking to suspend you for this game on Sunday. And the Meath county board were on and want half of this money … what did you get?"

'All this type of thing.

'I couldn't believe it. I went over to training and sat down with chairman,

Fintan Ginnity and Seán was there as well. I told them about it, that I was in the process of buying this house here at the time.

'I said, "Listen, I'm looking at getting a mortgage … I have to look after that type of thing. It's not as if I went looking for it … it was offered to me."

'I opened shops before and got a few quid. It's just that it wasn't publicly done. It fizzled out after that because I couldn't be seen to be doing anything.'

So Fay kept his cheque and waited for the publicity to die down. Since then, the GAA has clung resolutely to its amateur status, even as the door has opened to personal endorsements for players on a wide-ranging scale.

Fay believes it's only a matter of time before the dam breaks. 'The GAA was always aware that this sort of thing was going to happen but they were trying to block it as much as they can, as they always do. And you can understand why from their point of view.

'They're trying to block this professionalism coming in. But it's going to happen. Without a shadow of a doubt.'

Missing out on putting a National League title back-to-back with All-Ireland success was a blow, but the level of performance right through to the replayed final suggested Meath wouldn't let their grip on the Sam Maguire Cup go easily.

Fay's own personal sponsorship deal was an unnecessary distraction in the build-up. A newly remodelled jersey was another.

'The one thing I remember going into the Offaly game was that we changed our jerseys. We had this sleeveless monstrosity. A yoke that had a 'V' here with no sleeves to it.

'Meath introduced the sleeveless jersey as Trevor was cutting the sleeves off in '99. And every time he did, the Meath county board was being fined.

'The Meath county board were going mad and were on Seán's case. So it ended up they introduced the Meath jersey with no sleeves – it was a horrendous monstrosity of a yoke.'

'Seán introduced the jersey to us the night before the game, said, "This is what you're wearing." And John McDermott said, "Jesus Christ almighty lads, we're setting ourselves up for a right hiding tomorrow."

'Everyone was laughing at the jersey but he was the only serious one there.

And the mood completely changed. And he was right. He could see it.'

Sideshows apart, Meath's failed defence of their All-Ireland title hinged on a few simple truths: Offaly played with a hunger and intensity that the champions simply couldn't match.

'On the day against Offaly, they were just so much more up for it,' he admits.

That summer of 2000 was the last summer before the back door cushion of the qualifiers was introduced, meaning Meath had 12 months to lick their wounds.

The jerseys were packed away, never to be used again.

＊＊＊＊＊

On the same Sunday in June a year later, Darren Fay stood on the edge of the square and tried not to think of the consequences. To be part of the first Meath team to lose to Westmeath in a senior Championship encounter?

Well drilled and well coached by manager, Luke Dempsey, the underdogs were within touching distance of history. And then Meath did what Meath do; pulled the game out of the fire in the most dramatic of circumstances.

Twice trailing by six points, the trademark fight-back came via an Ollie Murphy special. Goal! Trevor Giles rounded off the great escape with a late free. Another comeback and last-gasp winner for Meath supporters to tell their grandkids about.

That afternoon, a young Dessie Dolan lined out at full-forward for Westmeath, a single point to show for an intriguing duel with Fay. It wasn't to be the last they'd see of each other over the course of the summer.

'The Westmeath game really stood to us that year. We were very lucky to get over them when we played them in the first round. That really gave us the kick up the arse that we needed.'

In the semi-final against Kildare, Trevor Giles once more pointed the way, his penalty and 1-5 haul setting up an old firm battle against Dublin.

Fay was back in the zone. 'That Leinster final was probably the best performance I was involved in against Dublin. We completely dominated them.'

Davy Byrne's spilled ball early on in goals saw Geraghty show his attacking instincts by punching to the net. Evan Kelly was the star man in the first half, and Richie Kealy's goal lent a routine air to the victory, despite the best efforts of Ciaran Whelan.

In three Leinster finals against the old enemy, Fay still didn't know what it felt like to lose.

'The three Leinsters I had won were all against Dublin,' he admits. 'It makes them more special because of that.'

In the first summer of the qualifiers, Westmeath set off on an unprecedented Championship odyssey, beating Wexford after extra-time, Louth, and then taking the prized scalp of Mayo.

The quarter-final draw then pitted them against Meath once more.

Fay though, had a date of a different kind on his mind. On Thursday, August 2, Darren Fay and Rhona Costello were married in the Church in the nun's convent in Trim. Jack Quinn and Mick Lyons were among the guests at the reception in the Old Darnley Lodge in Athboy, Jack no doubt recalling being best man at his brother's wedding the day before the 1970 final and everything that goes with such an occasion.

The date had a special resonance for Fay and his new bride. 'The reason why the wedding was on that date was because herself came and told me one day before Christmas, "We're getting married next August." It was her mother and father's wedding day.

'I went and enjoyed the day as much as if there was no football on Sunday. Some people say I was right; some people say I was wrong.

'It's your wedding day ... it's supposed to only happen once! You have to make the most of it. The Friday, the next day, we had the afters in a pub in Trim. Sure I ended up singing *'Wonderwall'* that night! The pub was packed.

'We trained then on the Saturday evening. I felt okay going into it. You have the fitness built up.'

Fay's nuptials hardly escaped Luke Dempsey's attention and Westmeath's plan seemed to involve Martin Flanagan taking the Meath full-back on a tour of Croke Park to test his constitution.

'I didn't feel like I was gasping early on but they dragged me out the pitch and suddenly they had three goals in the first half.'

At one stage the gap was a staggering nine points. When Dessie Dolan's looping shot dipped under the crossbar just before half-time, it looked like it was going to be one of those days. Surely Meath were a beaten docket?

Only one team in the country could have found a way back. 'We clawed it back ... and clawed it back,' says Fay.

Westmeath were like a big fish caught on a line, drawn inexorably in, no amount of flailing escaping the inevitable. Ollie Murphy copper-fastened his reputation as a goal scorer supreme with his second of the game in the final minute, somehow finding the net as he stumbled to force a replay. Incredible.

Any honeymoon would have to wait.

The replay had that same sense of inevitability about it. Despite Hank Traynor's 16th minute sending off, the frenzied pace that Meath played at made it look at times as if they had the extra man.

Fay puts it up there with one of the best team performances he was involved in.

'We watched the video of it even a couple of years after. It was probably the best hunting down by a Meath team that was ever in a game. Any time a Westmeath player got a ball, there were two players around him.'

When Fay thinks back to the drawn game in particular and yet another logic-defying comeback, in keeping with Meath's reputation as the comeback kings, he cites the influence of one man.

'There's one connection there – Seán Boylan. The one thing he instilled in the Meath team was to play to the final whistle ... the next ball that comes. I know it's a cliché and as a manager now I find myself saying it to teams but players have to realise what it is to play for the next ball, and only the next ball.

'The thing then was that even when Meath were so far behind, you felt you had the time to claw it back.'

What happened next in the All-Ireland semi-final against Kerry stunned the world of football. The scoreline says it all: Meath 2-14 Kerry 0-5. In the realm of GUBU. No Kerry player scored more than a single point.

And all the Kerry stars were there; Seamus Moynihan at full-back, Darragh Ó Sé at midfield, Dara Ó Cinnéide at full-forward. By the time Maurice

Fitzgerald came on as a substitute before half time, Kerry were taking on water, trailing 1-6 to 0-4 at the break.

'The first half was tight enough. It was nip and tuck. The balls were coming in and it was end-to-end stuff. Graham was struggling on Moynihan down the other end and he was our talisman.'

Seven unanswered points in the third quarter from Meath amounted to a wipeout. And it continued in a similar vein right 'til the end.

'We were so focused for that game. If we were honest about it, there was discontent in the Kerry camp. Wasn't Maurice Fitzgerald unhappy with Páidí Ó Sé? Because Maurice didn't start. They had come through a replay in their own quarter-final against Dublin, when he got the famous point from the sideline kick but there seemed to be problems.

'I marked him in the National League quarter-final down in Limerick in '99. I was looking forward to it because he was a top forward at the time.

'I definitely had the speed on him … but the speed didn't matter. It was amazing how he was able to move for a ball. He was just gone in his own head a second quicker than anyone else more than his legs. His reading of the game was special. Now he only scored a point in Limerick but I found it very tough.'

If marking Fitzgerald was like trying to solve a Sudoku puzzle, Fay felt he could always get his head around the type of forwards managers loved to throw at him to try and unsettle him.

'That's why I used to love marking the small, tricky fellas. Because all they had was speed. And they used to think I hadn't the speed … but I had.'

Dara Ó Cinnéide was another Kerry opponent for whom he had the greatest of respect.

'We used to play Kerry in challenge matches and even down in Thurles that time with all the goals [2000 National League semi-final], I was marking him. I could never get the better of him.

'Just so solid, so stocky … really strong on the ball. Very few people I came up against I thought, "I'm caught for strength here." It wasn't as if he was aggressive or dirty but any time he was running with the ball and you tried to tackle him, he was just all there.

'The only other person I felt like that was Colin Corkery. You think that it's going to be a handy day. But he had the strength as well, that you come off the pitch and think, "That was tough."

'Declan Browne had everything. He had the cleverness and he had the speed. He was like a Corkery and a Fitzgerald and an Alan Brogan all rolled into one. He was so difficult to mark.' In fact Fay once described him as, 'the most lethal forward I've ever come across'.

In that All-Ireland semi-final against Kerry though, no Kerry forward got a look-in, in what was one of the great Meath team performances. John McDermott nonchalantly drop-kicked a goal late in the first half to set his team on their way. Substitute Declan Quill accounted for Kerry's sole point of the entire second half.

Rather than being one of the high points of Meath football, Fay has an interesting theory about the county's subsequent fall from grace. He believes that second half was a watershed for another reason.

When the supporters started cheering every Meath pass, a part of Fay instinctively cringed. He genuinely feels the empire began to crumble at that very moment, that the values of honesty, hard work and particularly respect that Boylan lived his life by, and demanded from the players, were undercut with every light-hearted cheer to rub Kerry noses in it.

'With 10 minutes or so remaining this "Olé" started. Oh yeah … you could hear it on the pitch, sure the whole stadium nearly was doing it. It took the goodness out of it.

'For that 10 minutes, for the first time I've ever experienced, and probably the first time Meath football experienced, an arrogance became part of Meath football. An arrogance to the players from the supporters.

'It was never like that before.

'Meath always treated teams with respect.

'And the players bought into it. John Cullinane scored a goal and it was a nothing goal … I think we were 12 points up and it put us 15 points up. He was hit a little bit late and he just turned around and went like that into one of the Kerry player's faces,' says Fay, opening his arms out wide to illustrate as if to greet the crowd's acclaim. 'That summed up exactly what happened after the whole thing started.

'When the supporters did that in the last 10 minutes and the players bought into it, that's when Meath football starting showing an arrogance ... and it's never recovered from it.

'I remember we were walking out of Croke Park after the Kerry game and everyone was delighted saying, "No-one has ever done that to Kerry. Kerry did that to Roscommon and all these other teams in the 1970s ... this is an historic game."

'We were walking up ... myself, Mark O'Reilly, Trevor Giles and John McDermott. We were all delighted. Sure you'd have to be after beating Kerry by 15 points. As we were walking I remember John McDermott saying to all of us, "That is actually going to do Meath more harm than it will Kerry."

'And he didn't say us ... he said *Meath*.

'And you look at what happened. Meath haven't got within an ass's roar of winning an All-Ireland and Kerry have won what ... four?'

With Galway awaiting in the All-Ireland final, it was shades of 1966 all over again. A Meath team buoyed by one of the great semi-final displays by any team. Set up for the fall.

Thirty five years later, history was about to repeat itself.

Fay recalls the party atmosphere in the build-up, as if the Cup was already in transit.

'We used to train in Dunsany for our pitch work. Every single night, whether it was the Tuesday, the Thursday, or the Saturday, three, maybe four weeks to the All-Ireland final, the crowds of supporters were there, the media were there, everyone looking for an autograph or something.

'It used to be a once-off. A meet and greet with the players say on a Thursday night before an All-Ireland ... same for media.

'But every single session seemed to be like that. It was a carnival atmosphere. John O'Mahony most have been rubbing his hands down in Galway, no-one coming next nor near to them. He must have been absolutely delighted to see what was going on in Meath.'

Croke Park, Sunday, September 23, 2001.

It's a measure of Darren Fay that he brings the same level of critical analysis to his own game. Going into the final, he has one personal record that is creating a legend all of its own.

Twenty-five Championship matches now and counting. Still an average of roughly one point from play conceded to his direct opponents. No player ever to score more than one score from play off him. Kildare's Martin Lynch in 1998, the only player to thieve a goal off him.

As the Meath team exit the dressing room, Fay is one of the first out the door, ball in his left hand, blessing himself with his right.

Padraic Joyce walks over before the throw-in and shakes hands. This is it.

In a tense first half, with both teams struggling to find their 'A' game, nothing separates the sides. Galway are feeding the two-man inside line of Joyce and Derek Savage at every opportunity, but Fay and Mark O'Reilly are giving it back in spades.

For the first time, Fay reveals where it all went wrong, how Meath's season, and his own record, unravelled in the most dramatic fashion.

'We went in six points all. I was marking Joyce … everything was grand. He hadn't scored – now he'd missed a couple of easy frees. And he was completely off his game. He missed a free from 21 yards out nearly straight in front of the goal.

'I felt there was an uneasy feeling in the dressing room at half time. We were after kicking the s**t out of Kerry and all of a sudden we were drawing with Galway, and we can't find the switch to flick it on again. It just wasn't there. The cliché of you can't go into a game and suddenly flick a switch and away you go, that was true for us.

'It became a case then of "Did Galway want to win this game?" If they did, we weren't going to be able to stop them. That was the sense of it after half time. I remember sitting there thinking there's no way we're going to be able to kick into third gear, never mind fourth or fifth. The only way we were going to win that game was if Galway were afraid to win it. And let us win it.'

Less than a minute after the restart, Joyce gets in behind him and blazes over the bar with the goal at his mercy. Not long after that, Savage passes to Joyce who dodges one way, slips Fay, and scores. His second point from play. A defining moment.

'It was the first time ever in my playing career that someone had scored twice from play off me.'

Suddenly, the doubts swirled in Fay's mind. Right in that moment, something snapped in him.

'Talk about panic on a football pitch. I says to Mark O'Reilly, "Look, I'm being roasted here … you may have a go." That's what happened. I made the switch myself onto [Derek] Savage.

'The high standards I set for myself was my downfall that day.'

O'Reilly's low centre of gravity and reputation as one of the best man markers in the game means that he is the perfect fit for Savage. In size and physique, Fay squares off evenly with Joyce. Now Meath have two mismatches on their hands.

Everything that can go wrong is going wrong. Ollie Murphy retires with a broken wrist, Nigel Nestor is sent off for a second yellow card offence, and Trevor Giles misses a penalty. With Galway owning possession, they hit their inside line at will.

The second half turns into 'The Padraic Joyce Show'.

Joyce finishes with 10 points, five from play.

Galway run out easy winners, 0-17 to 0-8.

It's Fay's one big regret from a stellar career. The one thing that twists in his gut. If he could turn back time …

'I would love to go back to half time … stay in full-back. And for Joyce to kick 10 points off me … it would sit easier with me … instead of switching, because I thought I was getting a roasting after two. You know that kind of way? I'd love to do that. I wouldn't care about the 10 points. Just to stand beside him all the way through.

'That was the first five minutes or so of the second half where he kicked the two points. I'd say about 15 minutes later we switched back. But the damage was done. The game was gone.

'It's funny. It's amazing how the wheel goes full circle. The Galway fans were going, "Olé… Olé" … for the last 10 minutes of that game.'

For the next decade and more, Galway wouldn't win a senior Championship match at Croke Park.

Meath haven't been back in a final since.

Fay recounts his hardest day as a Meath footballer with a level of honesty that is as rare as it is admirable.

In a fresh twist on the Andy Warhol maxim, '15 minutes of madness' is how he describes his decision to switch himself off Joyce.

'I'd know Joyce well. We played International Rules together before and after. It's probably the hardest thing for me to live with. For the simple reason being that you've spent five or six seasons getting a reputation for yourself, five or six years building a standard for yourself … and then you ruin it all with 15 minutes of madness.'

'You lose the character of yourself by making a decision like that. You live and die by the decisions you make under pressure. And I made that decision under pressure. I made it when I wasn't in the right frame of mind. That was the hardest thing. If I was in the right frame of mind it would have been different.'

Claiming that he ruined his reputation though isn't true. The outstanding full-back of his generation just had a day when he was beaten by the better man.

As Mick Lyons put it once, the position of full-back is like 'always being one bullet away'. That day, he took a bullet.

Joyce played like a gunslinger with an itchy trigger finger.

Fay didn't 'ruin it all'. Six years later, he was still proving himself.

'The most honest performance I actually ever gave was, ironically enough, against Galway in 2007. In Portlaoise, in a qualifier. Joyce was actually dropped for that game. I was marking Michael Meehan. It was so hard; it was nearly like the same whole thing again. But I never once wavered from it. At the end of the game I was the one getting hands in on the ball. Even if he scored 1-5 that day – it was 1-2 from frees, and the goal was a penalty which shouldn't have been a penalty which is another story. But that was the most honest performance I ever gave. It was exactly the same situation but I handled it differently. I was so keyed up for that game.'

Plenty of times in his career, he'd switched off players when it was clear the tactic was to take him out of the game. But never when he was getting filleted. 'Not in that scenario. I played against numerous forwards who brought me out to the wing-forward position and basically stood there, with no intention of getting the ball. You'd make the switch then, for the good of the team.'

In truth, the reason for Joyce's tour de force was because of the pummelling Meath were taking all over the field. It was a rare systems failure. Compared to the semi-final, the players looked flat and heavy-legged. Fay blames it on the attitude that seeped from the stand in the semi-final.

'You could bring in other players if you want but the damage was done from what happened in the All-Ireland semi-final. You could bring in anyone you want but you'd be just changing players for the sake of players.

'Now looking back, there wasn't a hope in hell we would have won that game anyway. There was no-one firing that day. Trevor wasn't firing; Ollie Murphy wasn't firing … he broke his hand anyway. Nigel Nestor was sent off; nobody was firing. John McDermott I'd say was the only one who could have held his head up high that day.'

For a player who went through such an obsessive process in psyching himself up for big games, who literally found it hard to speak in the dressing room after – win, lose or draw – he took this defeat to heart. It shook him to his core.

'I was supposed to go into work on the Wednesday but I couldn't go in. I was just sitting at home here, thinking to myself, "This isn't happening." I shut myself out to the world.

Sitting here now and looking back you think, "It's only a game of football." But the decision I made was hard to take.'

The International Rules tour to Australia the following month would offer a sort of redemption, manager Brian McEniff and team captain Anthony Tohill going to the trouble of door-stepping him after he ducked Ireland team training. Boylan, typically, would also play a part in saving him, marking McEniff's card.

'I don't think I would ever have got over the decision I made in 2001, only Brian McEniff stood in this kitchen with Anthony Tohill,' he reveals. 'I didn't want to go anywhere because I was kind of depressed. I don't mind losing. But I hate losing when you didn't give everything you had.

'It was like, "Jesus Christ, how did I do that?" You kind of quit half way through the game. That's exactly what it was.'

'You know the way you set your own standards. Up until then, no-one had scored more than one score from play off me. When that goes, things just seemed to fall asunder. In your own head, you think that the record is gone.

'Maybe I'm being a bit hard on myself but I kind of quit when I was getting a roasting … when I should have dogged it out.'

He's being hard on himself. Touring Australia with Ireland would show that he was still the same player who could produce his best days under pressure.

He returned home after being named as Ireland's 'Player of the Series'. Determined to prove a point.

✦ ✦ ✦ ✦ ✦

Playing for Meath though was not without incident. A mundane National League encounter against Monaghan in February the following year came with a further sting in the tail, Fay fingered for his part in a melee.

Not one to throw his weight around unnecessarily, he says it all kicked off after a teammate was sucker punched.

'Richie Kealy was hit on the ground ... punched after a free was given. I ran in and rugby tackled the guy who did it to him. And a row ensued.

'But the fella who I did that to got up and started swinging boxes at me. So I started swinging back, no problem. But a Monaghan fella came from behind me and held my arms back. It was to restrain me but the other fella was still throwing boxes. I'd no way of defending myself so I drew a kick.

'It was just a reaction ... I couldn't do anything else.'

They threw the book at him.

Twelve weeks. Boylan railed against the injustice of the suspension and had a word of advice for his full-back. 'Seán says, "Go off and play soccer." Because I'd played during the winter with Trim Town. "Train with the team and keep yourself fit." A week into the soccer I got sent off in that too! I handled the ball on the goal-line to stop the ball going in! I had nothing to play then.'

He tells the story with such a sharp line in self-deprecation that it's hard not to see the funny side. But he believes that the events of the previous September's final had damaged Meath, even if the scars were barely visible to the eye.

'My edge at that time was gone. The real fine edge.

'What happened the previous year ... the whole edge had gone off Meath football. Off Seán ... off everybody. John McDermott had retired.

'Everyone saying, "If we had only turned up and treated Galway the same way as every other team, there is not a hope Galway would have won that All Ireland."'

As Offaly manager, Tommy Lyons masterminded the famous '97 Leinster final breakthrough, Fay was a hapless bystander in his civvies as Roy Malone and company ran riot. Now the Mayo native was back, putting the swagger back in Dublin football. Full of bold and colourful pronouncements, the charismatic Mayo native talked the talk. And Lyons had Meath in his sights once more, the draw ensuring a semi-final collision once Meath had brushed aside the challenge of Westmeath. On June 23 in Croke Park, his players walked the walk.

That summer, Ray Cosgrove would emerge as the capital's golden boy, the new darling of Hill 16, the goal king. Nearly everything he put his hands on that day turned to gold. Even now, Fay looks nonplussed describing his tussle.

'Ray Cosgrove touched the ball twice that day – got it in his hands twice – and got 'Man of the Match'. Basically, every time the ball went up the other end he went over and stood by the sideline and looked into the crowd. Every time I switched he went back into the middle; when I went out to meet him, he went back again.

'He got 2-3 that day but the three points were from frees and the two goals he actually punched into the net. I'll never forget it ... he actually physically only got the ball into his hands twice.'

It's one he can live with. Cosgrove finished the season as top Championship scorer with a sublime 6-23, his luck running out when his late free-kick rebounded off the upright in the All-Ireland semi-final against Armagh.

Meath had six days to pick themselves up for a derby date with Louth at Páirc Tailteann. Nobody in the county knew that this would be one of the great, great days. No qualifier before or after has matched it for drama.

It started with a helicopter ride.

Graham Geraghty, at a friend's wedding in Wexford that very day, was flown up the country. Landed down in Bellinter just in time to meet up with the rest of his teammates gathering for the short trip onwards to the Navan ground. A sight to lift Fay's mood immediately.

'I remember Graham coming in, dolled up in the suit from the wedding. Not even changing! He was doing best man and had a cravat thing going on ... dolled up to the nines! It was the first Championship match we ever played in Páirc Tailteann and it was jammed to the rafters. I'll never forget it.

'Meath players then hated playing in Páirc Tailteann whether it was League matches or whatever. Maybe it was too open and there was never enough people in it, but that day it was just a great place to play. It was hopping.'

Only once before in seven seasons of Championship football had Fay ever played a Championship match outside Croke Park - the Leinster quarter-final against Westmeath at the start of June. This felt different.

But Meath couldn't shrug off the hangover from their Leinster exit.

'It was all going wrong. Nigel Nestor played as a corner-forward coming back to play as a sweeper. It was the first time Seán would have played a sweeper to that extent. It ended up that I felt uncomfortable because even when the ball was down the other end or we had a free, Nigel was still standing in front of me. It seemed like a waste. It ended up that I might get Nigel to pick up my man if the ball was gone out to the wing; I felt in limbo then. Mark was there, Hank Traynor was there and were the same. Everyone was sharing the responsibility; nobody was taking it.

'Even though we were coping we were a little bit all over the place.'

Louth, with Ollie McDonnell and JP Rooney firing, took full advantage with goals. Richie Kealy, on as a second half substitute, banged home one for Meath but when Mark Stanfield floated over a glorious sideline ball, Louth were four ahead with full-time approaching.

What happened next is right up there with the endgame of 1991. Except this time the two scores that Meath conjured happened to be goals. The mother and father of all-comebacks.

First Richie Kealy finds the net for the second time with a venomous shot.

Then, a full three minutes and 45 seconds into injury time, Ollie Murphy cuts in along the end line and squares a ball across which Graham Geraghty plucks down. Behind by a point, knowing that it is pretty much the last kick of the game, the thought of an equaliser doesn't enter his head. Cool as you like, he slots a low shot past goalkeeper, Stuart Reynolds.

'Anyone else would have put it over the bar and taken the draw,' says Fay. 'The place went absolutely mental. I remember just going, "Whew!" ... just breathing a sigh of relief.

'With five minutes to go you're thinking, "Oh Jesus, this is gone." For it all to happen so late.

'Then Graham got the goal and came running down the pitch with his shirt off him. Took the jersey off and started swinging it around his head in front of the stand. Only Graham could do that.

'I think he hardly touched the ball before that. He was poor, and no wonder coming from the wedding. And to do that then in the last minute … that was Graham all over.

'Anyone else would have put it over the bar and been delighted with a replay or extra time. Graham probably thought, "I'm doing something else next week so I'd better stick this in the goals." That's the kind of attitude he had. And if it didn't go in he'd say, "fair enough".'

A strike of dizzying nerve and talent rounded off an epic night. A quick shower and Geraghty took off again, back for the 'afters' at the wedding.

The party didn't last too long.

After routinely dismissing Laois in the next round the following Saturday, Meath were beaten by a better Donegal side in a bruising round four meeting at Croke Park. At midfield that day was a certain Jim McGuinness.

Not that anyone knew it, but for Meath, the Louth match was like the last stand of the Roman Empire before it collapsed. The climax encapsulated Meath football; never-say-die, never over until the final whistle, and somehow fashioning an escape to victory.

The coming years would involve a slow, gradual slide, a litany of tough Championship exits.

'It just went very stale after that. Louth was probably the last great hurrah of the Meath team. From the 1986 breakthrough to that day was probably the modern era of Meath football.

'I don't think things were ever the same. I don't think Meath football was ever the same; I don't think Seán was ever the same - I don't think the Meath players ever believed in themselves the way they used to after that.

'Take Trevor Giles. Trevor is not relying on speed, just relying on his head. Someone who can split a pass 10 times out of 10 from 50 yards away into your chest. He retired in 2005.'

Fay's stock was such that he ended up having a familiar conversation with his manager in the off season.

'Seán rang me in the winter time and said, "I want to make you captain."
'I said, "That's grand", and he said, "Sure I'll talk to you about it." Listening to the radio then a few days later and it announced, "Darren Fay … captain of the Meath team." If Seán wants you to do something you do it!'

Just like 2001, Westmeath pushed them to the brink in the first round of the Leinster Championship. Another high scoring thriller. A shoulder injured forced him off early, with Dessie Dolan kicking up a storm in the corner, hitting 1-7, only spoiled by a late free in front of the posts that he somehow kicked wide.

Meath dominated the replay before Kildare edged them out by the narrowest of margins in the Leinster semi-final. A subsequent qualifier against Monaghan hinted at cracks in Meath's armour.

'We were 12 points up at half-time … cruising. And were lucky to hang on. We were in disarray. We became the team who were afraid … afraid of what was going to happen. We used to go and take every ball as it came.'

Losing to an emerging Fermanagh outfit in the next round at Clones wasn't quite the shock it seemed at the time, but it was hard to take for Fay as team captain. On the same July weekend, 12 months later, just to prove it was no fluke, Fermanagh repeated the trick in a see-saw qualifier at Brewster Park. Typically hard on himself, the one incident that circles around Fay's head is one right at the end of normal time.

By this stage, his hunger for the game was waning. He was beginning to feel a sense of entrapment, like a hamster endlessly spinning on a wheel. Only 28, he already had 10 years marked down as a senior inter-county footballer. The obsessive focus that he brought to big games took its toll and he could recognise the signs of burn-out towards the end of 2004.

For Fay, it was all or nothing. So he opted out. Took an extended break. In his stead, the young but imposing figure of Kevin Reilly filled the No.3 jersey.

'I didn't know whether I was going to come back that year. Kevin had come in … been playing well at full-back. Seán says, "Will you come back?" – this was late League – and I said, "yeah, sure". So I went back playing centre-back.'

But the summer took an all-too familiar twist. Squeezed out by Dublin in a Leinster quarter-final, a 5-12 cricket score put up against Antrim only papered over the cracks. In the next round of the qualifiers, extra time was needed to avoid the shock value of losing to Leitrim, before Cavan book-ended the Seán Boylan Years.

'That was the end of everything. The end of Seán. The end of Trevor. I retired as well.

'There was no doubt in my mind that I was gone. Gone! I had no appetite for football at all at that time. The last few years had gone so stale. Evan Kelly had gone. Mark O'Reilly … the whole lot.

'I'd no interest going training. In the years when things were going well, that we were winning All-Irelands, you couldn't wait to get to training. There was a buzz about the place.

'It just felt so stale the last few years. The enjoyment had gone out of it.'

Truly, it was the end of an era when on August 31, 2005, Seán Boylan stepped down. The man who made it all happen. Who oversaw the most successful era in the county's history. Four All-Irelands in 23 years. Eight Leinster titles. Three National Leagues. A Centenary Cup and plenty more besides. The man who rebuilt Meath football.

Fay followed suit.

'Once Seán left it was very easy for me to go. Eamonn Barry came out here to the house and asked me to play, but I said no. I'd no emotional attachment there so it was easy to say no.

'2006 was the one year I gave Trim everything I had and that was a huge thing for me as well.'

He stayed away from Croke Park as Meath beat Louth before crashing to a six-point defeat to Wexford. When Laois dumped Meath out of the qualifiers in front of their home support in Páirc Tailteann, Fay was down the town watching it all in a bar in Navan. He couldn't bring himself to go. And it didn't make comfortable viewing.

Within a matter of months, his sabbatical would be over.

'What changed then was that emotional attachment came into it again with Colm Coyle taking over the team.

'I had so much time for Colm Coyle. Now Colm Coyle wouldn't have been the best footballer that I ever played with but he'd be the first person I'd want the day of a Championship game, and that's the biggest compliment I could say about anybody.

'He was working as a sales rep for a kitchen accessory place and I used to buy off him. So he came in with a cup of coffee and a cream bun in his hand one day. I said, "Where are you going with the coffee and the feckin' cream bun?" He replied, "Oh, come in to the office. I'm looking to see if you're coming back playing."

'I stopped and thought about it for literally five seconds and said, "Yeah, okay."

"What?" he says. "I shouldn't have bothered buying myself the coffee and the bun if I'd known it would be this quick … I would have saved myself five quid. I suppose I'd better finish them now!"

'After the year off I had my appetite back. I never was as dedicated. We trained six nights a week from October through to March.

'We were given a programme and had access to a gym. It was the first time I ever came across where I was tested in terms of body fat, sprinting – you were given a chart and all this type of thing. You went up to DCU and you were sprinting at angles and getting the average of it; jumping in the same spot to see how high you could go – it was all alien. I was still old school.

'Seán had his own way and he didn't need that. But Meath were falling behind so they needed the scientific back-up. I didn't have to put myself up on the scales or check a chart to know when I was right. I knew instinctively.'

This time, he was happy in his own head going back. 'I can't do things by half … it's all or nothing. If I was going back for Colm Coyle, I was fecked if I was going to let him down.

'I'd say the gym was four times a week and then a collective session. The gym in the Knightsbrook hotel … that was our gym. There was a gym in Navan for the Navan lads; one in Dublin for the Dublin lads.

'I was 31, not 21. So I felt I had to do more to make sure I was right. Rather than just doing the four nights or whatever. So I did six or seven nights a week. When I left in 2005, I felt like I'd unfinished business. It was never going to happen but I still kinda felt I left things in a bad way. When Colm Coyle asked me to come back, I kinda said, "This is a second chance for me – and I'm going to take it."

Under Coyle, Meath had their edge back.

Coasting past Kildare in the first round of the Leinster Championship in 2007 was notable for Fay's first and only score for Meath after drifting upfield after his man: a goal into the same end where his Trim clubmate, Kevin Foley broke Dublin hearts back in 1991.

The quarter-final against Dublin needed a replay to find a winner. Cian Ward kicked five points from dead balls in a super-sub performance in the drawn game as Meath played with an intensity of old. In the repeat encounter a fortnight later, Dublin were just that bit better, edging it 0-16 to 0-12, Stephen Bray leading the charge up front for the losers.

After regrouping in the qualifiers with wins over Down and Fermanagh, the draw threw up a pairing with a fully-filled out back story. Meath versus Galway. A first Championship meeting since the 2001 All-Ireland final. In Michael Meehan, Galway had a ready-made heir to Padraic Joyce at full-forward.

And it was a cracker.

Stephen's Bray excellent brace of goals helped Meath hold sway on a day when Fay's duel with Meehan provided a fascinating sideshow.

By the end, both could be proud of their contribution to the cause. Meehan finished with 1-5, but just two points of that came from open play. Under pressure at times, Fay refused to back down from the challenge.

To him, that was the most important thing. 'It was my most honest performance. When my back was to the wall, I kept sticking at it.'

Intensely self-critical though, he was still torn up. His own view of his performance overall differed wildly from anyone else at the game. 'We won that game but I was so disgusted because, at the end of the day, I felt that Meehan had roasted me.

'I remember coming home – we'd met at the County Club – and I was in a jeep at the time. Myself and Brendan Murphy travelled together. I came down the road that fast that Brendan Murphy never thought he'd get out of it.

'He says to me a few days later, "I was never as afraid as in that jeep … I didn't know what you were going to f**kin' do." Because I absolutely tore down the road, out of pure thickness … wouldn't talk to anybody.

'There was lads ringing on the phone, my friends and his friends. They were wondering was he going out, he was asking me was I going out but I wouldn't even talk to him when he asked me a question.

"'Fayzer' are you going out?"

'I wouldn't – couldn't – even answer him. Eyes staring straight out onto the road, bombing down it.

'He was there into his phone, "Ah no, I don't think he's going out. Listen, I'd better go here."

'I was absolutely devastated.'

In his own head, the standards he set for himself 10 years earlier still applied. Already, he was psyching himself up for the next challenge against Tyrone at Croke Park.

'The friend that actually rang Brendan Murphy at the time is a good friend of the two of us. He said, "You weren't roasted ... you weren't roasted. He's a good footballer, Meehan."

'I just said, "I guarantee you. Wait and see ... I'll f**kin' do it in the next match."

'If you have the drive to do anything, *nothing* will get in your way.'

Driven. Obsessed. Focused.

Mickey Harte's Tyrone had two All-Irelands under their belt by that stage, revolutionising Gaelic football along the way. Conor Gormley, Philip Jordan, Seán Cavanagh, Brian Dooher, Owen Mulligan ... all the stars were present and correct. The following September they would make a large play for the Team of the Decade tag by adding a third. But on Saturday, August 4, 2007, Meath produced a vintage display, reminiscent of the great days under Boylan. And Fay's performance was warrior-like.

After the wilderness years and the gradual slide of the team that won two All-Irelands in 1996 and '99, the second act of his career will forever be remembered for that last stand.

The day could even be distilled down to one moment when Fay came bursting out of defence, spreading Tyrone players like skittles, sending Owen Mulligan flying before clearing downfield drawing a tremendous roar from the Croke Park crowd. 'When you feel so strong in yourself after all the weights training and everything else, you just go for it.'

Graham Geraghty too produced another memorable cameo, his improvised two-handed punch over John Devine a touch of sheer class as the ball bounced in front of the advancing goalkeeper.

When Fay walked back in to the sanctuary of the dressing room, he was physically and emotionally drained.

'I actually sat in the dressing room afterwards and Mark Ward says to me, "What's wrong with you?" I just needed an hour or so to come down. I had built myself up so much for it.

'I was building up for that game from the moment I walked off the pitch against Galway. And it was an intense build-up. Worrying about what I was going to do. Replaying it every night in my head what I was going to do … what the Tyrone game was going to be like. When you play every different scenario over in your head you just know that there's nothing going to be there … that you can't cope with.

'Absolutely spent. I took off my clothes and I was walking in to have a shower. The RTE fella comes in and says, "Darren, you got 'Man of the Match' here." I said, "Oh right." They wanted me out straight away. So I had to go back and put on my clothes again, do the interview.'

And he felt he had laid the ghost of 2001 to rest. 'I felt after that game a sense of everything being put to bed. I had proven to myself I still had it. I had come back, and no matter what happened, I was able to close a chapter. The Galway game enabled me to banish the memories of 2001 because I was able to stand up and be counted when the chips were down. I knew then it was just a moment of madness in 2001 … it wasn't who I am.

'I have to thank Colm Coyle for coming out and asking me back with a cream bun in his hand! He bought it to try and blackmail me … to entice me. He put both down on the counter to soften me up.'

Rarely was a fiver better spent.

It's that performance the captures the essence of his playing days. Meath were well beaten by a superior Cork team in the All-Ireland semi-final but there was a sense of a county's pride being restored again.

It also represented a personal landmark for Fay. 'I was only the fifth person ever to go by 50 Championship appearances for Meath. I ended up on 53. 2007, the Cork semi-final, was my fiftieth. So I was proud to pass that. That was a milestone. And it was after playing half my career with the knock-out format as well … no back door.'

And the end-of-season garlands flowed his way.

'In 2007 I ended up winning 'Footballer of the Year' in Meath which was a huge thing for me.

'Head the ball out here won 'Footballer of the Year' in 1981,' he says slagging his father Jimmy, who is outside in the kitchen entertaining the grandkids. 'He used always be slagging me, "You never won 'Footballer of the Year'!"

It was the one thing where I thought … I was never the best footballer in my club so obviously I'm not near being the best footballer in Meath. So to win that award and be on that scale was some achievement for me. I was so proud. I found it to be a massive thing.'

In Meath, there are two versions of the award, the other being the 'Supporters Footballer of the Year'.

'I won both of them that year. It was unanimous. I was disappointed enough I didn't win an All Star that year but it made no odds – I won a GPA All Star.

'Stephen Bray was fantastic that year. So to be the unanimous choice that year was huge for me.'

He should have walked away then. He wanted to walk away then. But a sense of loyalty to Coyle, to Meath, to the supporters kept him there – against his better judgement.

After 2007, he couldn't give any more.

'I switched off after 2007. That was it for me. Coming up to Christmas 2007, I was only doing two, three nights with the weights. And I was disgusted with that. Coming back, then going again after a year, I thought people wouldn't give you that respect. You have to have a bit of longevity.

'My head was *completely* retired … *completely* retired. But I felt that I was letting people down – Coyler to an extent, but mainly the supporters – if I didn't come back after having a good year.

'I went back then and I'll never forget it. We played at the opening of a pitch in Meath Hill. I was out there in the back garden and it was summer's evening before the Championship started. I was playing football with the kids and the game was at seven o'clock – it was about quarter to six. I was loving playing football with them. They were just at that age where they were able. I swore to myself I'd never, ever have to leave the kids again to go football training. It was the one time I hated going out the door. I had turned off completely.'

All the progress under Coyle was undone in a mad-cap second half in the Leinster quarter-final against Wexford, somehow conspiring to cough up a 10-point lead. It was like a thread had been pulled and pulled, and suddenly the whole fabric of Meath's season came apart at the seams. When Matty Forde kicked the winning point, there was a sense of shellshock.

'We were 10 points up against Wexford and lost – that shows you how fragile Meath football was.'

The radio dispatches from the Gaelic Grounds where Limerick hosted Meath in the subsequent first round qualifier had the hoax-like feel of a War of the Worlds broadcast. The scoreline with 15 minutes to go: Limerick 4-11 Meath 0-3. A difference of 20 points.

To Meath supporters listening at home, the shock value could hardly have been more if HG Wells himself had declared an alien invasion.

Ian Ryan lined out at full-forward for Limerick that day and finished with 3-7 in brackets beside his name. As a unit, the defence was torn asunder. Fay laughs gently as he tries to explain that it wasn't quite as bad as it looked on paper, particularly the damage done by his own man.

'We got two frees in our full-back line and they were kicked straight to him as I went out looking for the ball. That was 1-1. Now he scored another four or five from frees so it wasn't as bad as it looked. When I look back on my career, that game never flickers in my imagination. I was gone ... just waiting for it to finish. When you're turned off like that, whatever happens in that time doesn't affect you.

'Now the 2001 final does hurt me. It's always in my mind. I'm glad I banished a few of them memories by going to Australia with Ireland but the Limerick game never enters my head. Never.'

When Brian Farrell and Joe Sheridan rattled in a brace of goals each it at least reduced the embarrassment on the scoreboard to nine points.

But one of Boylan's old lieutenants, Colm Coyle knew something had been lost. Listening to the talk switch to the Blue Jeans Festival in Athboy crystalised the decision in his mind: it was time to step down as manager.

Fay and Geraghty would follow.

It is the way of inter-county football that careers generally don't end well. Only the rare, lucky few get out at the top. Because the view from the steps of the Hogan Stand in September is invariably too enchanting to leave behind.

Fay, like Paddy 'Hands' O'Brien, Jack Quinn and Mick Lyons, never had the comfort of walking away with applause ringing in his ears. It was just one thing more he shared with the county's celebrated full-backs.

In the 1955 Leinster final, Paddy O'Brien left the field, chastened by the experience of trying to keep tabs on Kevin Heffernan and a rampant Dublin.

In the 1976 Leinster final, the Meath selectors toyed with the idea of sending a crocked Jack Quinn in to try and rescue the game against the old enemy, but decided against it, leaving him to watch his last Championship match from the dug-out.

In 1992, Mick Lyons went for a pint with his old buddy Colm O'Rourke and confided his intention to retire the same evening Meath crashed out, defeat by Laois in the first round a bridge too far.

So Fay's off-Broadway ending followed a familiar theme.

Even the game's greats don't get to pick and choose their exits. But their legacies would remain unspoiled.

It's that refusal to walk away, that loyalty to the cause, that stubbornness, and intensely competitive spirit that helped each of them burn such a trail.

Four men who spanned the 50-year golden era of Meath's seven All-Irelands. Their reputation already cast in stone.

CHAPTER 7

FOR CLUB

In March 2012, a roll call of Skryne stars past and present took a nostalgic tour of Croke Park as part of the club's 125 anniversary celebrations and to mark the launch of Dave Carthy's lovingly crafted two-volume history of the club.

Brian Smyth and Micheál O'Brien from the famous '49ers' were there, with the author himself a part of the 1967 odyssey, while modern heroes such as John McDermott and Trevor Giles joined them.

Needless to say, Paddy O'Brien was there too, his early career fitting snugly into that proud history. His club career came in two acts. Skryne made him, before he put down roots and made history with Sean McDermotts in Dublin.

From being selected to represent Meath for the first time as a kid in school to togging out at senior level for the first time in 1942, when still just 16, he was always going places in a hurry.

In 1944, when Skryne won out after an epic three-match series in the county final against Navan Parnells, O'Brien belied his tender years, scoring a goal and a point in the decisive match. The following year the club put titles back-to-back with the same player now starring at midfield.

He could hurl too, lining out for Oberstown in the 1945 final only for Kilmessan to take the honours.

And then life took him further afield.

Skryne has a remarkable connection with the Meath senior football team. All seven All-Ireland winning teams, starting with Brian Smyth, the man who first lifted the Sam Maguire Cup in 1949, contained representatives from the club.

It was to Skryne he returned to finish out his club career and the parish maintains a special place in his heart, though he wears a wry smile as he tells the story of how his two county Championship medals disappeared from his possession.

'I was up here in Dublin one day and I had the medals on my person. Didn't I run out of cash and I hadn't my bus fare home. I went into a broker's shop and pawned the two medals. I forget what I got for them. When I went back to reclaim them they were missing, they hadn't got them.

'I told the lads in Skryne – I'm still involved with the club, they invite me to their functions every year – so I made an appeal at one of the functions a couple of years back that I'd love to get my hands on the medals. Didn't they send me these two.'

And he holds up two finely crafted replicas he is proud to display.

After his working life brought him to Dublin, he recalls his time with Sean McDermotts fondly. It's clear his second club has a special place in his heart too, the photograph of the 1947 Dublin county title winning team hanging proudly on the wall in his sitting room amidst all the decorations signifying a glittering Meath career.

His own Meath teammate, Christo Hand was right half-back and he lightens at the memory of the friends and characters on that team; Dick Bradley and Noel Crowley of Clare, Louth's Eddie Boyle, Joe O'Connor of Offaly, not to mention Tom Langan of Mayo.

To think that both himself and Langan would mark each other in the 1951 All-Ireland final.

Or make the 'Team of the Century' selection, at different ends of the field.

In an era when St Vincent's dominated the football landscape in Dublin, the 1947 title had a significance all of its own. 'I have known very few prouder moments,' he admits. Even if the post-match party took an unexpected twist.

'Our lads used to converse in the Scotch House on the quays, beside the

Liffey bridge. That's where they'd discuss their football on a Monday evening after a match. From Croke Park, I rang the Scotch House and told them that we'd be bringing down the Cup – would there be somebody there to look after us and fill it. It was owned by a Meath man at the time, from down Dunderry direction ... but they were all missing when we went down. We were disgusted.

'The chairman of the club was a fella called Martin Molloy, he was an Offaly man and he had a pub out in Tallaght. Now Tallaght was way out of town ... way out in the country back then. I rang Martin. "I'll tell you what you do, Paddy," he says. "Go on down and hire all the taxis that you can see. And bring them all out to Tallaght." And I did that. We had a whale of a time that night.'

Remember, this is the club who valued him so highly they sent a delegation to the airport to inveigle him to play a match as he walked through arrivals at Dublin airport with Kay, fresh from his honeymoon in France. Of course, he took a detour home via Jones' Road.

1947 too proved to be the high watermark of Sean McDermotts club history.

That title still stands alone.

+ + + + +

Join the dots of Kilbride's meteoric rise from junior ranks to the kingpins of senior football and the influence of the Quinn brothers is impossible to understate.

In fact, the arc of the club's golden era just happens to mirror the arc of Jack's flourishing county career.

Only officially formed in 1948, the record books show the swift ascent. Junior champions 1960. Intermediate champions 1962. Senior champions 1964, '67, '69, '70 and '71.

And all the while the Quinns at the heart of the success story. Martin, an iron-willed figure at full-back. Jimmy, the wing-back who boasted a terrific record on the best attackers that any other club could throw at him. Jack, majestic at midfield where he could show the full range of his talents. Gerry, the natural finisher up front.

A family affair. Especially when it came to the seven-a-side tournaments that had such cachet at the time.

When Meath made the breakthrough in 1964, beating Dublin on their way to a first Leinster title in a full decade, Martin, Jack and Gerry were central to the success, lining out on that emotionally charged weekend as their father lay ill and dying, determined to honour their county and the man who instilled their love of the game and who would live just long enough to see the cup brought to his bedside.

For the three brothers to be part of Meath's re-emergence as a power was a proud boast for the club, but to Jack it just felt normal. 'It just seemed to come naturally that you were on the team because you'd be playing with Kilbride and there'd be four of us on the seven-a-side teams and four of us on the Kilbride team that won the junior Championship, so it was a natural progression.'

When their father passed away, the club helped give them a sense of normality, a sense of place, especially after the All-Ireland semi-final defeat by Galway, overshadowed by Jack's controversially disallowed goal.

'We won a senior Championship for the first time,' explains Gerry. 'For a little club like Kilbride, it was unheard of.'

'It was always tinged with the sorrow that he was gone for the two biggest occasions, the Leinster final and winning the senior Championship, that he wasn't around to see either.'

'Jimmy was good enough to be on the county team, just wasn't that interested in county football,' says Jack of his brother. 'He was a smashing wing-back. I've never seen a half-forward in Meath get the better of him.'

For other forwards, taking a ball through the heart of the Kilbride defence was at times the equivalent of running with the bulls at Pamplona; an adrenaline ride that had an outside chance of ending badly.

Apart from Jack, Gerry and Martin, the six strong Kilbride contingent on the Meath squad that captured the Sam Maguire Cup in 1967 also included Pat Rooney, Pat Bruton and Murty O'Sullivan, all captured together in a lovely photo taken on the eve of the All-Ireland final and reproduced in *The Irish Times*.

With such a county contingent, a second senior Championship title followed. 'We won the senior Championship that year and that was the year to win it,' says Gerry. 'If you were the champion club in the champion county...'

Of the ones that got away – the final defeats of 1965 and '66 sandwiched between those historic senior titles - the latter has its own place in Meath county Championship history, requiring three games to find a winner.

Gerry has his own reason to remember that series of games distinctly.

'I played in the first one ... watched one from hospital. I got a bad knee injury. Three months not only out of football but not being able to walk properly.' Even lying in a hospital bed in Navan, a stone's throw from Meath's county ground, he set up a system of communication which enabled him to keep track of the score.

And the series of runners who kept him in touch with constant updates?

'Nurses!' he laughs. 'I was in the orthopaedic in Navan. The match was on in Páirc Tailteann. It was a bit like listening to the old All-Ireland finals on radio with the running commentary I was getting.

'Kilbride were playing well and Kells kept getting goals. The first one was a draw ... that one was a draw, Kells won the third one. I've a nice record; I never played in a losing final!

'I went back on the Meath panel and Meath kept winning. A few trials were held coming up to Leinster final time and I managed to hold my place on the panel. I never got back on the team though after that injury.'

In 1970, after winning their fourth senior title, the half-way point of a glorious three-in-a-row, Kilbride became the first club to represent Meath in Leinster club competition.

Not content with that distinction, Kilbride decided to spread its wings. America called! And so Kilbride became the first club team from Meath to tour the United States.

Jack played for Monaghan over there, won two Championships. Won 'Footballer of the Year' twice in America.

'Tells a great story about the last year they beat Kerry. About John Kerry O'Donnell, the man who owned Gaelic Park, and Alan Clancy who lived down the road here. They began to bring Jack out constantly.

'The side bet between Alan Clancy and John Kerry O'Donnell was a top of the range Merc. A personal bet between the two lads who were multi-millionaires. That's how they paid for these things … the lads in the pubs put money into the pool to bring players from Ireland. So the more money they put into bringing players, the more certain they'd be that their team would win. So they'd back their team.

'I was selected to go the year I got married: 1970. Building a house. Martin had six tickets … he picked the players who were going. And he came to me.

'I was paying for my house and I'd a good contract for bailing hay and straw that year. So I couldn't go, because I'd lose too much money from being away for the week. As it turned out, the match over there was a draw. They were kept over there for a week. Paid as electricians while they were away to work on the famous Twin Towers. Came back with loads of money, and the rule was that if you didn't play in that round, you couldn't play in the following round … you could only bring those players back again.

'Meanwhile, in Ireland, it rained for the week!' He cracks up laughing as he delivers the punchline: 'No bailing!'

And so he missed out on the trip, the craic, and all the financial trimmings to boot.

But Gerry would get his chance to go Stateside again. In 1973, the Kilbride team set off themselves, their tour starting in New York. 'At that time, that was some city. What a place to be … Century Paramount Hotel …. Forty Second Street …. right off Times Square. Twenty-three Kilbride fellas there for a week!

'Played in Gaelic Park, Philadelphia. Finished up in Washington.'

It was like a like a valedictory tour to mark the end of the club's proudest era. The club dropped to intermediate ranks in 1979, and to junior grade in 1984, and is still trying to climb back up the ranks once more.

Back in the 1960s, seven-a-side football was hugely popular. As a club on the Dublin border, one tournament in particular in nearby St Margaret's became famous. And this when Kilbride was only establishing itself.

'The local rivalry then was unbelievable,' explains Gerry. St Margaret's were desperate to win it and had a packed team. So we met them in the final.

'Here we were, then a junior team, going to play a senior team. It was a very tough match. Oh my God! The referee who had refereed most of the other matches wouldn't referee the final. So Father Shine had to ref it … the parish priest.

'At half time even he was losing control. So he decided to take steps … rang the gardai in Finglas. And they came down and helped keep the line, and keep the peace. Father Shine was a man who didn't take no for the answer.

'Kilbride won well in the finish and the presentation was that night in St Margaret's. But we were advised not to come back.' Have a guess which one of the Quinns decided to ignore that advice.

'Martin went back. With Jack Sweeney and a few other fellas … they were going back to collect the Cup! And no-one hassled them.'

There is one other incident involving Martin that has developed a folklore all of its own. The 1965 county final between Kilbride and Skryne. The abandoned match. Martin's 12-month suspension that caused ructions and had a ripple effect on the county team, and Meath's failed All-Ireland bid of the following September.

For the first time, Martin, Gerry and Jack give the full story of what actually happened. The telling of it leaves each of them in a state of animation that shows exactly how the incident and its aftermath will never be forgotten.

With 12 minutes to go, 14-man Kilbride were clinging to a 1-4 to 1-3 lead against Skryne. Jack takes up the story.

'Martin caught a high ball in the square. A chap came in and challenged him. Now Martin did a lovely thing – he let your man by him like a bull charging at you.

'He actually hopped the ball like that … your man went charging by. And then he caught the ball and cleared it. And the referee gave a free in.

'So Martin grabbed the ball and said, "What's the f**kin free for?"

'"You did this, that and the other," the referee said.

'"I did nothing wrong," said Martin. 'Which he hadn't. So he sat down on the ball.'

It was an instinctive act of defiance that would become known countrywide.

'The reaction of the latter was to sit down on the pitch in boxing fashion by waving his arms to indicate that it was all over,' reported the *Drogheda*

Independent. In his words with the referee though just before that, he brushed against the official Seamus Duff, who tried to order him off on that basis.

It says everything about Martin's fearsome reputation that no Skryne player made a serious attempt to shift him. So the referee abandoned the match.

Martin's recall of the incident is unequivocal. 'Sean Smith and Mickey Lynch and myself went for that ball. They were two big men on the Skryne team. And I won the ball and came out. I went about five, 10 yards on a solo run and was clearing the ball when I heard the whistle blow.

'My first reaction was, "What the hell is he giving a free out for?" And I turned around and suddenly it was, "You're off!"

'"OFF?"

'FOR WHAT? It has to be for catching the ball because that's all that happened.'

Martin becomes very animated discussing it, all too obvious that it still strikes a chord to this day.

'So the referee blew. "You've two minutes to get off the field," he says.

'"If you're here in two hours I'll be still standing here," I says.'

And promptly sat down near his own goalmouth.

'I remember at the county board meeting, the '49 captain Brian Smyth speaking,' says Gerry. 'He stood up and said, "If Martin Quinn made that catch and clearance in Croke Park for Meath he'd be a hero."

'He wanted to know why he was sent off and he brushed against the referee. They said he shouldered him. He wasn't going off because he didn't deserve to go off. I suppose Kilbride were getting a tough reputation and it was a very tough match.

'It was unbelievable. The match was abandoned then. I never had any hard feelings about Skryne, their players or any officials. But I thought Martin's treatment was outrageous.

'To get 12 months? That was 1966. They let guys out of Mountjoy because of the 50th anniversary of 1916 – and Martin couldn't get back to play football for a year.'

Believe it or not, the drama of the day was far from over. While all of this went on, the Cup stood out on the display on the sideline.

'Paddy Cromwell was the Meath goalie at the time and Paddy's brother

Colm was coaching the team,' says Gerry. 'Colm would know the rules of football so he shouted to Paddy, "Get the Cup … it's ours. We won it."

'That caused a sprint for the cup! A couple from each side.'

Jack explodes the chief myth about that day, that it was Martin who got there first and took it away into the dressing room, the Kilbride team closeting themselves then as consternation reigned.

'It was around all over the place that Martin Quinn grabbed the Cup and ran into the dressing room with it,' says Jack. 'Which is not true … not true.

'What did happen was, when we were coming by, there was a lad called Val White playing corner-back for us. A real quiet chap. … good footballer. He grabbed the Cup. And he gave the table it was on a good kick, and busted it into bits. And brought the Cup into the dressing room. But it couldn't be him in the famous story, because he wasn't a well-known footballer. So it had to be Martin Quinn.'

And that's the legend that has lived on to this day.

'There was nobody going to come in for the Cup. When [Meath county secretary] Liam Creavin who everybody had great respect for … when Liam came in and things cooled down and the supporters outside went away, then it was decided to give them back the Cup, that we'd get it again in the replay anyway.'

But there was to be no replay, Skryne settling for being crowned winners subsequently by a boardroom committee.

'We've a great old bond with Skryne now,' says Jack. 'There's no problems. We just had our day of destiny.'

As for his reputation as one of the hard men of Gaelic football, did Martin deserve it?

'When you get that reputation, everyone has to have a go at you. What do you do? You can't stand there, take it and not give it back?'

And for those who would have accused him of taking the law into his own hands at times, it doesn't bother him. 'Not in the slightest. I'd lads telling me they'd never see me leave here alive.

'Well I always managed to get out alive anyway!'

+ + + + +

For Mick Lyons, football begins and ends with Summerhill. With Meath at such a low ebb when he broke onto the county team, he wore his club crest as his badge of honour.

'Playing for Summerhill was as good as anything back then,' he says.

If the 1960s belonged to Kilbride, the '70s were Summerhill's to cherish. And the curve mirrored the former's. Intermediate champions in 1972. Then senior champions for four years in a row, 1974-77, an incredible run of success.

In fact 1977 stands apart. A teenage Lyons – named the club's 'Young Player of the Year' three years before – was now involved as Summerhill became the first Meath club to be crowned Leinster champions. To do it against a famed St Vincent's outfit, bristling with Dublin All-Ireland winners, elevated it to another level in a famously tough game. 'There was a bit of a melee,' admits Lyons in typically understated fashion. 'A bit of trouble.'

Against a team that included Brian Mullins, Jimmy Keaveney, Fran Ryder, Bobby Doyle, Tony Hanahoe and Gay O'Driscoll, the Meath champions hit a staggering five goals, including a hat-trick in a two minute spell during the first-half. A 5-4 to 0-6 victory remains a landmark in the club's history, captain Padraig Gray lifting the trophy.

'All the Dublin lads were on that team. It was a huge thing for Summerhill to win that. Massive.

'Played St John's then up in Belfast. That didn't go down too well because at that time the Troubles were making headlines. I think I was midfield that day.' Summerhill were beaten, but Lyons has happy memories of playing football around different counties, just like the Quinns.

'You'd be going around playing tournaments in all different places … which is great for clubs to go play a different type of football in different counties. You'd be going to Kildare, play in the Na Fianna tournament up in Dublin, play in Monaghan, Cavan … Offaly.

'The county Championship then was fierce. Fierce competitive.'

Paraic Lyons has his own memories of those great days. 'Summerhill through the 1970s were in six finals on the trot. Won the first four, should have won the fifth – had a perfectly legitimate goal disallowed that Austin Lyons scored. He was done for being in the square and a picture came up in

The Meath Chronicle the following week showing him a yard outside it flicking the ball on. That would have been their fifth title.

'I would have been young in the mid-70s and I'll always remember the bonfires. They'd all be celebrating and all that would be in your head was, "Will the schools be closed tomorrow?" There was great hoo-ha in the village the night they won.'

Three years younger than Mick, he had to wait until 1986 to captain Summerhill to their next success after the run of titles in the 1970s, his younger brother Terry a central figure at full-back as well as Mick, Terry too representing Meath during his time.

With Paddy Lyons a selector, the family influence was writ large.

When Paraic picked up a leg injury later in his career in 1991, he discovered a new calling as club goalkeeper. 'I actually got a great buzz out of it. Mattie Kerrigan was involved again around then. I said to him, "I won't make too many promises but I'll say this: I'll catch anything that will come my way and I'll kick it out a long way. We'll see how the rest of it goes."'

Ten years later, he signed off in style. 'It was 2001 I finished. A relegation match versus Navan O'Mahonys over in Dunsany.

'I wasn't playing well leading up to that match. All that was going through my head in the build-up; "You don't want to be the reason Summerhill go down to intermediate." I was afraid of my life of making the mistake that would send Summerhill down. That bothered me.'

But Paraic kept his end of the bargain up as his team stayed up. With that, he took his leave.

'I left my football bag in the dressing room. Left the whole lot behind me. I'd bought a new pair of gloves for that and I gave them to the sub keeper. I left bag, boots, togs everything in the dressing room ... walked off.

'I actually played my first senior game in goals in 1979. Just by chance. I wasn't a regular by any stretch of the imagination ... the senior team were short. And they put me in goals for a senior Championship match. I finished up in 2001.

'When I'd be having a few pints with the lads I'd be telling them I played in four decades!'

Since then, both Mick and himself have been at the coalface coaching and managing various teams with the club, from senior right down through the under-age ranks.

Still giving it back.

✦ ✦ ✦ ✦ ✦

Peter Darby lifting the Sam Maguire Cup as Meath captain in 1967. Darren Fay's uncle Mickey kicking 10 points in the 1970 All-Ireland final against Kerry, his father Jimmy part of the squad that day too as Jack Quinn led them into action.

Two-time All-Ireland winner, Kevin Foley firing home one of the greatest goals Croke Park has ever seen to put an unforgettable final twist to the four-match saga against Dublin in 1991.

And then Darren Fay coming along to blaze his own trail.

Trim's contribution to the history of Meath football is a proud one, but at club level it has been a case of so near yet so far.

Darren has two county senior medals alright – in hurling. Trim's history of success centres largely around the small ball code. Eight senior hurling Championships were annexed between 1949 and 1960, for example, but the 1962 county football title stands alone.

'Underage ... I was always a hurler. Trim were very strong and you're winning every second year. We won the county final in '98.

'When I came onto the Meath set-up I kinda put hurling aside. Really only played when Meath were knocked out of the Championship early. I won in '98 and 2000. I have two Championship medals without playing a whole lot.'

On the football field, the Holy Grail of a county senior medal eluded him.

'I played my first senior game with Trim in 1992. I was 16 ... Liam Hayes was playing for Skryne and it was just a huge thing for me. Traditionally, Trim were a hurling club. Never really had much football success. But we then had a great underage crew coming through around '97.

'We reached the county final ... played O'Mahonys who hadn't a great team around that stage, but they knew how to win county finals.

'We just froze on the day.'

And too many big days followed a similar pattern. Five semi-finals went west. And another county final in 2002, this time against Dunshaughlin.

'I was usually midfield or centre-back – never full-back with Trim,' he explains. 'The Trim team that came along in 2002 to 2005 was probably the best team in the county at the time.

'We just couldn't get over the line. Just didn't know how to win the important games.

'We had what I consider the best team out there at the time. We just hadn't the winning mentality.

'We just hadn't the tradition.'

The club is still trying its best to change that.

CHAPTER 8

FOR COUNTRY

Apart from sharing the Meath No.3 jersey over the course of Meath's seven All-Irelands, Paddy 'Hands' O'Brien, Jack Quinn, Mick Lyons and Darren Fay have another thing in common: they all represented Ireland with distinction. In Jack Quinn's case it was in an ambassadorial role for his country along with the rest of his Meath teammates in a pioneering round the world trip, travelling Down Under to take on the pick of the Australian Rules Football in a five-match tour.

Before the Compromise or International Rules was ever conceived, the Tailteann Games of 1924, 1928 and 1932 brought together the greatest players of the time to take on the cream of America or, in one case, England.

In Paddy O'Brien's time, the equivalent of a modern All Star selection was picked for Ireland to play against the Combined Universities. When Meath made the big breakthrough in 1949, the 'Old Firm' full-back line of Micheál O'Brien, Paddy O'Brien and Kevin McConnell provided a key part of the jigsaw, a famed partnership that lasted more than six seasons.

All three, though never all together, donned the Irish jersey.

In February 1950, the first of the Ireland versus Combined Universities games was played, with a strong Meath element. All-Ireland winning captain, Brian Smyth took on the same leadership role with the team, with O'Brien full-back and Kevin Smyth selected as goalkeeper. A fellow Meath man, Dr

John O'Brien happened to be captain of the students fifteen.

After no less than eight Meath men featured on the Leinster Railway Cup team earlier in the year, this was another show of strength.

To pull on an Ireland jersey carried a distinction all of its own, recalls O'Brien. 'We honoured every jersey we pulled on, but of course it was special. The game featured some stirring duels between my old midfield partner, Victor Sherlock, who was left half-forward for Ireland, and another Cavan star, the dashing PJ Duke, at right half-back for the Universities.'

Ireland won 1-12 to 2-3 at Croke Park.

By the time Meath and Jack Quinn climbed the steps of the Hogan Stand in 1967, a tour of Australia to play the pick of the AFL was being mooted, the brainchild of Australian promoter Harry Beitzel.

But fortune ruled against O'Brien taking a seat on the plane in the capacity of supporter. 'I was very busy at the time. I had opened the first self-service supermarket on the north side of Dublin. It was going very well at the time, I was deeply involved in it, so it was hard to get away.

'I could have gone. I changed my mind but it was too late. There were no seats left on the plane.'

Little did he know, those who flew out were in for the trip of a lifetime.

Meath were about to play the lead part as Gaelic football went truly global.

+++++

On Saturday, March 2, 1968, a Meath team carrying the tag of 'Champions of Ireland' gathered at Dublin Airport to begin the first leg of a pioneering 30,000 mile round-the-world trip with a five-match series against various Australian selections at the heart of it.

As All-Ireland winners in 1967, the county squad had the honour of travelling out. The Quinn brothers, Jack, Martin and Gerry were among a six-strong Kilbride contingent that set out on a trip that would last three weeks, span four different continents and create a legend all of its own.

'There's a great photograph of the team boarding the Aer Lingus flight to Rome,' explains Gerry, 'and the six first onto the plane were the six Kilbride lads! Just in case it took off without us!'

It all started with a phone call to the 'Man in the Cap' Peter McDermott, who had played a key role in managing Meath to the summit in 1967.

Harry Beitzel, the Melbourne promoter, was the driving force behind a world tour for a selection of star Australian Rules footballers from the State of Victoria and it was intended to round off the tour with a unique exhibition match in Croke Park.

Meath, as reigning champions, were to be the opposition. Never mind that the party was still in full flow – the carrot of a return trip Down Under was dangled to sweeten the deal.

'When we won the All-Ireland in '67, they came over here on a trip while we were still celebrating the All-Ireland,' recalls Jack Quinn. 'They played the Civil Service in Dublin in an exhibition match to get the hang of it. We weren't at it but Peter McDermott went up to watch. Civil Service nearly beat them. Sure they were taking it easy … weren't bothering themselves.

'We played them in Croke Park. Before the match we were all yapping and talking. I remember we were in shocking bad shape after all the drinking and celebrating. A lot of us were going out and I'd say there were a fair few hangovers.

'Peter McDermott actually said it to us in the dressing room beforehand. "I want you to do one thing lads; don't beat these by too much. Take it easy. Don't go hard on them because there is a great chance of a trip to Australia. We want to make this a bit of game."

'Sure we were f**kin' 10 or 15 points behind before the game had barely started!' says Quinn laughing hard. 'They kicked the lard clean out of us. Sure we thought, "That's Australia gone now!"'

Not quite. 'A humiliating hour,' is how McDermott described it himself. But Beitzel had announced over the PA before the throw-in that he was inviting Meath to Australia. And so the offer would still stand.

The tour schedule for March 1968 would not just take in Australia, but Rome, Singapore, Hawaii, and America – and involve a massive fund-raising process, McDermott driving it all.

In the spring of 1968, a round-the-world trip carried the whiff of adventure and exoticism. To some of the locals in Kilbride, it was all too much to handle.

'I remember local people coming to the house before we flew out and they were crying,' says Jack. 'It was like going to the moon!

'Some people we didn't even know were coming to shake hands ... crying, thinking they might never see you again. And my mother was looking at them wondering, "What are they crying for? Sure they'll be back in a matter of weeks."'

It didn't end with the crying.

Some neighbours up the road caused a further stir. 'There were protestant people just down the road,' recalls Gerry. 'They didn't know anything about GAA ... had no interest in GAA, and they arrived with a mass card to my mother! Imagine getting a mass card and you going to Australia!'

At a farewell function in the Beechmount Ballroom in Navan, after 'Red' Collier sang his now famous party piece *'Wild Rover'*, another one of the players, Mick Mellett announced that he had written his own song that would become the tour's anthem as they criss-crossed the world.

WE WILL NOT LET YOU DOWN
To the air of *'Come Back to Erin'* from an LP by Larry Cunningham.

They sing of famous happenings that happen every year,
And this is about a football team who've proved themselves so dear
To every football follower far away and near at hand,
Now pioneering GAA in far-off Aussie land.

We beat the men from County Louth and the boys from County Cork,
Westmeath, Offaly and Mayo, then the 'Yankees' from New York,
Then there came Australia and they made us bit the dust,
Now we go out to play them there and beat them there we must.

We owe it to our supporters, to our trainer and our coach,
And when we beat Australia we'll surely drink a toast,
We want to prove the experts wrong, they don't give us a chance,

And a win for Meath would be for them a great kick in the pants.

So we are the men from Royal Meath, we're a very lucky band,
Now going to represent our games in far-off Aussie land,
And to all you faithful followers gathered here in Navan town
This we promise you tonight
WE-WILL-NOT-LET-YOU-DOWN

And so they met at Dublin Airport on the first Saturday in March, the Kilbride lads jockeying for prime position on the steps of the plane.

'Our first flight was to Rome,' recalls Jack. 'We stayed a night there. We went down to the Cathedral and were there for the Pope's blessing on the Basilica. We didn't meet the Pope but were out there as part of his Papal audience.'

From an audience with the Pope to an audience with Marlene Dietrich.

En route from Rome to Singapore, the Hollywood film actress and singer was spotted. Travelling first-class, she was at a remove. But at the various pit-stops along the way, she had the admiring eyes of a selection of star-struck Meath players.

By this stage, McDermott had already taken to chronicling the whole adventure, his superbly detailed diary later published in book form, 'Gaels in the Sun'.

He recalls tailing her around Bangkok looking for a memento only for her to wave off all entreaties for a photograph or autograph.

'Please don't bother me' she insisted.

Jack Quinn tells of how she eventually warmed to the more boisterous crew of players who were making their own on-flight entertainment. 'She was on the plane alright ... someone did recognise her. The thing about her was, she was sitting up at the front. I remember a few fellas were looking for autographs. Of course she didn't really want the autograph craic.

'So we had a few beers with us on the plane going, and a sing-song got going. Up she gets then from her first grade seat and sat down with us. Sang songs with us the whole way over.

'When we were getting off the plane she went round every single one of us and shook hands … said it was the best trip she was ever on, that she'd never forget it!

'She was at the end of her film career I'd say at that stage but she was a serious actress and a fabulous looking woman. Ah, it was great craic.'

Just picture it? Hollywood royalty and Pat 'Red' Collier banging out the tunes. Jack Quinn doesn't remember if they sang, *'We will not let you down'*, the theme tune adopted for the historic trip or if she knew much about the intricacies of full-back play, only that they had a ball.

From the stop-off in Bangkok then to Singapore, where team manager, Father Tully stood up to warn the players of the perils of the city, particularly its nightlife. Certainly well-intended, Gerry explains how his words had the reverse effect on the players.

'He addressed the players and warned them; "All of ye have been to London last year and most of ye have been to New York already … but this is the most corrupt city in the world."

'Fellas who were half asleep after 20 hours flying suddenly perked up; "We gotta see this!"'

Jack describes the culture shock of the lurid nightlife for a bunch of wide-eyed Meath lads.

'We went to Singapore and stayed for a night. There was great craic in it … if you keep the young ones away from you. There were pimps coming at you from everywhere. All you could hear was, "You like to meet Singapore nice girl?" They were mad for sex.'

Against the backdrop of the Vietnam War, there was a different kind of edge to the city as well. 'In Singapore, it was there you really noticed the army. When you had the army there you'd always be afraid that something might happen.'

It opened the players' eyes to another side of life they hadn't seen as well. 'You went from a five star hotel to out on the street through the city where the abject poverty was just incredible,' adds Gerry. 'It was certainly an education.'

Back at the hotel, where the players sought out the swimming pool to dodge the oppressive heat, a serious incident threatened to bring the trip to a shocking end.

As Kevin McConnell found himself in trouble in the pool, Paddy

Cromwell and Jimmy Walsh were suddenly spotted on the floor of the pool after getting into difficulty unnoticed.

A Mr Jansen from Denmark dived in and brought the two men up.

Jack remembers the sense of shock at the time. '

'It was serious. We were very worried about Jimmy. But the army fella was very quick. Dived in, took him out ... gave him the kiss of life or whatever and there was no problem.'

So much drama ... before the plane had even touched down in Australia.

First stop was Perth.

Up on the viewing balcony at the airport, two pipers dressed in kilts played Irish airs as the players came through customs, the welcoming party including dozens of newspapers, radio and television reporters.

'I do remember when we started off, we arrived early morning, had a couple of hours sleep. Then went out and did a first bit of training in the afternoon ... about four o'clock, because you couldn't train too early with the heat. It was 105, 110 degrees in Perth.

'Sure we didn't last 10 minutes ... we weren't able to stand up. There were a few Aussie lads looking at us training, and they clearly decided, "These lads are a bunch of wasters! It won't be too hard to beat this bunch."

'We went out the next day then and trained for about 15 or 16 minutes and we were little better. Then we trained the next day and we were a lot better. It just took a bit of time to acclimatise. It wasn't long though that we were flying.'

The locals watching the first couple of sessions clearly felt cheated.

It took the first test against a West Australia selection of AFL players to show the tourists meant business. 'We played our game more or less with the round ball. There were a few little concessions – you could pick the ball off the ground, things like that.'

The start of the game had to be delayed after a mix-up saw Jack's boots left behind, before a brand of crisp, free-flowing football robbed the fire from the bellies of the bedazzled hosts - 6-6 to 0-3 it ended, in front of 11,000 spectators, Mick Mellett presented with a trophy to mark his nomination as the 'Best and Fairest' on the Meath team.

'You sure sold us a pup about your fitness,' exclaimed Australian player-coach, Polly Farmer afterwards.

It was the first of five tests that would be played out in Perth, the Melbourne Cricket Ground, Sydney, Adelaide, and finally the Carlton Ground in Melbourne.

Five wins cemented the legend. Australia had stars like Ron Barassi leading the charge.

'For the fifth game, they put all their big guns together,' says Jack. 'The final game was in Melbourne. That was the real big one. Because we'd won all our games they decided to get their bloody best team out ... they picked their best players from each city.

'Melbourne was the main area where all the big teams were based but they decided to get two or three of the best from Sydney and other places.

'And it was a dinger.

'But we bet them again!'

But boy did they have to work for each and every victory. 'Oh God they were tough. I was full-back generally. They'd certainly let you have it once you got the ball. But I wasn't hit beforehand or anything like that.'

Martin played in Sydney and all three featured in the bruising Adelaide test. 'The Adelaide test was particularly tough,' explains Gerry, 'because there were a lot of Irish lads on the Australian team ... Irish immigrants. They knew how to hit and take care of the Meath fellas.

'I was playing on a fella that I knew; I knew him from Meath club football. It was one of the only times in my whole football career that I was warned what was going to happen at the throw-in. He said he was going to give me a nice welcome! That was a very tough match.'

Off the field, the reception couldn't have been warmer.

A snapshot from one night at the Rembrandt Rooms in Perth tells its own tale: Joe Walsh (on trumpet), Jack Quinn (clarinet), Peter Moore (sax), Tony Brennan (maracas) and Pat 'Red' Collier (electric organ). Meath's answer to the Beatles.

Ripping it up.

'We were good ambassadors for our country!' laughs Martin. 'Fellas were given a lot of freedom to enjoy themselves and I think that's why they played so well. As long as they kept reasonable hours and there was no mad drinking sessions.

'To win the five matches was massive.'

Jack grins ear-to-ear as he remembers the sense of culture shock. 'We were staying in a place called Coogee Bay in Sydney. I'd say it was only 150 yards down to the beach. And you want to see the talent!'

Gerry recalls the reception they received across Australia as heart-warming. 'Meeting so many Irish people. Unlike nowadays, when people emigrated to Australia they weren't coming home. So you were meeting people who were longing to talk about their relatives and relations back in Ireland. That's what you met everywhere you went.'

The Meath team then was split up into groups to go to different functions in different parts of the city, same in Melbourne and Sydney. 'Everywhere we went, it was indescribable. Every pub we went to, every club we went to. There was only one thing wrong with Australia, the pubs close at what … nine o'clock?'

On then to Hawaii where the players were feted for their exploits in Australia.

The Meath travelling party was captured on their arrival in a lovely shot in 'Gaels in the Sun', all 56 identified by McDermott with his meticulous eye for detail. Except one person is missing from the group … Jack Quinn.

'This is when we arrived in Hawaii and my feckin' bags didn't come through,' he says, studying the picture once more. 'I was back waiting at the airport.

'I came out of it lucky. You see all the garlands on the lads, they're ordinary flowers. I got a neck bracelet with lovely stuff on it because I was last, because of what happened. I gave it to my sister. Sure I said to the lads then, "Sure those flowers are nearly wilting already!"'

Everywhere they went they were treated like kings.

'There was an American sergeant who was very high in the army. He was very friendly with Liam Creavin here, the county board secretary. He invited the whole bunch … the Meath team and the supporters who came with us, down to the beach, down to Pearl Harbour.

'We were up in this place on a huge hill looking down on Pearl Harbour. They were obviously very wealthy people around the island, multi … multi-millionaires. And we went in to this place and I'll never forget it.

'Do you remember the old stacks of corn, the way they used to put them one on top of the other? Well they had bottles of champagne built up like that. So it was all laid on. "Open as many as you want lads."

'Glasses there everywhere. Sure we went back scuttered.

'I've a lovely photograph in a case somewhere. Your man from the army said, "I want somebody to give me an exhibition of how to catch a football." So a coconut was thrown up in the air and I'm there jumping to catch it.'

It's a priceless shot. Pat Collier, with a traditional Hawaiian garland around his neck, throwing the coconut high so Jack can go at it full-stretch.

The biggest concern at that stage was having enough money to last the trip. 'I remember in Hawaii you'd be very careful in the bars you'd go to because the drink was so bloody dear and the money would be running low, and you'd be saying, "Jaysus, we still have to go to America!"'

And yet, in the background there were constant reminders throughout their trip of a world in turmoil over America's involvement in the Vietnam war.

'It was a base for American soldiers on holiday from Vietnam,' says Gerry. 'As was Sydney. We stopped in Karachi, Calcutta, Bangkok – everywhere we stopped there were American soldiers, GIs on holidays. The fear in those guys was unbelievable.

'I remember sharing a taxi in Sydney. I was going to see an old nun – she was one of the Sweeneys from Kilbride. I was asked to go and visit her … which I did. Now it was about an hour's drive in a taxi and I shared it with a black American solider. He was telling me about the carry-on. And he was so scared.'

His tales of the war in Vietnam chilled the blood. 'What they were doing … that they didn't know who they were fighting … that they were just blowing villages out of it. And Americans were being slaughtered or were being captured. The only way they could fight the Vietnam war was to let them have it left, right and centre … it didn't matter who was in the way. The result was that he was a very scared guy. In fact, he wasn't sure whether he could go back to it.

'From a Meath players' point of view, anywhere you went, any club, hotel or nightclub, these guys were there and they were ripping it up. That was their holidays. We went to a place in Singapore and it was jam-packed as well … they were just everywhere.'

From Honolulu it was on to San Francisco for the American leg of the tour.

'To come in to San Francisco … it was beautiful,' says Gerry. 'Even the streets were magic. And the atmosphere and reaction in the pubs … and it was the same everywhere we went.

'Once you had your blazer on you were instantly recognisable, particularly in Australia.

'Pat Reynolds and 'Red' Collier were great entertainers. They often had to go to five or six different venues the one night, whereas other fellas would be going to eat. Those two lads and a few others might be heading off to sing for their supper.'

An invitation came to dine one evening at Harrington's bar and grill where each of the party were presented with an inscribed pen, a wallet and a key ring. Proprietor Harry Harrington even went so far as to present Jack Quinn with a trophy as a testament to his ability. Clearly a fan!

And then, a special visit in the early hours of the morning roused a group of players from their beds. A visit by the local sheriff can do that. But this was a hospitality call. The sheriff of San Mateo county, California, was one Brendan Maguire - who lined out for Meath in the 1952 All-Ireland final and replay, his two brothers on the opposite side.

'We knew he was there,' explains Jack, 'and we'd heard about the history of playing the matches with Meath and against the brothers. So we were hoping he'd drop in.'

On again then to Los Angeles and New York where they met with John 'Lefty' Devine, the man who christened Paddy O'Brien 'Hands' all those years before. And finally, three weeks after leaving Dublin airport, they returned to a colourful reception, the president of the GAA on hand to greet them individually – and members of the Trim CBS band together with a troupe of girl dancers from the Convent of Mercy providing an upbeat backing track.

'You went out and threw down the gauntlet in a setting completely strange to you,' declared president, Seamus Ó Riain. 'And you not only disproved those who said you had no chance; you proved yourself worthy All-Ireland champions and outstanding ambassadors for this country. We are proud to welcome you back.'

Home then at last.

Just to round it all off, a civic reception took place in Navan the following evening with a special dinner in the players' honour.

At the very back of 'Gaels of the Sun', the subscription list for the 'Meath-Australian tour fund' is listed, an extensive roll call of names, addresses and the amount of the donation.

It's like a Who's Who of Meath football, with a few unexpected names added to the eclectic list.

Fourth to be recorded is *'Mr Sean Boylan, Edenmore, Dunboyne'*, a man whose investment in Meath football would be incalculable.

Then there's *'Mr J May, The Ward P.O, Co Dublin'*, the self-same former Meath footballer Jackie May, owner of the shop where Paddy O'Brien helped pick out Gerry Quinn's first pair of boots.

'Dr Jim Brosnan, Dingle, Co Kerry', the famous footballer, manager and administrator.

'"Eight Boozers", c/o The Central Bar, Dundalk' who, together, donated the princely sum of a pound.

'Mr J Dowling, Sec, Offaly Co board', the same man whom Liam Harnan and Gerry McEntee would refuse to accept their All-Ireland medals from, was then very much a friend of Meath football, giving five pounds.

Or how about one *'Mr C.J. Haughey, Minister for Finance'* who contributed another fiver to the cause.

The *'Meath Chronicle, Ltd., Navan'* gave a sizeable £50 donation, so too the one and only *'Peter McDermott, Navan'*

'God rest him, he was brilliant,' says Jack of the man who made the whole tour happen. 'He got everyone to do something. Left no stone unturned …

and did a big job himself.'

On a Sunday in early July, 1968, Meath faced Longford in the semi-final of the Leinster Championship at Mullingar. 'It's some comedown to travel around the world, see those sights, win all our games and then come back,' admits Gerry.

Longford won, 0-12 to 0-7.

Back to reality.

＋＋＋＋＋

The way Sean Boylan tells it, Mick Lyons' career in an Ireland shirt played a part in shaping his whole reputation.

'Mick Lyons had an aura and a presence about him. What really made him stand out, what created the legend of him, was the 1984 International Rules. He got knocked out down below in Cork but after everything that went on there's a bigger crowd at Croke Park the following Sunday. The Big Dipper and company.

'The second match is only on, the ball breaks, towards where the old tunnel was, the corner of the Canal and the old Hogan Stand. And Mick and the Dipper and another Aussie player went for it.

'Ohhh! It looked like Mick was going to be destroyed in the sandwich. And whatever happened Mick came out with the ball and the two boys were left on the ground. From then on, because your normal Dublin supporters were at it, they called it "The Lyons Den". That created the myth from there. It became legendary.'

First test.

Cork, October 21, 1984.

Mick Lyons stands in the parade for Amhran na bhFiann.

'Bring it on,' he thinks.

He can handle this. In a year when a broken thumb ruled him out of the Leinster final, Meath going down narrowly to Dublin, his level of performances were such that he made the cut as the All Star full-back.

When Meath's esteemed Peter McDermott and Liam Sammon from Galway, joint Irish managers, tipped their hats to him to play for Ireland, he jumped at the chance.

For the first time since Meath's famous tour of 1968, a 'Compromise Rules' series had been organised with the Aussies travelling over for the three tests.

So Lyons stands, sizing up the visitors, all hulking, barrel chested specimens. Just minutes in and he goes for a ball. Bang! Lights out.

Carted from the field unconscious.

'Knocked clean out,' he says.

'Lost two chunks out of the back two teeth.'

He made a point of finding out his assailant. 'Mark Lee is his name,' he says, able to smile about it now. 'I wouldn't normally be out in front but I was this time and I remember getting my hands on the ball and nothing else. I remember being back in the dressing room and the ceiling just going round and round on me.'

The Aussies bulldozed a path to a 70-57 victory. When it came to the following Sunday, he was burning to play. Not to settle a score but to play for his country with pride – at least long enough that he could remember.

'I suppose it's a stupid thing but like any lad … that's the one thing the GAA missed, not having the chance to represent your country. We don't fight wars anymore so it's the nearest thing you can get!' he says, chuckling away.

The tests then had an errant lawlessness about them that turned them into a part-circus act, except with plenty of blood on the floor. The second test provided plenty of rough and tumble, that one incident that Boylan recalls helping to add to the Lyons' myth.

Ireland hung tough to level the series at one apiece, 80-76, before Australia took an equally helter-skelter third test and the series' bragging rights.

Lyons felt honoured to share a dressing room with some of the game's greats. And it gave him a chance to see the level Boylan's emerging Meath team had to attain. 'Another thing was … it was nice to play with players who you'd be plotting against for so long. To actually play with them. To see how you matched up; to see how you'd learn more. It was all a learning curve.'

Two years later, the learning curve continued in the shape of a return trip Down Under. Eighteen years after Jack Quinn and the trailblazing Meath team took on an AFL selection in that tour, Ireland travelled to take on the pick of Australia.

Just like 1968, Perth hosted the first test.

For the Lyons family, the squad selection represented a badge of pride. Both Mick and Paraic were asked to answer their country's call.

Summerhill, after all, was on the crest of a wave. Paraic had just captained the club to a first senior county title since 1977 and even now, it's easy to detect the sense of pride in Paraic's voice at being involved.

'It was probably one of the biggest buzzes I got out of football. I would have considered Kevin Heffernan to be ahead of his time. I had him very high up as a manager. For him to deem me good enough to travel, that was just...

'My father told me I was in. We were down in Summerhill and he told me, "You've been picked to go to Australia." It must have been on the radio. Sure I think we went for a few pints in Shaws afterwards to celebrate.

'There were trials. I could never say at any stage that I was looking good for the trip. But he would have liked the way we played football at the time ... and the way that Kevin Heffernan would want football to be played. That might have helped get me the nod.

'I was injured going out, that was the only thing. That was a disaster. The county final was on the Sunday before we left. And I got a dead leg.

'I'd say travelling long-haul didn't help; I'd say my preparation the night after winning the county final didn't help. I knew all about it the next morning.'

The brothers' father, Paddy travelled over for the series as well.

For both Mick and Paraic, to watch Kevin Heffernan up close and personal, to see how he ran a team, was fascinating in and of itself. Meath's intense rivalry with Dublin was underpinned by a mutual respect and admiration. The lads had Kevin Heffernan up on a pedestal.

'Kevin Heffernan was class,' reveals Mick. 'Top drawer stuff. He was a huge man in terms of organisation ... massive. He had a sense about him ... that aura around him. If you messed about, there was no way back in.

'He had everything done on the Australian players. Every player ... what he does ... where he runs. Full breakdown. What I want you to do; what I want that fella to do. They do it now on all the teams … back then it wasn't done.

'He did the same with Dublin. So you knew what you were up against.'

The first test though didn't go to plan, Australia taking it 64-57.

Going into the second, Mick says Heffernan came into his own. Radically altered the team selection to neutralise Australia's strengths. 'Kevin turned the whole thing around. I used to play on and off. In here, out here. He put full-forwards playing full-back … turned everything around.'

It wasn't a question of whether he was happy or not to fit that role. When Heffernan asked you to do something, it was like a direct order from an army commander where the chain of command simply had to be followed.

'There was no point being there, going up to Kevin Heffernan and saying, "I'm not doing that," explains Mick simply. 'Because you'd be out.'

For the third test, Heffernan cast him as the villain in the piece, sent in to 'do a job' as they say in the business.

'That would be close to it alright. You knew in no uncertain manner that if it happened to come your way, to be ready. Because that's what they were doing. They were no angels.'

Boylan puts his own colourful spin on how it all unfolded.

'There's a great story told of when the lads were out in Australia in '86. Third test. Australia were really having a go at Ireland in a big way. Kevin Heffernan called Mick, told him he was putting him in, and said to him, "Mick, just go out there and rough them." That was the instruction. So he went out and there was hell to pay. Sure they were queuing up to hit him because he was a legend from '84 … they couldn't wait!

'Things like that would never worry Mick. He'd be ready to do what you wanted.'

'Paddy Lyons the father, was out there. Paddy went over and said, "Congratulations Michael."

'"Thanks very much, daddy."

'"I'll say this Michael, I wasn't too happy with the way you were out there."

'"Daddy, I was given a job to do."

'"Aw, that's alright Michael."'

And, says, Boylan, 'That was it!'

Paraic confirms the instruction from Heffernan as well. 'I remember Maurice Rioli that he high tackled. But Heffernan told him that's what he wanted done. They were at it. The series wouldn't have lasted too long if what went on then went on in all the matches.

'There were all out fights. It wasn't pushing around the fringes and lads just holding on, it was proper boxing. It wasn't hand-bag stuff.

'Pat O'Byrne was telling us afterwards he had his nose broken.

'I says, "What did you do then, Pat?"

'"I did that," he says ... Paraic twisting his hands around his nose in imitation of O'Byrne.

'"I just got my hands on it, straightened it up, and kept going."

'And that's exactly how it was out there.'

For Paraic, the injury sustained in the county final ruined his tour from a playing point of view. 'I couldn't train for a while out there. I'm not sure whether I would have been picked or not but I wasn't ready for the first test. Then there was a Gaelic football match. I played in that, against a local GAA side.

'Not long into that, near the end of the first half, I kicked the ball and I felt something in the leg again ... I'd say a scar tissue tear. And that put me back to square one. That was the second test gone.

'At the end of it, we played an exhibition match in Sydney and I played in that. But that was it.'

Still, he is proud to say he was selected to represent his country and he puts the whole experience among his career highs. 'It was like being a professional sportsperson for a month. You could be training in the day and then again in the evening.

'One of the biggest buzzes I got out of playing... whether with club or county. It's up there with winning All-Irelands, right up there. Just getting the nod to go. ... being deemed good enough to represent your country.'

Mick didn't need to go scuba diving or skydiving to get his kicks. 'No, I didn't go skydiving. Ah, we'd have great craic. After a match you'd be told, "Right lads, you have two days." You just went off. Went mad for a couple of days.

'Socialising with lads who you'd never get a chance to normally. We'd great fun alright with Pat O'Byrne. Pat was fearless … not too many of the Australian lads wanted to go near him.'

For all the sense of achievement in a bunch of amateurs stealing a series win, Lyons never felt the Compromise Rules game was sustainable.

'We won over there and it was great. But there is no future in it. Australia is huge. There is so much going on, you'd get a little piece in the paper. That's all. A little piece on the back somewhere. You'd be thinking, "Ah Jesus, c'mon." If it was on here in Ireland it would be all over the back page.'

When Australia came to Ireland a year later, Meath were All-Ireland champions.

This time, Australia took the series 2-1.

Relations with the Aussie players tended to be strained, given the hot and heavy nature of play during the tests.

'We didn't socialise together,' explains Mick. 'Would that not tell the tale! We didn't really want to socialise with them.'

✦✦✦✦✦

After another blood and bandages type of tour Down Under in 1990, the series was put into cold storage. For Darren Fay, it's revival in 1998 couldn't have come at a better time.

Still only 24, he feels now that he was dining out too much on his reputation.

'I suppose the moment came towards the end of '98. Colm O'Rourke was appointed as the manager of the International Rules and it was the first time it started back up. This was another legendary thing from yesteryear. You were going to be playing for your country.

'Trevor [Giles] was injured at the time. We all got trials and myself and John [McDermott] were picked. That was the moment that I said to myself, "Hang on a minute here. I need to cop on to myself."

'Colm picked me a little bit on reputation because from '96 I was probably regarded as the best full-back in the country. O'Rourke would have been …

I wouldn't say a critic of mine, but he knew the auld lad and played with the auld lad who liked a bit of a good-time.

'He definitely would have painted me with the same brush.

'It went well for me playing against Australia, a hugely proud moment representing my country. And it made me knuckle down again and get ready for '99. Luckily, everyone else knuckled down as well.'

The 1998 series was a compromise in a literal sense in that it was only a two-test tour for visiting Australia, the aggregate of two Croke Park matches deciding the winner.

Ireland won 128 to 118.

'The whole novelty of playing for your country … having your name across the back of the jersey was so strange.

'D Fay.

'Even wearing a different number. After wearing No.3 all the time, now I was nine or 10 because it was going alphabetically. Being part of the Irish squad definitely put me on the right road for '99. It was an amazing experience.

'And the fella that came in and marked me the first game was six foot eight inch "Spider" Everitt. I marked Wayne Carey who would have been the star player in Australian Rules at the same time.

'I found it a very easy game to play. And I loved it. It wasn't as frantic as Gaelic football. It was like a game of chess in a way. You get a ball and you have to pin-point a pass.

'It was great having the tackle. You could tackle them any way you wanted, once it wasn't too high … like a rugby tackle. And it was great to be able to do that because in Gaelic football, there's a lot of … "What's a tackle … what's not a tackle?"

'And it was the underdog thing again. Here's Australia. They're more powerful than us, earning savage amounts of money to play the game while we're earning nothing. It was great to be able to pit yourself against these people.'

He found that it always seemed to be about the bottom dollar for the Australians from the conversations he had with them.

'Afterwards, you'd notice that they'd be talking down to you: "Well, y'know, I'd be on 250 grand a year. And you've to go to work in the morning?"

'I've played against them eight times and they've always been like that. It's great because you go out the next day on the pitch and it's equal. You can really prove how equal you are.

'We won the International Rules which was massive. I felt a huge sense of pride and said to myself … '"I have to cop myself on now."'

With Meath clinching a seventh All-Ireland and bridging a 50-year link to the famous '49ers', the 1999 tour to Australia rounded off the perfect year.

It opened Fay's eyes to the life of a professional athlete. 'After 99 it was a great thing to go to Australia and represent Ireland again.

'We were three and a half weeks down there and we were actually treated like professional sportsmen. You're actually given money every day … daily expenses. It was as close as I'm ever going to get to being a professional footballer.

'You trained twice a day; had your meals at a certain time; told to stay in your room at a certain time. There were bananas thrown into the room at hourly intervals.'

And Fay made good use of those daily expenses when he landed home. 'It was actually good because I came home and tarmacked the drive with it! I think it was 125 dollars per day. You wouldn't spend it because you wouldn't be out anywhere. I ended up coming back with two or three grand.'

O'Rourke manager. John McDermott captain. Fay and Graham Geraghty also flying the flag for Meath … life could not have been better, or more homely, for Darren Fay.

Also, Ireland won the first test at the famous MCG, Melbourne Cricket Ground, 70-62. And then drew the second test, 52-apiece in Adelaide, to ensure victory belonged to the touring side.

All told, Fay played in four consecutive series; 1998, 1999, 2000, 2001.

It's no exaggeration to say that the 2001 series saved him. Pulled him from the fog of depression that enveloped him after the All-Ireland final and the '15 minutes of madness' when he took himself off a rampant Padraic Joyce.

He took the defeat so personal he ducked work and brooded around the house with the 1,000-yard stare of a shell-shocked soldier returning from duty. He didn't want to see a football or put himself through the process of a trial for the International Rules.

He felt he let his county down; the last thing he wanted to do was let his country down as well.

No surprise Sean Boylan had a hand in shaking him from his stupor. In 'Total Fitness' in Blanchardstown where his kids were taking swimming lessons, he bumped into Brian McEniff who had the Ireland squad in for a pool session. The man who guided Donegal to their breakthrough All-Ireland was now in charge of the International Rules, with Anthony Tohill a selector alongside him. Boylan gave McEniff directions to Fay's front door when he heard Darren wasn't answering his phone.

'I was supposed to go training on the Thursday with the International Rules. They were in Simonstown because it was the middle of the country. And I didn't arrive.

'Graham rang me. I told him, "Tell him I'm not playing … I'm not f**kin going out there. And don't tell him where I live either!"

'"Right," says he. So that was grand.

'That night McEniff and Tohill came out to the house and basically stood here until I changed my mind.

'Tohill had to go off but McEniff stood listening to me … "I'm not going… I'm not going… I'm not going."

'And he pleaded with me and begged me, "It will be good for you…"

'I said, "F**k it then … I'll f**kin go." And I was thick saying it. But he wouldn't leave the house until I said "yeah". And I'll be so indebted to him for the rest of my life. Going out there and having another focus and another goal, and not wallowing in self-pity here!

'It was actually only two weeks on from the All-Ireland that we went out.

'And Australia changed everything. I loved playing International Rules anyway. I went out there totally focused. I said to myself, "I'm going to give this everything."

'It felt like a second chance.

'You know the way you fall off a horse and get up on it a week later … I wouldn't have been able to get up on that horse if I left it for six months with

Meath or waited for Championship even later.

Also on the tour was one Padraic Joyce. One night out on the town did more than any therapy session, the pair forging an unlikely bond.

'Myself and Joyce hung around together and I remember one evening it was only the two of us in the pub and we were chatting about everything ... chatting about the All-Ireland final. It's amazing when you're chatting to the fella who did the damage.

'It was great to get it off my chest with the player I needed to say it to.'

As for Joyce's response?

'He just said, "I was glad you were moved off me!"'

Ireland won both tests with Fay a tower of strength in defence.

When it came to the selection of the Irish 'Player of the Series', he was bowled over to be honoured.

'Player of the Series in a sport against a bunch of professionals ... I felt a huge sense of pride. I won All Stars but I never won 'Footballer of the Year' or anything like that. I was so proud of the couple of 'Man of the Matches' I got because you're playing with players who are far more talented than you but on that day you were better than them.'

Back in 1996, he declared his intention to win three All-Ireland medals.

He grins when he is reminded of that statement.

'Look,' he says, pulling out some of the mementoes of his career. Turns out, the 'Player of the Series' in 2001 was fashioned in a very particular way, a Celtic Cross to match the style of the pair of medals from 1996 and 1999.

'It's actually an All-Ireland medal that you get so technically I have three of them,' he says, proudly turning it over in his hand.

Another dream fulfilled.

Redemption.

EPILOGUE

It's not always easy being the son of a living legend.

Paddy O'Brien's wife, Kay tells the story of an incident at school that was to shape the path of one of her four sons, Gabriel.

'Gabriel was very fond of playing sport. He was playing tennis with a young lad out in the yard one day. This big Christian Brother came out and said, "Oh, a young lad like you, a son of Paddy O'Brien's playing tennis? Go down and get your football boots!" Kay doing a grand imitation of the brother's outraged demeanour.

'He was real rough with him. Well Gabriel came home and the tears were in his eyes. I felt very sorry for him. But he was as determined as could be … just put down his books and said, "If I have to play football just because you were the best footballer, I'll never put a football boot on me again." And he never did. That's what the Christian Brothers did for him.'

'He's not a sports person at all,' adds Paddy. 'He works on films. He flew out to London this morning.'

Turns out Gabriel O'Brien had other talents, winning himself an actual Emmy award, for his work on the hugely successful television series *The Tudors*.

Padraic and Garry laugh off any claims to sporting greatness themselves on a football field but Tony is the one who carved out a reputation for himself on the field, playing under-21 for Dublin and earning a few senior run-outs in the early-1980s - and winning two county senior Championships with Scoil

Uí Chonaill, also captaining the team.

His son Conor played centre-back on the Dublin junior team in 2011 as well as winning a Dublin Intermediate Championship medal with Skerries Harps the same year in the company of county captain, Bryan Cullen. Tony's daughter, Claire also captained Skerries Harps to a Dublin Championship in 2008.

For Paddy, in looking for a competitive edge after he retired from the game, he found a familiar haven for ex inter-county players.

'I suppose I did miss football to a certain extent. I took up golf then and I used that as a sport.'

On the living room wall beside his medal collection is a lovely photograph of him standing on the first tee at Rush Golf Club in south Dublin before taking the traditional captain's drive. Except instead of a golf ball on the tee-box, he is in mid run-up as he prepares to boot an 'O'Neills' down the fairway. What he achieved on the field had a lasting legacy.

Kay too later became ladies captain.

When he thinks of those who shaped his football life, he picks out two men of the cloth.

Fr McManus, who played such a part in the emergence of Skryne, he once described as 'possibly the best midfielder who ever wore the jersey' and then there was Father Tully, 'an inspiring guide, philosopher and friend.'

Others names that captured his imagination in the early days were 'Ned Giles, Bill Dillon, the full-back of the wonder kick-out Matt Rogers, Bill Shaw, Christy Doran and a host of others.'

Like Jack Quinn, Mick Lyons and Darren Fay, he is loathe at times to single out teammates, because the team was everything. Everything he achieved on the field was because of a special group dynamic.

As for the opposition, he is a bit more forthcoming. 'I may as well be candid and admit that the full-forward I feared most when I was in my prime was the big, unassuming policeman, Tom Langan,' the Mayo man and clubmate for a time at Sean McDermotts who made the 'Team of the Century' at the other end of the field.

The St Vincent's team that went on to dominate Dublin football he has great respect for. 'In team work and combination I have not seen their equal.'

Top of the list of Kerry greats he faced off against comes the likes of Paddy Kennedy, Jackie Lyne, Gega O'Connor and Tadghy Lyne. Kevin Armstrong of Antrim too. 'Unassuming, but remarkable … would have graced any All-Ireland team.'

Kevin Heffernan's passing in January 2013 evoked memories of that last fateful day in a Meath jersey in the 1955 Leinster final and of how many of his own compatriots have passed on.

What they achieved on the field together though will forever be remembered.

✦✦✦✦✦

Jack Quinn runs the popular self-titled pub in Scurlogstown just outside Trim with his wife, Mary and still has the lean and fit look of his playing days.

Their son John, now living in Kilkenny, played club football with Trim and they have two daughters as well, Sheila and Ann.

Football has given Jack Quinn so much but life has had its knocks too.

Walk through the campus of Dublin City University and one bench is inscribed with the name of Maeve Quinn, in remembrance of their daughter who lost her life tragically to cancer.

'Oh … it was shocking. Everyone was brilliant, they did all they could. But when a daughter dies, there's nothing anyone can do. Maeve was a young girl … lymphoma … twenty and a half exactly. She passed away in 1996.'

And he leads you through to the living room where a photo of her in the full flush of youth hangs.

The pub attached to the house remains a hub of football conversation and while a big admirer of what Meath have achieved since he finished playing, he is no big fan of the modern game of Gaelic football.

'I still go to it but to me, this handpassing has destroyed football. It has taken all the skill out of it. Top class fielding is now a dying art. All you want now is someone who can run. It won't happen ever again but I couldn't see what was wrong with football in the '60s and '70s.

'It's all change, change, change. I'd play the game as it was played before.'

For all the Quinns, the reminders of the great days on the field come from the unlikeliest of places.

Martin Quinn has two daughters living in Australia and decided in April, 2013 to travel over to visit. It was his first time to return since the famous tour of 1968, a full 45 years earlier.

Just to show how the world really is a small place, he describes a fateful encounter his daughter, Orla had 12 months previously.

'She is a nurse in a hospital in Melbourne. The matron called her down to say there was a celebrity coming in and she was to look after him ... her alone was to look after him. Nobody was to be let in to see him. No phone calls. No press. No photographers ... no nothing.

'She was expecting a film star or a singer, or someone. The next thing who arrived but this auld fella ... grumpy as anything. He used lie on the bed, and the moans and the groans out of him. They got him down to X-ray and he had a dislocated collar bone, five or six ribs broken, a lot of bad injuries. She was looking after him for a couple of days before he even got to talk to her.

'He said, "Where are you from?"

'"Ah, from Ireland."

'"Oh I know that place."

'It wasn't until afterwards that we found out it was Ron Barrassi. Captain of their team in '68 and who played in all the matches.

'I'll tell you what happened him. He was going down the street on his bicycle. There was an accident on the far side of the street and he was looking over at it – a couple of ambulances, fire brigade were there – and he went straight into a pole!

'That happened him on a weekend. The following weekend he was getting on the 'Team of the Century' ... or he was being picked as the 'Footballer of the Century'. His wife told Orla that she had to have him right to go to this 'do' – of all the 'dos' he was ever at, he couldn't miss this one!

'What they had to do was put a pillow up along his side, strapped it right around him, so no-one would touch him. And that's the way he went off.

'It was only after that she told me.

'If I'd only known.'

+ + + + +

Mick Lyons can be found these days in Rathcore Golf Club, about three miles out the road from Enfield which he owns and runs, along with his first cousin, Austin.

'We started the golf course about 12 years ago. We wanted to get involved in sports, always had a grá to do it. A piece of ground came up in Rathcore. It's a lovely piece of natural land, rolling hills … uncommon in Meath.'

'We always tripped around the course in Trim when we were young … played golf when we weren't playing football. Most lads who stop playing football play golf, and talk about football. It's the same down here … it's all football.

'Once you've played sports and you've been in an arena and there's 60, 70, 80,000 people looking at you … if you go for a drink somewhere and someone comes up and says something to you, you can't just say "good luck".

'You have to give a bit of time … but … if lads are annoying you… different matter.'

Mick and his wife Helen have raised four children, three boys following the eldest of the brood Michelle. All three have already made their mark with Summerhill, Alan centre-back on the senior team that reached the 2013 county final with Kevin and Conor coming quickly on his heels. Paraic's son, Declan too was part of the 2011 county title winning panel.

Before Mick and Austin took up their business together, Paraic recalls the days the brothers used to work together. 'I was there with him when we were involved in plant hire. We had machinery and that. You'd always know if there was a row coming - we'd let a couple of f**ks at each other, then we'd part, come back again an hour later and it was as though it never happened. That's the way it was.'

Now, Paraic breeds thoroughbred horses for the flat.

'I got into it by chance. Michael and Austin were doing a bit of it. I got one mare back in 2002 and I just got lucky with her. I've seven mares now; so far so good. It's a fairly fickle business. If you get lucky you can get a right pay-off. You might have a great year out of the blue. Things can happen in pedigrees that you've no control over.'

Their lifelong attachment to Summerhill GFC continues and their exploits on the field with Meath are still celebrated. On All-Ireland final day in 2012, the double-winning team of 1987-88 was honoured as part of the annual jubilee celebrations. Mick and his good buddy, Joe Cassells, the two captains, led the respective panels onto the Croke Park pitch, the pair still instantly recognisable even though sporting a shirt and tie.

He looks at the changed football landscape and wonders whether history would have unfolded differently if the qualifier system was in place during his time.

'Cork were a very good side. We had it so hard to get by Dublin; they had it so hard to get past Kerry. If the backdoor system was in operation back then I'd say Kerry wouldn't have as many All-Irelands. Now the Kerry lads might disagree.'

The role of full-back too has changed with the times. 'Back then you needed to be good in the air to play full-back. Nowadays you don't.'

But he is no big fan of how the game has evolved.

'It's hard to watch sometimes. It's vastly different. People are still going to see it I suppose.

'At the end of the day it's an Irish sport. It's too organised. Too … keep, keep, keep ball … too structured. I'm not saying Gaelic football doesn't have to evolve; it does. Everything evolves. But who wants to be a defender any more? Because you can't tackle. You can't shoulder a fella because he'll sidestep you or it's a yellow card. Put out your hands and it's a free. It's a forward's game. I wouldn't like to be a defender anymore.

'They're on about black cards in the game yet there is still no defined tackle. Cynical fouling … certainly get rid of it. But I think they are taking the hardness out of Gaelic football. I'm not saying the lads now are any weaker. They're travelling faster, probably stronger too. But it's the way the game is going.

'I think the sin bin in rugby is brilliant. They should have stuck with that.'

Yet he is no misty-eyed romantic when it comes to the football of his own era.

'I'm not one of these lads who says it should be played the way we played it. Football will change again in 10 years' time.'

Even in his hey-day, Lyons enjoyed the banter with the Dublin supporters, Tommy Dowd once telling a story of the love-hate relationship.

'I remember talking to a couple of Dublin supporters one time,' remarked Dowd. '… and I remember them saying, "The only things wrong is that Mick Lyons was born in the wrong f‴kin' Summerhill."'

How they wished he grew up in the version within sight of Croke Park, rather than the Meath outpost.

Con Houlihan's gift of capturing the essence of life extended to the Meath full-back. *'I wouldn't be surprised to hear that there are small boys in Dublin who believe that Mick Lyons is kept in a cage in Summerhill and fed with raw meat. In fact, Mick is as mild a man as you could find in the world outside football. Many people think of Mick Lyons as a hard man – I think of him as a footballer, first class.'*

No wonder Mick has a soft spot for the late, great Kerry wordsmith.

Between 1984 and 1991, Meath and Dublin met in the Leinster championship 10 different times. On the two occasions Dublin won, Mick Lyons was missing due to injury.

'I'd have great fun with the Dublin lads, especially with the supporters. When I finished I'd go in for a drink in the pubs in Dublin and there would be great craic. No malice. It's like a war. You fight lads for long enough and you gain respect.'

✦✦✦✦✦

Darren Fay thinks back to the younger version of himself that barrelled through the early years of his Meath career without a care in the world. As to what has changed since he answered a Q&A for a local newspaper with a sharp line in humour – he listed a 'Keg of Guinness and Anna Kournikova' as his 'desert island necessities' – he quips, 'I'm not drinking Guinness anymore.'

But so much has changed off the field. A venture into the home kitchen business came just before the Celtic Tiger bubble burst and he later found that the pub trade wasn't for him either after opening one in Trim.

So in June 2012, the 36-year-old married father of three entered St Patrick's Classical School in Navan to re-sit a Leaving Certificate biology paper. As the man with two All-Irelands, three Leinster titles, and three All-Stars made his way to the very top of the hall, he could sense the heads turning.

'It was a bit surreal sitting down and you've 17 or 18-year-olds running around the place. Typical O'Rourke. He put my chair right up to the top of the hall so I had to walk the whole length of it. I was nervous enough about the exam that I didn't pass too many remarks.'

Passing the exam with distinction made it all worthwhile. He credits the Gaelic Players Association for their hugely important work in guiding and advising past county players and found them invaluable in trying to plan a new career.

It worked both ways too, Fay getting a big reaction to a talk he did for the GPA to the next generation of rising stars about the importance of a career and a life outside of football.

He recalls his own school years, looking to earn a bit of extra pocket money. 'I started collecting milk money on a Saturday … there was a lot of lads doing it.

'There was delivery runs then at night – not anymore – so when people woke up in the morning the milk would be there. Everyone buys their milk in the shop now. The fella who we did the round with asked me, "Do you want to do the Sunday night run?"

'I said "grand".

'I did it all through my secondary school in the early '90s. Going out in the middle of the night delivering milk – 1am til 8am! And then I'd try and go to school then. I never really went in on a Monday. No wonder I failed my Leaving Cert!'

On resitting it nearly 20 years later, he got what he wanted in terms of a college course. And so he started a five-year Masters in Science Education at Maynooth College in September 2013.

'That would lead to being a teacher in biology and chemistry in secondary school. But it leaves my options wide open for the industry as well. There are a load of opportunities there.'

A new chapter in his life is only beginning.

✦ ✦ ✦ ✦ ✦

Funny how their paths have intersected, in ways none of them even knew.

The Lyons brothers didn't realise Paddy O'Brien's son, Garry is living in Kilcock, a stone's throw out the road. Paraic's daughter, Joann didn't realise that the Tomás O'Brien in her biology class at Scoil Dara in Kilcock is Garry's own son.

Back in February, 2013, the school won the North Leinster senior schools football title.

Garry shows a photo on his mobile phone of Tomas lifting the trophy. His father smiles as he describes how his local coach has only recently bestowed a new nickname on his son … 'Hands'.

Paddy himself smiles proudly at the mention of it.

The legacy of a golden era of Meath football, of a golden era of full-backs, lives on.